Advances

in COMPUTERS
VOLUME 67

Advances in

COMPUTERS

Web Technology

EDITED BY

MARVIN V. ZELKOWITZ

Department of Computer Science
and Institute for Advanced Computer Studies
University of Maryland
College Park, Maryland

VOLUME 67

AMSTERDAM ● BOSTON ● HEIDELBERG ● LONDON ● NEW YORK ● OXFORD
PARIS ● SAN DIEGO ● SAN FRANCISCO ● SINGAPORE ● SYDNEY ● TOKYO
Academic Press is an imprint of Elsevier

ELSEVIER

ACADEMIC
PRESS

Academic Press is an imprint of Elsevier
525 B Street, Suite 1900, San Diego, California 92101-4495, USA
84 Theobald's Road, London WC1X 8RR, UK
Radarweg 29, PO Box 211, 1000 AE, Amsterdam, The Netherlands
30 Corporate Drive, Suite 400, Burlington, MA 01803, USA

Library of Congress Cataloging in Publication Data

British Library Cataloguing in Publication Data

ISBN-13: 978-0-12-012167-0
ISBN-10: 0-12-012167-0
ISSN (Series): 0065-2458

For information on all Academic Press publications
visit our web site at http://books.elsevier.com

Printed and bound by CPI Group (UK) Ltd, Croydon, CR0 4YY
Transfered to Digital Printing, 2013

Contents

Broadcasting a Means to Disseminate Public Data in a Wireless Environment— Issues and Solutions

A.R. Hurson, Y. Jiao, and B.A. Shirazi

Programming Models and Synchronization Techniques for Disconnected Business Applications

Avraham Leff and James T. Rayfield

Academic Electronic Journals: Past, Present, and Future

Anat Hovav and Paul Gray

Web Testing for Reliability Improvement

Jeff Tian and Li Ma

Wireless Insecurities

Michael Sthultz, Jacob Uecker, and Hal Berghel

The State of the Art in Digital Forensics

Dario Forte

Contributors

Professor Hal Berghel is Associate Dean of the Howard R. Hughes College of Engineering at the University of Nevada, Las Vegas, and Erskine Fellow at the University of Canterbury. He is also Director of the Center for Cybermedia Research, and Associate Director of the Identity Theft and Financial Fraud Research and Operations Center. He has held a variety of research and administrative positions in industry and academia during his twenty-five year career in computing. His current research focuses on Internet security and forensics, interactive and participatory computing environments, and dynamic models for cyberpublishing. His research work appears frequently in a variety of scientific and technical venues, and his columns, editorials, and articles appear regularly in such publications as Computer and the Communications of the ACM. He is a Fellow of both the ACM and IEEE. He can be reached at hlb@acm.org.

Dario V. Forte, CFE, CISM, has been active in the information security field since 1992. He has almost 15 years experience as a police investigator. He is a member of the TC11 Workgroup of Digital Forensics. His technical articles have been published in a host of international journals and he has spoken at numerous international conferences on information warfare and digital forensics. He worked with international governmental agencies such as NASA, and the US Army and Navy, providing support in incident response and forensic procedures and has resolved many important hacking-related investigations. He has lectured at the Computer Security Institute, the United States D.H.S. and D.o.D., the Blackhat Conference, the DFRWS (US Air Force Rome Labs), and POLICYB (Canada). Dario has given interviews with Voice of America, Newsweek, the Washington Times and CSO Magazine. At the moment he is Adjunct Faculty at University of Milano at Crema and provides security/incident response and forensics consulting services to the government, law enforcement and corporate worlds. He can be reached at www.dflabs.com.

Professor Paul Gray is Professor Emeritus and Founding Chair of Information Science at Claremont Graduate University. He specializes in information systems, particularly decision support systems, knowledge management, data warehousing and electronic publication. Before coming to Claremont in 1983, he was a professor at Stanford University, the Georgia Institute of Technology, the University of Southern California, and Southern Methodist University. Prof. Gray retired in May 2001, but continues to teach, do research, consult, and edit the electronic journal *Communications of the Association for Information Systems* (CAIS). He is the winner of the LEO award for lifetime achievement from the Association for Information Systems, a fellow of AIS and INFORMS, a past president of The Institute of Management Sciences, and the author of over 120 papers and 13 books.

Professor Anat Hovav is a visiting Professor at Korea University in Seoul, South Korea. She also taught at Temple University, University of Southern California and Cal-Poly. Her research interests include electronic publishing, Internet standards adoption, Risk assessment and Internet security. Dr. Hovav holds a Ph.D. in Management Information Systems from Claremont University. She also has over 15 years of industry experience in Information Systems management and strategic planning. Dr. Hovav published articles in journals such as *Communications of the ACM, Information Systems Journal* (ISJ), *Information Systems Frontiers* (ISF) *and Communications of AIS* (CAIS).

Professor A.R. Hurson is a Computer Science and Engineering Faculty at The Pennsylvania State University. His research for the past 23 years has been directed toward the design and analysis of general as well as special purpose computer architectures. He has published over 230 technical papers in areas including database systems, multidatabases, global information sharing processing, application of mobile agent technology, object oriented databases, Mobile computing environment, computer architecture parallel and distributed processing. Dr. Hurson served as the Guest Co-Editor of special issues of the *IEEE Proceedings on Supercomputing Technology*, the *Journal of Parallel and Distributed Computing on Load Balancing and Scheduling*, the *Journal of Integrated Computer-Aided Engineering on Multidatabase and Interoperable Systems, IEEE Transactions on Computers on Parallel Architectures and Compilation Techniques, Journal of Multimedia Tools and Applications, and Journal of Pervasive and Mobile Computing*. He served as a member of the IEEE Computer Society Press Editorial Board, an IEEE Distinguished speaker, editor of IEEE transactions on computers, and IEEE/ACM Computer Sciences Accreditation Board. Currently, he is serving as an ACM lecturer and editor of Journal of Pervasive and Mobile Computing. He can be reached at hurson@cse.psu.edu.

Dr. Yu Jiao is a postdoctoral researcher at the Oak Ridge National Laboratory. She received the B.Sc. degree in computer science from the Civil Aviation Institute of China in 1997. She received her M.Sc. and Ph.D. degrees from The Pennsylvania

State University, in 2002 and 2005, respectively, both in computer science. Her main research interests include software agents, pervasive computing and secure global information system design. She can be reached at yjiao@cse.psu.edu.

Dr. Avraham Leff is a Research Staff Member in the e-Business Frameworks department of IBM. He joined IBM in 1991. His research interests include distributed components and distributed application development. He received a B.A. in Computer Science and Mathematical Statistics from Columbia University in 1984, and an M.S. and PhD. in Computer Science from Columbia University in 1985 and 1992, respectively. Dr. Leff has been issued six patents, and has five patents pending.

Li Ma received the B.S. and M.S. degrees in Computer Science from Xi'an Jiaotong University, China, in 1998 and 2001, respectively. She is currently working toward the PhD degree in Computer Science at Southern Methodist University, Dallas, Texas. Her research area includes software quality and reliability, software testing, software measurement and web engineering. She is a student member of the IEEE Computer Society.

Dr. James T. Rayfield is a Research Staff Member in the e-Business Frameworks department of IBM. He joined IBM in 1989. His research interests include object-oriented transaction-processing systems and database systems. He received an Sc.B. in 1983, an Sc.M. in 1985, and a Ph.D. in 1988, all in Electrical Engineering from Brown University. Dr. Rayfield has six patents issued and seven patents pending.

Professor Behrooz A. Shirazi is the Huie-Rogers Chair Professor and the Director of the School of Electrical Engineering and Computer Science at Washington State University. Prior to joining WSU in 2005 he was on the faculty of Computer Science and Engineering at the University of Texas at Arlington and served as the department chair from 1999 to 2005. Dr. Shirazi has conducted research in the areas of pervasive computing, software tools, distributed real-time systems, and parallel and distributed systems over the past eighteen years. Dr. Shirazi is currently serving as the Editor-in-Chief for Special Issues for Pervasive and Mobile Computing (PMC) Journal and has served on the editorial boards of the IEEE Transactions on Computers and Journal of Parallel and Distributed Computing in the past. He is a co-founder of the IEEE International Conference on Pervasive Computing and Communications (PerCom). He has received numerous teaching and research awards and has served as an IEEE Distinguished Visitor (1993–96) as well as an ACM Lecturer (1993–97). He can be reached at shirazi@eecs.wsu.edu.

Michael Sthultz is the Associate Director of the Center for Cybermedia Research at the University of Nevada, Las Vegas. He received his undergraduate education at Claremont Men's College and the University of California, Berkeley. His M.S. in Computer Science was completed at UNLV. Mr. Sthultz has extensive industry experience in the areas of systems engineering, programming, network administration, management, and consulting. His most recent experience has been in post-secondary education at both private and public colleges.

Professor Jeff (Jianhui) Tian received a B.S. degree in Electrical Engineering from Xi'an Jiaotong University in 1982, an M.S. degree in Engineering Science from Harvard University in 1986, and a PhD degree in Computer Science from the University of Maryland in 1992. He worked for the IBM Software Solutions Toronto Laboratory between 1992 and 1995 as a software quality and process analyst. Since 1995, he has been with Southern Methodist University, Dallas, Texas, now as an Associate Professor of Computer Science and Engineering, with joint appointment at the Dept. of Engineering Management, Information and Systems. His current research interests include software testing, measurement, reliability, safety, complexity, and applications in commercial, web-based, telecommunication, and embedded software and systems. He is a member of IEEE, ACM, and ASQ Software Division. He can be reached at tian@engr.smu.edu.

Jacob Uecker is a Senior Network Engineer for Cox Communications in Las Vegas, NV and a Research Associate at the Center for Cybermedia Research at the University of Nevada, Las Vegas.

Preface

This volume is number 67 in the series *Advances in Computers* that began back in 1960. This is the longest continuously published series of books that chronicles the evolution of the computer industry. Each year three volumes are produced presenting approximately 20 chapters that describe the latest technology in the use of computers today. Volume 67, subtitled "Web Technology," presents 6 chapters that show the impact that the World Wide Web is having on our society today.

As I write this, I only returned from a 10,000 mile trip to Australia just two days ago. I can clearly remember my last trip to Australia in 1996, only 9 years ago. On that earlier trip I managed to make hotel reservations "on the Internet" for the first time. As a Computer Science faculty member for over 30 years, I had networking access via the original ARPAnet since 1979. While it was a valuable tool for accessing computer science computers, it was a mysterious "high technology" academic gadget for most of the 1980s. However, early in the 1990s you started to see strange symbols on television ads; things that began www.something.... Finally, in 1996 I was able to make a connection with hotels some 10,000 miles away—businesses that had no real need for research computer technology, only a marketing need to reach its customers. The Internet had arrived!

Looking back, it is amazing to see that change in only 9 years. The first web browser is only 15 years old. Today, a company would soon go out of business without web access. In the chapters that follow in this book, we try to cover many of the changes that this web technology has brought to our society, and anticipate what further changes may occur in the near future.

A current focus of interest in Web technology is in wireless devices. Cell phones have become ubiquitous and many have Web interfaces. Almost every laptop computer is now sold with a wireless interface. Connectivity to the Internet can occur at home, at work, and just about anywhere else—airports, coffee shops, libraries, etc. Given this complex structure where devices attach and remove themselves from the network frequently, how do you ensure the integrity of data needed by multiple devices. In Chapter 1, A.R. Hurson, Y. Jiao, and B.A. Shirazi in "Broadcasting a Means to Disseminate Public Data in a Wireless Environment—Issues and Solutions" explore this problem. "In the mobile computing environment, the characteristics of mobile devices and limitations of wireless communication technology pose challenges on broadcasting strategy as well as methods to retrieve data" write the authors. Their chapter reviews and addresses solutions to many of these challenges.

In Chapter 2, "Programming Models and Synchronization Techniques for Disconnected Business Applications" by A. Leff and J.T. Rayfield, the authors address a related problem brought on by the ubiquity of mobile devices. Many applications are now distributed over multiple sites, communicating via the Internet. How does one structure a program to effectively use this connectivity and still achieve a reliable implementation? The authors discuss several strategies for creating distributed business applications and argue that a connected programming model is appropriate even in a distributed environment.

Chapter 3, "Academic Electronic Journals: Past, Present, and Future" by A. Hovav and P. Gray concerns a topic of immense interest to most readers, the authors, and the publisher of these volumes—how is the publishing industry going to evolve? More and more technology is presented online. Several journals only distribute content electronically. Journals printed on paper may become an artifact of history. Electronic distribution is faster than paper and at lower cost to produce. But with these advantages are some problems. How will these electronic journals preserve quality? Keep high standards? Maintenance of archives? etc. These and other questions are the focus of this chapter.

With all of these new web applications of the first 3 chapters come some technological problems. For one, how do we know that the resulting web application is reliable? How do we test the program to ensure it works as required? These topics are the focus of Jeff Tian's and Li Ma's chapter "Web Testing for Reliability Improvement." They look at the various methods for testing programs and focus on those applicable for web applications. They address testing, defect analysis, and reliability improvement issues for the constantly evolving web as a whole by analyzing the dynamic web contents and other information sources.

With all of the advantages of the World Wide Web come problems. Any new technology brings with it those who seek to profit illegally from its use. Use of the Web has an economic value and there are those who either seek to steal some of that value or simply destroy the value that others have in the web. This brings up the entire area of web security. Many computers have credit card information and other personal information about their owners or passwords to various other machines. How do you protect that information from unauthorized access? In Chapter 5, M. Sthultz, J. Uecker, and H. Berghel discuss "Wireless Insecurities." What features have been built into wireless networks to prevent others from exploiting weaknesses in individual computers to prevent the unauthorized theft of valuable Web resources?

In Chapter 6, Dario Forte discusses "The State of the Art in Digital Forensics." When someone does succeed in breaking into a computer system and steal valuable information, can you figure out who did it and how? The owner of the system has to know what information has been compromised and the legal system needs a mechanism for proving that a theft did indeed occur and that a certain person committed it. What are the ways to provide this information? Using the Unix system as an example, the author describes many ways to detect the occurrence of such theft. He describes his own efforts with the IRItaly Project at the Università Statale di Milano in Crema, Italy.

The World Wide Web is continuing to evolve at an extremely rapid rate. I hope that you still find these chapters of use to you when they finally appear in print about a year after they were written. In order to produce these books, I have to stay about 3 years ahead of the technology. If you have any suggestions of topics for future chapters, or if you wish to contribute such a chapter, I can be reached at mvz@cs.umd.edu.

Marvin Zelkowitz
College Park, Maryland

Broadcasting a Means to Disseminate Public Data in a Wireless Environment— Issues and Solutions

A.R. HURSON, Y. JIAO

Department of Computer Science and Engineering
The Pennsylvania State University
University Park, PA 16802
USA

B.A. SHIRAZI

School of Electrical Engineering and Computer Science
Washington State University
Pullman, WA 99163
USA

Abstract

In today's heavily networked society, there is an increasing demand for fast and reliable access to information. It is believed that for many application domains, the information superhighway contains much of the needed information and is capable of delivering it at extremely high speeds. However, the information may not be available at the users' fingertips. In other words, we no longer need to question the availability of information; however, the information is not readily accessible. What needed are means to:

- Locate the relevant information intelligently, efficiently, and transparently;
- Extract, process, and integrate relevant information efficiently and securely; and
- Interpret the processed information intelligently and efficiently.

Within this infrastructure, two types of services are available to the user: on-demand base services and broadcast-based services. Private and shared data are usually subject of on-demand-based services, while public data can be most effectively disseminated using broadcasting.

ADVANCES IN COMPUTERS, VOL. 67
ISSN: 0065-2458/DOI 10.1016/S0065-2458(05)67001-5

1

In the mobile computing environment, the characteristics of mobile devices and limitations of wireless communication technology pose challenges on broadcasting strategy as well as methods to retrieve data. Major issues of concern include reducing power consumption, reducing access latency, and disseminating relevant data of interest to the public user. User profiling, monitoring the access patterns, application of indexing, broadcasting over parallel channels, data distribution and replication strategy, conflict resolution, and scheduling of data retrieval are solutions to these issues that have advanced in the literature.

This chapter is intended to review and analyze these solutions. Comprehensive simulation results to demonstrate the effectiveness of each solution based on performance metrics such as access time and power consumption are presented and analyzed.

1. Introduction

A mobile computing environment involves accessing information through a wireless network connection. The mobile unit may be stationary, in motion, and/or intermittently connected to a fixed (wired) network. The increasing development and spread of computer networks, and the extensive need for information sharing have created a considerable demand for cooperation among pre-existing, distributed, heterogeneous, and autonomous information sources. In addition, users have become more demanding in that they desire and sometimes even require access to information "anytime, anywhere." The growing diversity in the range of information that is accessible to a user at any given time and the rapidly expanding technology that makes available a wide breadth of devices, with different physical characteristics, have changed the traditional notion of timely and reliable access to global information in a distributed system. Growth and success of such an environment depends on two fundamental issues—efficient management of information systems and availability of reliable communications infrastructure.

Remote access to data is a rapidly expanding and it has become increasingly important aspect of computing. Remote access to data refers to both mobile nodes and fixed nodes accessing heterogeneous and autonomous data sources in an infrastructure that is identified by the following parameters:

- Low bandwidth;
- Frequent disconnection;
- High error rates;
- Limited processing resources; and
- Limited power sources.

Nevertheless, regardless of the access devices and connection medium, users require anytime, anywhere, fast, transparent, intelligent, secure, and cost efficient access to information repositories that are classified as:

(i) Private data, i.e., personal daily schedules, phone numbers, etc.
(ii) Public data, i.e., news, weather information, traffic information, flight information, etc.
(iii) Shared data, i.e., traditional databases, distributed, replicated, and/or fragmented across different geographic locations—a collection of processing nodes may contribute, cooperate, and complete with each other to maintain consistency and participate in distributed decision making operations.

The desire to support timely and reliable access to the information sources is not an entirely new concept. Traditional databases based on fixed clients and servers connected over a reliable network infrastructure have addressed the issues involved in accessing various types of information in the form of relational, object-oriented, distributed, federated, and multidatabase management systems. However, the concept of mobility, where a user accesses information through a remote connection with a portable device, has posed several challenges on traditional database management systems (DBMS). Within the scope of this infrastructure, two types of services are available to the user:

- On demand-based services; and
- Broadcast-based requests.

1.1   On Demand-Based Services

Private data and shared data are the subject of these services in which users obtain answers to requests through a two-way communication with the database server—the user request is pushed to the system, data sources are accessed, query operations are performed, partial results are collected and integrated, and generated information is communicated back to the user. This requires a suitable solution that addresses issues such as:

- Security and access control—methods to guarantee authorized access to the resources. This includes protocols for authentication, access control, inferential security, and integrity.
- Isolation—methods to deal with a degraded network connection. This should also include a means to work off-line if an intentional/unintentional disconnection has occurred. Furthermore, if the connection is too slow or unreliable to work fully on-line, the user may intentionally choose to work off-line due to bandwidth restrictions.
- Semantic heterogeneity—methods to handle differences in representation, format, structure, conflict, and meaning among information sources and hence to establish interoperability among different information sources. Techniques such

as the United Nations or the Bilateral Approach could be used to accomplish this task [56].

- Autonomy—methods to allow different information sources to join and depart the global information sharing environment at will. Autonomy comes in the form of design autonomy, communication autonomy, execution autonomy, and association autonomy.

- Query processing and query optimization—methods to efficiently partition a global query into sub-queries to allow parallel execution.

- Transaction processing and concurrency control—methods to allow simultaneous execution of independent transactions and interleaving interrelated transactions in the face of both global and local conflicts.

- Data integration—methods to fuse partial results in order to draw global result. This is particularly important because of the limited resources and capabilities of mobile devices. With a very large amount of information available, the entire set of data cannot be kept locally.

- Browsing—methods to allow the user to search and look at the available information in an efficient manner without any information processing. This is needed due to an enormous amount of information available to the user.

- Distribution and location transparency—methods that allow efficient heterogeneous remote access to data sources while hiding the network topology and the placement of the data. This is particularly important for wireless devices, which have considerable communication cost. In addition, a high degree of mobility argues for a high degree of heterogeneity—a mobile user can potentially access a much wider variety of systems and data sources.

- Limited resources—methods to accommodate computing devices with limited capabilities. This includes memory, storage, display, and power.

Further discussion about these issues and their solutions is beyond the scope of this chapter, however, research has extensively studied the aforementioned issues and their solutions either within the scope of heterogeneous distributed systems [10,11] or mobile applications [22,25,26,39,42,44,46,47,57,58].

1.2   Broadcast-Based Services

Many applications are directed towards public information that are characterized by (i) the massive number of users, (ii) the similarity and simplicity in the requests solicited by the users, and (iii) the fact that data is modified by a few. The reduced bandwidth attributed to the wireless environment places limitations on the rate and amount of communication. Broadcasting is a potential solution to this limitation. In broadcasting, information is generated and broadcast to all users on the air channels. Mobile users are capable of searching the air channels and pulling their required information. The main advantage of broadcasting is due to the fact that it scales up as the number of users increases, eliminating the need to multiplex the bandwidth among users accessing the air channel. In addition, broadcast channel can be considered as an additional storage available over the air for the mobile clients. Finally, it is shown that pulling information from the air channel consumes less power than pushing information to the air channel. Broadcasting is an attractive solution, because of the limited storage, processing capability, and power sources of the mobile unit. Within the scope of broadcasting one needs to address three issues:

- Broadcast contents;
- Network latency; and
- Power consumption of the mobile unit.

For broadcasting applications, in general, the information to be broadcast is of multimedia or hypertext nature originated from an information source(s) governed by multiple, possibly heterogeneous, database management systems. The object-oriented paradigm has proven to be a suitable methodology for modeling multimedia databases [6,23,32,43]. In addition, in a distributed environment, object-oriented methodology provides a systematic mechanism to model the association and translation of the data from multiple sites [10,11,33]. Therefore, in this chapter, we model the information units on the air channel(s) as objects. Within the scope of object-oriented database systems, object clustering has proven to be an effective means of reducing response times [7,13,17,19,20,45]. The employment of broadcasting in the mobile-computing environment motivates the need to study the proper organization of objects along the air channel(s). Due to the natural differences between the serial air channel and the random-access disk, one has to look at different and efficient methodologies to organize and cluster objects on the air channels in order to reduce the response time. In addition, the network latency (response time) is the major source of power consumption at the mobile unit [35–38,65]. The reduction in response time translates into the reduced amount of time a mobile unit spends accessing the channel(s) and thus, it has its impact on conserving energy at the mobile unit. It is the goal of this chapter to address issues pertinent to broadcasting in a mobile environment.

Section 2 briefly addresses the background material on mobile systems. Technological limitations are outlined and their effects on the global information sharing environment are discussed. Issues such as data selection methodologies, semantic

data items on single and parallel channel(s), application of index-
d parallel channel(s), data replication, data distribution, conflict, and
ata accesses are enumerated and analyzed in Section 3. Solutions to
h respect to the

tency;

ncy; and

agement

nd analyzed in Sections 4–8. Finally, Section 9 concludes the chapter
me future research directions.

2.   Mobile Computing

omputing environment is based on wireless communication that al-
access information anywhere at anytime without any direct physical
ork. The wireless network (Fig. 1) is composed of:

of network servers enhanced with wireless transceivers—mobile sup-
s (MSS)—scattered along a geographical area; and

number of mobile hosts (MHs) free to move at will.

vides a link between the wireless network and the wired network.
n a MSS and the wired network could be either wireless (shown as
wire based. The area covered by the individual transceiver is referred
size of the area covered by each cell varies widely, depending on the
g used.
latively small, light weight, and portable. It is designed to preserve
y. Most of the time, the MH relies on temporary power sources such
s main power source. To save energy, the MH is designed to operate
rational modes (i.e., active doze, sleep, nap) that consume different

.1   Wireless Communication Technology

munication is accomplished via modulating radio waves or pulsing

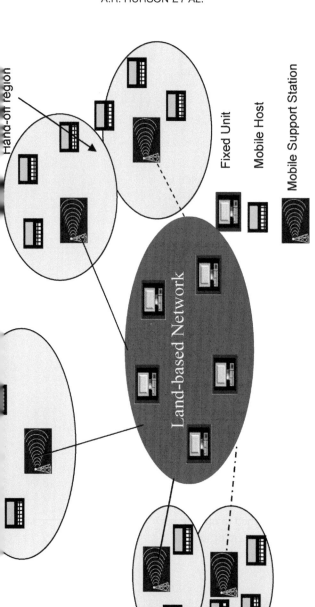

FIG. 1. Architecture of the mobile computing environment.

2.2   Characteristics of the Mobile Environment

Mainly, three characteristics distinguish the mobile environment; namely, wireless medium, mobility, and portability. Table I summarizes the characteristics of the mobile computing environment and some of the resulting challenges.

2.2.1   Wireless Medium

Whether the communication is based on the satellite link that spans one third of the earth or a wireless LAN within a building, the common ground among all wireless systems is the fact that communication is done via the air (and not via cables). This fact changes a major underlying assumption that was the basis for conventional distributed algorithms. The physical layer of the connection is no longer the reliable coaxial or optic cable that has been assumed all along. Communication over the air is identified by frequent disconnections, low data-rate, high cost, and lack of security [4,5,21,36–38,65].

TABLE I
CHARACTERISTICS OF MOBILE ENVIRONMENT AND RESULTING ISSUES

Mobile environment characteristics	Resulting issues
Wireless connection	Frequent disconnection
	Communication channel
	High cost
	Low bandwidth
	Network measurement
	Low data rate
	High error rate
	Security (eavesdropping)
Mobility	Frequent disconnection
	Motion management
	Location-dependent data
	Heterogeneous networks
	Interfacing
	Data rate variability
	Security (privacy)
Portability	Security (vandalism)
	Limited resources
	Limited energy source
	User interface

2.2.2 Mobility

Mobility is the second characteristic that distinguishes the mobile environment and poses challenges beyond the scope of traditional environment. This is due to the fact that processing units in the mobile environment can be used at multiple locations and in transition between these locations. Mobility results in several issues including disconnections due to hand-off processes, motion management, location dependent information, heterogeneous and fragmented network, security, and privacy.

2.2.3 Portability

There are many variations of portable computer systems with different physical characteristics and capabilities. However, all these portable units share many common features such as limited memory, processing power, user interface, and power source. The ideal goal would be to develop a device that is compact, durable, and light that consumes a minimum amount of power.

3. Broadcasting Issues

In a mobile computing environment, desire to have "timely and reliable" access to information is compromised by the power consumption and network latency. The necessity of minimizing power consumption and network latency lies in the limitation of current technology—the expected increase of the capacity of batteries is at much lower rate than the increase of the chip density [35,36]. The hardware of the mobile units has been designed to overcome this limitation by operating in various operational modes such as active, doze, sleep, nap, etc., to conserve energy. A mobile unit can be in active mode (maximum power consumption) while it is searching or accessing data objects; otherwise, it can be in doze mode (reduced power consumption) when the unit is not performing any computation.

Along with the architectural and hardware enhancements, efficient power management and energy aware algorithms can be devised to (i) organize and cluster related data entities on broadcast channel(s) and (ii) schedule data retrieval from broadcast channel(s). It is the major theme of this chapter to articulate some of these efforts.

The cost of communication is normally asymmetric—sending information requires, in general, 2–10 times more energy than receiving the information. As a result, for public information, popular information can be generated and disseminated over the air channel. The mobile user looking for certain information can tune to the broadcast channel(s) and access the desired information from the air in an orderly manner. This scenario, however, brings out three issues:

- How to determine the data contents of the broadcast channel(s). This is of important due to several factors as such, network bandwidth and scalability.

- The mobile unit should not waste its energy in constantly monitoring the air channel(s) to search for information—techniques should be developed to allow the mobile user to remain in low operational power mode while waiting for the desired information on the broadcast channel(s). This implies a disciplined order to organize information on the air channel(s) and to hint the availability of the desired data element. If the data element is available, the mobile unit will be instructed to the exact location of the data element on the broadcast.

- An attempt should be made to minimize the response time either by shortening the broadcast length and/or the number of passes over the air channels.

Broadcasting is an elegant solution to the limitations of wireless environment. Within the constraint of a limited bandwidth, the main advantage of broadcasting is the fact that it scales as the number of users increases, and thus eliminates the need to divide or multiplex the bandwidth among the users accessing the air channel(s). Furthermore, since the information on the air could be considered "storage on the air," broadcasting can be considered as a solution to compensate for the limited resources (storage) at the mobile unit.

Broadcasting information is not a new concept: Whether through a guided or unguided medium, the general concept is based on the encoding and transmission of the desired signal (analog or digital) on a certain frequency—the information is supplied by one source and read by multiple receivers. In general, data can be broadcast either on one or several channels. A broadcast is performed in a cyclic manner. The MH can only pull the information from the broadcast, whereas the database server is the only entity that can push information to the broadcast. Since dependencies can exist among the data items within the broadcast, and since data items might be replicated within a broadcast, it is assumed that updates of data are only reflected at the following cycle. This constraint enforces the integrity among the data elements within a broadcast.

3.1 Broadcast Contents

The literature has addressed several methods to determine and generate data contents on the broadcast channel(s). Some methods are classified as push-based techniques, where the users are passive listeners and the server assumes a priori client access patterns that does not change during the course of broadcast—i.e., strict static client access patterns. Based on this assumption, the server repeatedly broadcast a set of selected data items. This allows scalability and simplicity at the expense of limitation on the application domain. Alternatively, the dynamic and adaptive methods (pull-based methods) assume the clients' access patterns are either un-known in advance or changes relatively frequently during the course of broadcast. Finally, hybrid schemes assume a backchannel for users to explicitly request data items that are not included in the standard broadcast cycle. As a result, the push mode and on-demand data are interleaved on a broadcast cycle. As noted in Section 1.1, on-demand-based methods (pull-based methods) are beyond the scope of this work. Within the scope of push-based methods and hybrid methods, parameters such as the data type and data size can be used to further distinguish different solutions.

3.1.1   Push-Based Schemes

3.1.1.1   *Flat Broadcast.*   Flat broadcasting of data is the most basic way to distribute public data. All data within a database is statically and sequentially broadcast to the users of the network—server broadcasts the union of the data of interest to a user population. The users retrieve data from the air channels when it is available. There are no requests made by the users to the server database, and hence, data is made available to the users through the push method. Consequently, the wait time for data is relatively long and proportional to the half of the broadcast length on the average—data is not scheduled on the broadcast. However, flat broadcast does ensure that all users will get the data they require eventually as all data has equal priority of being broadcast [1].

3.1.1.2   *Broadcast Disks.*   Broadcast disks are similar to flat broadcast in that they broadcast all of the information in the database [2,12,64]. Broadcast disks improve upon flat broadcasting by attempting to reduce the waiting time for retrieving popular data. Instead of using one spinning disk to broadcast all of the data, broadcast disks distribute data among multiple disks with varying sizes and spinning speeds. As a result, pages available on faster spinning disks get mapped more frequently than those available on slower disks. Figure 2 illustrates this concept. Assume the list of ten pages to be broadcast (Fig. 2(a)). Further assume that these pages are partitioned and distributed among three disks where $disk_1$ is twice faster than $disk_2$, and $disk_2$ is twice faster than $disk_3$ (Fig. 2(b)). Figure 2(c) shows the allocation of the aforementioned database pages on a broadcast channel. Note that the broadcast cycle now is composed of smaller chunks (minor cycle).

The disks create a "memory hierarchy" for the data items. Data items move up and down in the memory hierarchy based on their frequency of access. The effect of varying the disk spinning speeds and number of disks used on the response time at the MHs was investigated and a threshold, above which increasing the number of faster disks degraded the overall response time, was found.

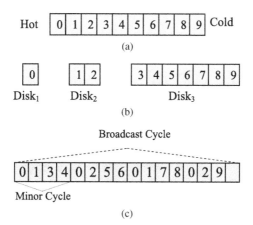

FIG. 2. Broadcast organization in *Broadcast Disks*. (a) Data base pages. (b) Distribution of data base pages. (c) Distribution of data base pages.

Broadcast disks solve some very basic problems in the broadcasting of public data but they have several limitations. Like flat broadcasting, they are intended to broadcast all of the data items in the database. This is impractical, unrealistic, and unnecessary. Since in reality, a single public data could satisfy a large number of clients and all data items in a database are not of interest to the clients at the same time. In addition, they assume the same granularity for the data items on air channel and disk pages—if a data item is to be broadcast more frequently (replicated), then the entire page has to be replicated. Moreover, due to the plain structural nature of the page-based environment, the research looked at the pages as abstract entities and was not meant to consider the contents of the pages (data and its semantics) as a means to order the pages. In object-oriented systems, directed semantics among objects greatly influence the method in which objects are retrieved, and thus, have their direct impact on the ordering of these objects/pages. In addition, the replication should be performed at the object-level granularity.

3.1.1.3 Hierarchical Broadcast.

The concept of the broadcast disks discussed in Section 3.1.2 was extended by Peng and Chen [54] to parallel broadcast channels with different speeds. In addition, they used the access frequency of a data item as a means to allocate the data item on a broadcast channel—hot data items are allocated to the faster channel. Given a set of data items with different access frequencies and several broadcast channels of different speed, the so called Variant–Fanout with the constraint K (VF^K) heuristically allocates data items to different channels in order to minimize the average expected delay of all data items. Fig-

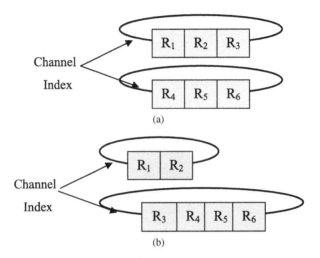

FIG. 3. Two allocation schemes. (a) Flat broadcast allocation. (b) Hierarchical broadcast allocation.

ure 3 is intended to distinguish this scheme from the flat broadcast allocation scheme discussed in Section 3.1.1. Assume six data items to be allocated to two broadcast channels. Figure 3(a) shows the flat broadcast allocation of the data items of two broadcast channels of the same speed. Alternatively, Fig. 3(b) depicts the allocation of the aforementioned data items on two broadcast channels where the first channel is twice faster than the second one.

3.1.1.4 *Square-Root Based Allocation.*   Acharya et al. [1] made an observation that in a broadcasting scenario minimum overall mean access time is achieved when the instances of hot data items are equally spaced. Based on this observation, Vaida and Hameed [62] proposed the so called square-root based allocation algorithm that based on the demand probability (access frequency), the length of the data item, and location of the broadcast data items in the past, determines what data item from the data base should be broadcast next. Assume M, p_i, and l_i, respectively stand for the number of the data items in the data base, demand probability of item i, and the length of the item i. Furthermore, let R_i stand for the time at which an instance of item i was most recently appeared on the broadcast. Then

$$\text{MAX}(G_i) = \left((Q - R_i)^2 * p_i\right)/l_i, \quad 1 \leqslant i \leqslant M,$$

determines the next data item to be broadcast (Q is the present time).

Assume the database is composed of three data items with (p_1, l_1), (p_2, l_2), and (p_3, l_3) of $(1/2, 1)$, $(3/8, 2)$, and $(1/8, 4)$. Figure 4 depicts the broadcast schedule

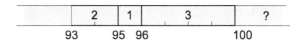

FIG. 4. A broadcast sequence.

up to the present time, i.e., 100. Applying the aforementioned equation will result in $G_1 = 12.5$, $G_2 = 9.18$, and $G_3 = .5$. As a result, item 1 is the next item to be broadcast.

Finally, the scope of this allocation algorithm has also been extended to the domain of the multiple broadcast channels.

3.1.2 Hybrid-Based Schemes

Studies reported in [8,52] have shown that push based model and pull-based model have complementary properties. In general, two conditions support a push-based model: (i) strict coherency requirements and/or (ii) the communication bottleneck. On the other hand, a pull-based model is suited in an environment where: (i) client has relaxed coherency requirements, (ii) the servers are heavily loaded, or (iii) fault tolerance is important. This study motivates the hybrid data dissemination, where the push and pull techniques for data dissemination are mixed. The users in the network play a more active role in deciding which data to be broadcast. The pushed data items are still the main means to disseminate public data. However, with the integration of an independent back channel, clients can directly query the server database and pull the requested data from the air channel. It should be noted that, in this class of data dissemination methods, unlike flat broadcasting and broadcast disks, all of the data base contents are not broadcast during a broadcast cycle.

The hybrid broadcasting of data items was originally proposed and employed in the Boston Community Information System [24]—broadcast and interactive communication to provide up-to-the-minute information to an entire metropolitan area. The experiment showed that users valued both components of the hybrid organization. Wong and Dykeman [63] also proposed hybrid teletext–videotex platform for both periodically pushed and upon-request pulled data items with some ad hoc partition of the data into two groups. Acharya et al. [3] proposed a back channel to allow the clients to explicitly request data items on the broadcast channel.

3.1.2.1 Adaptive Data Broadcast. This work was motivated by two issues; the dynamic nature of the clients' needs and requests and the passive nature of the clients receiving the broadcast. Similar to the concept of cache memories that is adaptive to the changing workload, the push-pull based broadcast model [60]

dynamically determines the state of the database items and adapts the broadcast contents by monitoring the broadcast misses. As a result, the "hot" data items are being pushed and the pull-based data items are being unicast based on individual requests. Similar to the states of water, the database items are classified into three groups: Vapor, Liquid, and Frigid. Vapor represents the class of the data items that are hot and therefore, they are being broadcast. However, due to the passive nature of the clients, the server does not receive any feedback regarding these data items and hence, gradually they will cool down and turn into liquid. Liquid represents the class of data items that are directly requested by the clients and as a result they are being unicast. These data are either being requested more and more and after passing a threshold level become hot, or they are not going to be requested and hence freeze. Data in frigid state either stay in that state or migrate to the liquid state.

3.1.2.2 Adaptive Push-Pull.
Bhide et al. [8] proposed a scheme that, based on parameters such as the network condition, scalability, degree of coherency, and resiliency to failure, intelligently and adaptively determines the degree of push and pull data that are disseminated.

A Time-to-Refresh (TTR) value is assigned and calculated by the proxy for each cached data item. The TTR determines the next time that the proxy should poll the server in order to refresh the cache contents. The TTR is computed based on the rate of changes of data and the degree of coherency required by the client. A smaller TTR shows a rapidly changing data and/or strict coherency requirement. A larger TTR, on the other hand, represent infrequent changes and/or relaxed coherency requirement. Two algorithms have been proposed, namely Push-and-Pull (PaP) and Push-or-pull (PoP).

In PaP, the proxy is responsible to pull changes to the data, and the server is allowed to push additional updates undetected by the proxy. In PoP, the server is allowed to adaptively choose between push and pull-based dissemination schemes.

3.1.2.3 Dynamic Leveling.
Dynamic leveling scheme [55] is a natural extension of the hierarchical broadcast model discussed in Section 3.1.1.3. Recall that the hierarchical model allocates frequently accessed data items on faster broadcast channels. However, the access frequency is dynamic and time dependent. The proposed dynamic leveling algorithm adjusts data items among the broadcast channels when the access frequency changes. Experimental results have shown greater effectiveness of the dynamic leveling algorithm relative to the VF^K algorithm, in term of execution time when the database size and the number of broadcast channels increase.

The hybrid method also has several drawbacks. Querying the database to pull data interrupts the server and consumes bandwidth and power that could otherwise be used for pushing data on the broadcast. As a result, one can conclude that the backchannel should not be used excessively.

3.2   Indexing Objects on the Broadcast Channel

Retrieving information from the air channel has two requirements:

- Minimizing the overall response time at the mobile unit; and
- Minimizing the amount of power consumed in the retrieval process at the mobile unit.

The concept of index has been extensively studied and applied in traditional file and database systems. It is a function that takes a key value and provides an address referring to the location of the associated data. Its main advantage lies in the fact that it eliminates the need for an exhaustive search through the pages of data on the storage medium. B-trees, B+-trees, and hash tables are some of the most common index structures that have been used in practice. An index is also used as a tool to facilitate the query optimization. Similarly, within the scope of broadcasting, an index can be used to point to the location or possible availability of a data item on the broadcast and allowing the mobile unit to predict the arrival time of the data item requested. This enables the mobile unit to switch its operational mode into an energy-saving mode and minimize energy consumption. It should be noted that the advantages of indexing comes at the expense of computational overhead and increased length of the broadcast, which increases the response time.

3.2.1   Signature-Based Indexing

The basic idea behind the application and use of signatures in a broadcast channel is to add a control part to the contents of an information frame [27–30,60]—a hash function is applied to the contents of the information frame to generating a bit vector that is superimposed on the data frame. As a result, a signature partially reflects the data content of a frame. In short, this technique creates a set of signatures for data frames on a broadcast and interleaves them with their associated data frame. Different allocations of signatures on a broadcast channel have been studied, including: *single signature*, *integrated signature*, and *multi-level signature* [28–30].

In the single signature scheme, the signature frame is broadcast before the corresponding data frame. In the integrated signature scheme, a signature is constructed for a group of consecutive frames called a frame group. The multi-level signature scheme is a combination of the simple and integrated signature methods in which the upper level signatures are integrated signatures and the lower level signatures are simple signatures [29].

During the retrieval process, a query is resolved by generating a signature based on the user's request. The query signature is then compared against the signatures of the data frames in the broadcast. A successful match indicates a potential hit. Consequently, the content of the corresponding information frame is checked against the query to verify that it corresponds to the user's demands. If the data of the frame corresponds to the user's request, the data is recovered; otherwise, the corresponding information frame is ignored. This reduces the access time and the tune-in time.

As part of the studies done on signature-based indexing schemes, the three afore-mentioned signature-based schemes have been analyzed with respect to each other using the access time and tune-in time as the performance metrics [28–30]. The results showed that, with fixed signature size, the multi-level scheme has the best tune-in time performance at the expense of a longer access time. The integrated scheme, on the other hand, has the best average access time, but its tune-in time depends on the similarity among the information frames. And finally, the simple scheme has an adequate access time and tune-in time. This study concluded that in comparison to broadcasting without using indexing, all three signature-based schemes improved tune-in time performance significantly with a reasonable access time overhead.

3.2.2 Tree-Based Indexing

An index is a meta data representing one or several data attributes pointing to the location of data collection (i.e., information frames) sharing the same common attribute value(s). This auxiliary information is usually organized as a tree in which the lowest level of the tree points to the location of the information frames on the broadcast channel. With this concept in mind, the frames on the broadcast are of two kinds: data frames and index frames.

A broadcast channel is a sequential medium and hence, to reduce the mobile unit active and tune-in time, and consequently to reduce the power consumption, the index frames are usually replicated and interleaved with the data frames. Otherwise, the request would have to wait for the beginning of the next broadcast cycle—an increase in the query response time. Two index replication schemes (namely, *distributed indexing* and $(1, m)$[1] *indexing*) have been studied [38]. In distributed indexing, the index is partitioned and interleaved in the broadcast cycle. Each part of the index in the broadcast is followed by its corresponding data frame(s). In $(1, m)$ indexing, the entire index is interleaved m times during the broadcast cycle—the whole index is broadcast before every $1/m$ fraction of the cycle. A series of analyses for both methods were carried out and compared with the scenarios that provided the best

---

[1] m represents the number of times the index is replicated during one broadcast cycle.

case for tune-in time and response time. It was concluded that, in general, the $(1, m)$ indexing scheme reduces power consumption at the expense of an increase in the response time; and the distributed indexing scheme, relative to the $(1, m)$ indexing scheme, increases the response time at a much lower rate at the expense of higher power consumption.

Access frequencies of the data items have been used to generate an index tree. Shivakumar and Venkatasubramanian [59] proposed application of tree-based indexing using Huffman-encoding scheme that is sensitive to data access patterns. The work proposed in [18] constructs an index tree based on the data access skew. To reduce the number of index probes, this work considered two cases: fixed index fan-out and variant index fan-outs. It was shown that the cost of index probes can be minimized if imbalanced index tree based on skewed data access is employed. This reduces the number of index probes for hot data items at the expense of more index probe for less frequently accessed data items (cold data items).

To conclude, the tree-based indexing schemes are more suitable for application domains where information is accessed from the broadcast channel randomly, and the signature-based indexing schemes are more suitable in retrieving sequentially structured data elements [29,30]. In addition, tree-based indexing schemes have shown superiority over the signature-based indexing schemes when the user request is directed towards interrelated objects clustered on the broadcast channel(s). Furthermore, tree-based indexing schemes relative to signature-based indexing schemes are more suitable in reducing the overall power consumption. This is due to the fact that a tree-based indexing provides global information regarding the physical location of the data frames on the broadcast channel. On the other hand, signature-based indexing schemes are more effective in retrieving data frames based on multiple attributes.

3.3   Single Broadcast Channel Organization

Organization of data objects as a means of reducing access latency has been the subject of intensive research in the past. Whether the physical storage medium is a flat memory or a disk rack structure, an appropriate data placement algorithm should attempt to detect data locality and cluster related data close to one another. The objects in an object-oriented paradigm are normally associated with one another through semantic links—inheritance, aggregation, or association. An object-clustering algorithm maps a complex object into a linear sequence of objects along these semantic links. A complex object can be expressed as a hierarchy or a directed acyclic graph (DAG) in which objects are represented as the vertexes (or nodes) and edges (or links) are the relationships among these objects. Such clustering can improve the response time by an order of magnitude [7,13,19].

Banerjee et al. [7] suggested three types of clustering sequences in a CAD object-oriented database—*depth first*, *breadth first*, and *children-depth-first*. Chang and Katz [13] developed a clustering algorithm for objects with multiple relationships and different access frequencies among objects. Based on the notion provided by [13], Cheng and Hurson [19] analyzed the clustering technique by studying the effect of object updating when tuning the disk page *read/write* ratio. A cost estimation of the gain achieved by a dynamic re-clustering scheme was investigated. It was concluded that, in general, as the read/write ratio increases, re-clustering should be performed more frequently. Inspired by Kruskal's minimum-cost spanning tree algorithm, the work was enhanced by proposing a level clustering algorithm. The algorithm takes a weighted DAG as its input, and provides a level-clustering sequence as its output based on the degree of connectivity among the objects— objects related through stronger semantic links (higher weights on the edges) are clustered closer to one another. Chehadeh et al. [17] investigated object clustering in a parallel disk environment. Finally, Lim et al. [45] studied the employment of the clustering scheme of Cheng and Hurson [19] in a distributed environment.

Figure 5 depicts a weighted DAG and the resulting clustering sequences achieved when different clustering techniques are applied. It should be noted that the techniques proposed in [7] are only applicable to non-weighted DAG and that the techniques proposed in [17,19] generate the same clustering sequence.

Similar concept can be adapted to organize information on the air channel. The object organization on an air channel has to meet the following three criteria [14,16]:

- *Linear ordering*: The air channel is a one-dimensional sequential access structure. This fact requires that the linear object ordering. In a DAG representation of a complex object, an edge between two nodes could signify an access pattern among the two nodes; retrieving the object represented by the first node could trigger the retrieval of the second object. Therefore, if an edge exists from object a to object b, then to achieve minimum delays between the retrieval of objects, a has to appear before b. The *linearity* property is defined as: if an edge exists between two objects o_1 and o_2 and in the direction $o_1 \rightarrow o_2$, then o_1 should be placed prior to o_2.

- *Minimum linear distance between related objects*: Reducing the distance among interrelated objects along the broadcast reduces the response time and power consumption.

- *More availability for popular objects*: Considering the sequential access pattern of the broadcast channel, providing more availability for popular objects can be achieved by simply replicating such objects.

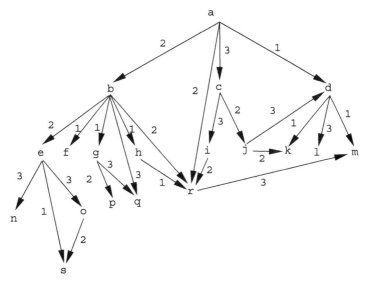

Clustering Method	Resulting Sequence
Depth First	abensofgpqhrmcijdkl
Breadth First	abrcdefgqhijklmnsop
Children-Depth First	abrcdefgqhmnsopijkl
Level Clustering	acibgqprmenosjdlkfh

FIG. 5. Various clustering of a sample graph.

Figure 6 depicts a directed graph and multiple linear sequences that satisfy the linear ordering property. The individual middle columns represent the cost of delays between every two objects connected via an edge. For the sake of simplicity and without loss of generality, an *object* unit is used as a unit of measurement. Furthermore, it is assumed that all objects are of equal size. The cost associated with an edge between a pair of objects is calculated by counting the number of objects that separate these two objects in the linear sequence. For example, in the **abfgchdeij** sequence objects *a* and *d* are separated by the sequence *bfgch* and thus have a cost of 6. The right-most column represents the total cost associated with each individual linear sequence. An optimal sequence is the linear sequence with the minimum total sum. In a query where multiple related objects are retrieved, a minimum average linear distance translates into smaller average response time. In this example, the optimum linear sequence achieves a total sum of 26.

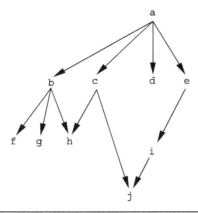

	Linear					Individual Costs							Total
	Sequence	ab	ac	ad	ae	bf	bg	bh	ch	cj	ei	ij	Cost
1	abfgchdeij	1	4	6	7	1	2	4	1	5	1	1	33
2	abfgcheijd	1	4	9	6	1	2	4	1	4	1	1	34
3	abcdefghij	1	2	3	4	4	5	6	5	7	4	1	42
4	abgfeichjd	1	6	9	4	2	1	6	1	2	1	3	36
5	acdeijbhgf	6	1	2	3	3	2	1	6	4	1	1	30
6	adeicjbhgf	6	4	1	2	3	2	1	3	1	1	2	26
7	adecbihgfj	4	3	1	2	4	3	2	3	6	3	4	35
8	adecbhgfij	4	3	1	2	3	2	1	2	6	6	1	31
9	adecijbhgf	6	3	1	2	3	2	1	4	2	2	1	27
10	adbfgcheij	2	5	1	7	1	2	4	1	4	1	1	29
11	adceijbhgf	6	2	1	3	3	2	1	5	3	1	1	28
12	aeidcjbhgf	6	4	3	1	3	2	1	3	1	1	3	28
13	aedcbihgfj	4	3	2	1	4	3	2	3	6	4	4	36
14	aedcijbhgf	6	3	2	1	3	2	1	4	2	3	1	28

FIG. 6. A graph, its linear sequences, and associated retrieval costs.

One method in obtaining an optimal linear sequence is to enumerate and calculate all possible linear sequences with their associated costs and then choose the sequence with the minimum cost. Naturally, such a solution, though simple, is computationally impractical. Hence, in practice heuristic rules are used to generate a linear sequence with a reasonable cost.

The average response time is a function of the broadcast length—reducing the broadcast length could also reduce the response time. The broadcast length can be reduced if objects are broadcast along parallel air channels. To follow our clustering policy the objects from a weighted DAG are assigned to multiple channels in such a fashion that (i) dependency implied by the edges are preserved, (ii) the overall broadcast time (load balancing), and (iii) clustering related objects close to one another. This problem can be mapped to the static task scheduling in a multiprocessor environment [31].

3.4   Parallel Broadcast Channel Organization

A static scheduling protocol within a multiprocessor environment attempts to find the minimum time in which n dependent tasks can be completed on m PEs. An optimal solution to such a problem is proven to be *NP* hard. However, heuristic rules can be employed to find sub-optimal solutions. Similar techniques can be developed to assign interrelated objects closely over parallel channels.

As one could conclude, distribution of objects over the broadcast parallel air channels reduces the broadcast length and hence could reduce the average access time. In addition, shorter access time could translate into lower power consumption. However, application of parallel channels brings the issue of access conflicts between requested objects that are distributed among different channels. Access conflicts require multiple passes over the broadcast channels and this has adverse impact on the response time and power consumption.

3.5   Access Conflict

Definition 1. A K-object request is an application request intended to retrieve K objects from a broadcast.

Without loss of generality, we assume that each channel has the same number of pages (frames) of equal length and each object resides on only a single page. Consequently, a parallel broadcast can be viewed as a two-dimensional array $N \times M$, where N is the number of pages per broadcast, and M is the number of channels. In this grid, K objects $(0 \leqslant K \leqslant MN)$ are randomly distributed throughout the MN positions of the grid. The mobile unit can only tune into one channel at a time and can switch channels with time and power penalties. Based on the common page size and the network speed, the time required to switch from one channel to another is equivalent to the time it takes for one page to pass in the broadcast. Thus, it is impossible for the mobile unit to retrieve both the ith page on channel A and $(i+1)$th page on channel B (where $A \neq B$).

Definition 2. Two objects are defined to be in conflict if it is impossible to retrieve both objects on the same broadcast.

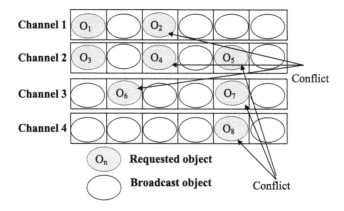

FIG. 7. A parallel broadcast of 4 channels with eight requested objects.

The access latency is directly dependent on the number passes over the broadcast channels. One method of calculating the number of required passes over the broadcast channels is to analyze the conflicts between objects. For any particular object, all objects in the same or succeeding page (column) and on a different row (channel) will be in conflict. Thus, for any specific page (object) in the grid, there are $(2M-2)$ conflicting pages (objects) in the broadcast except the last column (Fig. 7 depicts a request for eight objects from 4 parallel broadcast channels).

3.6 Access Patterns

The conflicts affect both the response time and power consumption. To reduce the impact of conflicts, retrieval procedures should be enhanced by a scheduling protocol that allows orderly retrieval of the requested objects during each broadcast cycle. One could define a set of heuristics as follows to achieve this goal:

- *Eliminate the number of conflicts.*
- *Retrieve the maximum number of objects.*
- *Minimize the number of channel switches.*

As can be noted, the aforementioned set of heuristics sacrifices the number of channel switches, hence power consumption, for reduced access latency. However, there is always a trade off between the access time and power consumption. Therefore, it would be interesting to investigate the effect of the reordered heuristic rules on the power consumption and access latency.

3.6.1 Generation of Access Patterns—A Bottom Up Retrieval Approach

The scheduling algorithm generates an *access forest*—a collection of trees (*access trees*), where each *access tree* represents all possible access patterns during a broadcast cycle [48,49]. An *access tree* is composed of two elements: nodes and arcs.

- *Node*: A node represents a requested object. Nodes are labeled to indicate their conflict status: mnemonically, "C_1" represents if the object is in conflict with another object(s) in the broadcast; and "C_0" indicates the lack of conflict. Each access tree in the access forest has a different node as a root—the root is the first accessible requested object on a broadcast cycle. This simply implies that an access forest can have at most n trees where n is the number of broadcast channels.

- *Arcs*: The arcs of the trees are weighted arcs. A weight denotes whether or not channel switching is required in order to retrieve the next scheduled object in the access pattern. A branch in a tree represents a possible access pattern of objects during a broadcast cycle with no conflicts. Starting from the root, the total number of branches in the tree represents all possible access patterns during a broadcast cycle.

Using the access forest, all possible non-conflicting weighted access patterns are generated and ranked based on their weights. A suitable access pattern for each broadcast cycle is the one that retrieves the maximum number of object with minimum number of channel switches. Figure 7 is used as a sample example to detail the generation of the access patterns for each broadcast cycle:

(1) *Search*: Based on the user's query, this step determines the offset and the channel number of the requested objects on the broadcast channels.

(2) *Generation of the access forest*: For each broadcast channel, search for the requested object with the smallest offset (these objects represent the roots of access tree). For the example, the objects with the smallest offsets are O_1, O_3, O_6 and O_8.

(3) *Root assignment*: For each channel with at least one object requested, generate a tree with root node as determined in step 2. The roots are temporarily tagged as "C_0."

(4) *Child assignment*: For each root, and relative to its position on the air channel, determine the closest non-conflicting objects on each channel. With respect to an object $O_{i,x}$ at location X on air channel i ($1 \leqslant i \leqslant n$) the closest non-conflicting object is either the object $O_{i,x+1}$ or the object $O_{j,x+2}$, $j \neq i$. If the child is in the same broadcast channel as the root, the arc is

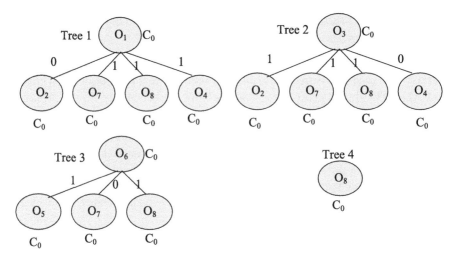

FIG. 8. Children of each root.

weighted as "0;" otherwise, it is weighted as "1." Each added node is temporarily tagged as "C_0." Figure 8 shows a snap shot of the example after this step.

(5) *Root label update*: Once the whole set of requested objects is analyzed and the access forest is generated, the conflict labels of the nodes of each tree are updated. This process starts with the root of each tree. If a root is in conflict with any other root(s), a label of "C_1" is assigned to all the roots involved in the conflict. Otherwise the preset value of "C_0" is maintained.

(6) *Node label update*: Step 5 will be applied to the nodes in the same level of each access tree in the access forest. As in step 5, a value of "C_1" is assigned to the nodes in conflict.

(7) *Sequence selection*: The generation of the access forest then allows the selection of the suitable access patterns in an attempt to reduce the network latency and power consumption. A suitable access pattern is equivalent to the selection of a tree branch that

- Has the most conflicts with other branches;
- Allows more objects to be pulled off the air channels; and
- Requires the least number of channel switches.

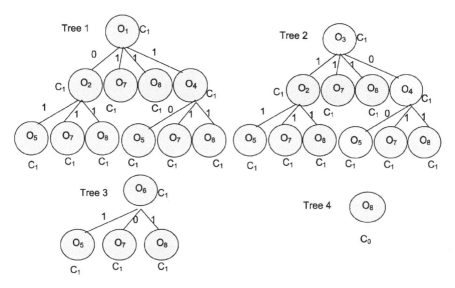

FIG. 9. Generation of the access pattern for the first broadcast cycle.

The O_3, O_4 and O_5 sequence represents a suitable access pattern for our running example during the first broadcast cycle (Fig. 9). Step 7 will be repeated to generate access patterns for different broadcast cycles. The algorithm terminates when all the requested objects are covered in different access patterns. The object sequence O_1, O_2 and O_7 and object sequence O_6 and O_8 represent the last two patterns for retrieving all of the objects requested in the example (Fig. 10).

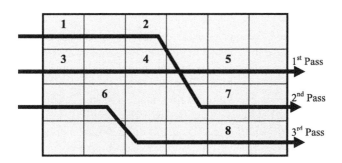

FIG. 10. Generation of the access patterns for our running example.

3.6.2   Generation of Access Patterns—A Top Down Retrieval Approach

The retrieval method discussed in the previous section produces access patterns with excessive channel switches. This in turn increases the energy consumption at the mobile unit. In addition, to determine "the best" access pattern, it generates a complete weighted access forest prior to the path selection step and then in a bottom up fashion it ranks all the potential access patterns along the access forest. This increases the execution time and space requirements. To overcome these limitations, the priority list of heuristics was revised as follows:

- Eliminate the number of conflicts;
- Minimize the number of channel switches;
- Retrieve the maximum number of objects;

and "Least-Cost Path" method was employed to generate the access patterns [53].

Similar to our discussion in Section 3.6.1, the temporal and spatial information provided by the index is used to plot an access pattern for the requested objects. The index is used to generate a weighted tree consisting of nodes as data objects and arcs. However, to improve the efficiency and effectiveness of the access pattern generation process, a top-down "best-first search" method is employed—heuristic information is used to assess the cost of every search avenue and the search continues down the path with the lowest cost. By nature of the search algorithm, nodes on the same level in a tree that possess a higher cost will produce non-ideal patterns. Thus, higher cost nodes are eliminated, and only those nodes that provide a potential least-cost path are expanded and searched further. For large user requests, the least-cost path approach provides a means for reducing the number of branches to be searched, thus having potential to reduce the overall searching time for an ideal access pattern. Our previous running example (Fig. 7) will be used to clarify the process.

(1) *Probe the index*: The index containing the user's requests is retrieved, and is used to determine the channel number and offset of each requested item.
(2) *Generate access forest*: For each channel, find the first object to be broadcast. The root nodes in the running example are O_1, O_3, O_6, and O_8.
(3) *Root node assignment*: For each root node from step 2, temporarily assign a tag of "C_0" and create an access tree with the root.
(4) *Children assignment*: For each node, find the closest non-conflicting objects that may be accessed later on in the broadcast by the node. Label the arc for each child respectively—"1" if the child is on a different channel, "0" if the child is on the same channel. All child nodes are temporarily assigned a tag of

"C_0." Figure 8 shows the state of the access trees after generating the children of the roots.

It is at this point in the algorithm where the new method differs from the one presented in Section 3.6.1.

(5) *Node label update*: After the generation of the children, they are examined and assessed for conflicts. If the parents of the children are the root nodes the root nodes are also examined for conflicts. A node that is in conflict with at least one other node is labeled as "C_1," and a node that is not in conflict with any node is labeled as "C_0."

A special case occurs if there is only one requested object on a channel. The tree of this root node is assigned a channel switch cost of "1" to signify that an extra broadcast pass is required to retrieve that object if its access tree is used. If a cost of "1" was not assigned, an attempt might be made to only use that tree because that path has a switching cost of "0." Therefore, it is desirable to attempt to retrieve this item using a channel switch during the retrieval of some other objects first. In the running example, O_8 is an example of this special case.

(6) *Cost evaluation*: At this stage of the retrieval method, the children are examined to determine the least-cost path of the tree. Using the weights assigned to the arcs of each child, the switching cost of each node is calculated. The node with the lowest switching cost (arc with label "0") will be expanded in step 7. If more than one node has the lowest switching cost, then all paths are to be expanded.

(7) *Expansion*: Using the node with the lowest switching cost found in step 6, the children of that node are determined to expand the least-cost path. The children are added as defined in step 4. Step 5 is repeated to further define the least-cost path.

(8) *Repeat*: Step 7 is repeated until all least-cost paths can no longer be expanded. The fully expanded least-cost paths for the running example are depicted in Fig. 11.

(9) *Compare*: If more than one least-cost path is determined for each tree, the heuristics are used to determine the most ideal path to follow. The least-cost path to use will be the access pattern that:

- Eliminates the most conflicts (has highest number of "C_1" nodes);
- Uses the least channel switches (the path whose arcs are weighted with the most "0"s;
- Retrieves the most objects (the highest node count).

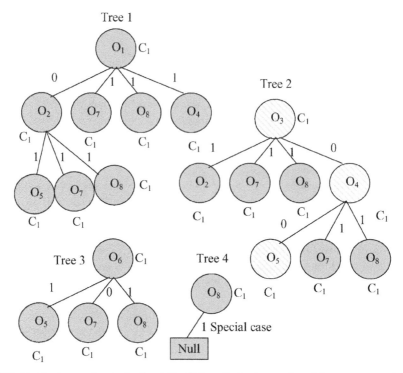

FIG. 11. Final access forest using Least-Cost Path method and generation of the access pattern for the first broadcast cycle.

After the access pattern for the first broadcast pass is determined, steps 2–9 are repeated to generate a new updated forest until every object in the user's request is scheduled for retrieval. Once all objects are covered by access patterns, the algorithm is complete, and the objects may be retrieved from the broadcast using the determined order. Figure 12 shows the complete access patterns of our running example.

4. Object Organization on Single Broadcast Channel

In this section we investigate two heuristic-based data allocation strategies. The first strategy assumes a strict linearity requirement and deals with non-weighted DAGs. The second approach relaxes such strictness in favor of clustering strongly related objects closer to one another and consequently deals with weighted DAGs.

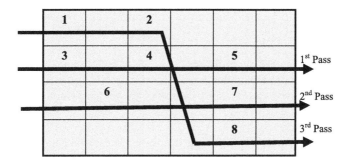

FIG. 12. Access patterns for our running example using the Least-Cost Path method.

4.1   ApproximateLinearOrder Algorithm

Definition 3. In a DAG representation of a complex object, an independent node is a node that has either one or no parent. In Fig. 6, node e is an independent node whereas node h is not. A graph containing only independent nodes makes up a forest.

Heuristic rules:

- Order the children of a node based on their number of descendants in ascending order—the child with the least number of descendants is placed first in the sequence.

- Once a node is selected, all of its descendants should be visited and placed on the sequence in a depth first manner, without any interruption from breadth siblings.

- If a node has a non-independent child, with all of its parents already visited, the non-independent child should be inserted in the linear sequence before any independent child.

The ApproximateLinearOrder is a greedy algorithm based on the aforementioned heuristic rules. It starts by selecting a node with an in-degree of zero and out-degree of at least one [16].

ApproximateLinearOrder Algorithm

1) traverse DAG using DFS traversal and as each node is traversed
2) append the traversed node N to the sequence
3) remove N from {nodes to be traversed}
4) **if** {non-independent children of N having all their parents in the sequence} $\neq \emptyset$

5)   *Set* ← {non-independent children of *N* having all their parents in the
       sequence}
6) **else**
7)   **if** {independent children of *N*} ≠ ∅
8)   *Set* ← {independent children of *N*}
9) *NextNode* ← node ∈ *Set* | node has least # of descendants among the nodes
   in *Set*

The depth-first search (DFS) in line 1 satisfies the second heuristic. The first
if statement (line 4) guarantees the third heuristic, and finally, the node selection
process in line 9 satisfies the first heuristic.

Applying this algorithm to the graph of Fig. 6, we can generate either the fifth
or eleventh sequence. This is dependent on whether *c* or *d* was chosen first as the
child with the least number of independent-children. It should be noted that neither
of these sequences is the optimal sequence. However, they are reasonably better than
other sequences and are obtained in polynomial time. Nodes with in-degree and out-
degree of zero are considered harmful and thus are not handled by the algorithm.
Having them in the middle of the sequence introduces delays between objects along
the sequence. Therefore, they are excluded from the set of nodes to be traversed and
handled by being appended to the end of the sequence. In addition, when multiple
DAGs are to be mapped along the air channel, the mapping should be done with no
interleaving between the nodes of the DAGs.

4.2   PartiallyLinearOrder Algorithm

In a DAG representation of a complex objects, nodes are connected through semantic links with different degrees of connectivity—the frequency of access pattern [23]. This observation is the basis of the PartiallyLinearOrder algorithm that
clusters strongly connected objects closer to each other. This algorithm assumes a
weighted DAG as its input and produces a linear sequence. It combines the nodes
(single_node) of the graph into multi_nodes in a descending order of their connectivity (semantic links). The insertion of single_nodes within a multi_node respects
the linear order at the granularity level of the single_nodes. The multi_nodes are
merged (with multi_nodes or single_nodes) at the multi_node granularity, without
interfering with internal ordering sequences of a multi_node [14].

PartiallyLinearOrder Algorithm

1) **for** every weight w_s in descending order
2)   **for** every two nodes N_1 & N_2 connected by w_s
3)   merge N_i & N_j into one multi_node

4)   **for** every multi_node *MN*
5) $w_m = w_s - 1$
6)   **for** every weight w_m in descending order
7)   **while** ∃ adjacent_node *AN* connected to *MN*
8)   **if** ∃ an edge in both directions between *MN* & *AN*
9)   compute *WeightedLinearDistance$_{MN\_AN}$* &
                   WeightedLinearDistance$_{AN\_MN}$
10)   merge *MN* & *AN* into one multi_node, based on the appropriate
                   direction

In the algorithm, the **for loop** in line 2 merges single_nodes together to generate multi_nodes. The **for loop** starting at line 4 merges the multi_nodes with adjacent multi_nodes or single_nodes (note that *AN* could be either a multi_node or a single_node). To guarantee a minimum distance among related objects, the ordering of a merge between a multi_node and an adjacent node is based on the shorter weighted linear distances between the two of them in both directions. Figure 13 depicts an example of the running process of this algorithm.

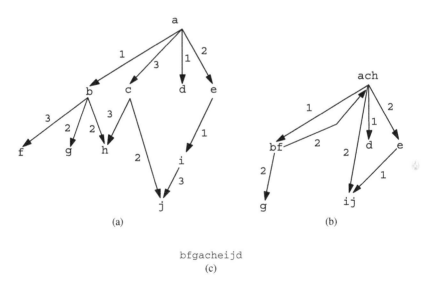

bfgacheijd
(c)

FIG. 13. Application of PartiallyLinearOrder algorithm. (a) Original graph; (b) First and second iterations; (c) Third iteration.

4.3   Performance Evaluation

4.3.1   *Parameters*

A simulator was developed to study the behavior of the aforementioned mapping algorithms, based on a set of rich statistical parameters. The OO7 benchmark was chosen to generate the access pattern graphs because of its rich schema graph for a general object-oriented database application. The NASDAQ exchange [50] was used as the base model, where data is in both textual and multimedia (graphics— i.e., graphs and tables). Table II shows a brief description of the input and output parameters. The simulator is designed to measure the average access delay for the various input parameters. Table III provides a listing of the input parameters, along with their default values and possible ranges. The default values are set as the value of the parameter when other parameters are varied during the course of the simulation. The ranges are used when the parameter itself is varied.

4.3.2   *Results*

4.3.2.1   *Impact of Number of Objects.*   Number of the objects on the broadcast has effect on the broadcast length and consequently, affects the access time—more nodes on the broadcast introduce additional distance between the randomly requested objects. Figure 14 shows the effect of varying the number of requested objects on the average access delay. As expected in all three cases, the average access delay increased as the total number of objects increased. ApproximateLinearOrder and PartiallyLinearOrder schemes performed better than the conventional children-depth first by taking linearity issue into consideration. Since the

TABLE II
DESCRIPTION OF PARAMETERS

Parameter	Description
	Input parameters
Number of nodes	Number of objects within the graph (excluding replication)
Object size	Sizes of objects (small/medium/large)
Object-size distribution	Distribution of the sizes of objects within the database
Next-node ratio	Connectivity to next node (random or connection)
Out-degree distribution	Distribution of the type of nodes based on their out-degrees
Level distribution	Semantic connectivity of two objects (weak/normal/strong)
Percentage of popular objects	Percentage of objects requested more often than others
Replication frequency	The number of times a popular object is to be replicated
	Output parameter
Average access delay	In a single query, the average delay between accessing two objects

TABLE III
INPUT PARAMETER VALUES

Parameter	Default value	Ranges
Number of nodes	5000	400–8000
Object size (in bytes)		
• Small	$2 \leqslant o < 20$	2–20
• Medium	$20 \leqslant o < 7K$	20–7K
• Large	$7K \leqslant o < 50K$	7–50K
Object-size distribution [S : M : L]	1 : 1 : 1	0–6 : 0–6 : 0–6
Next-node ratio [C : R]	8 : 2	0–10 : 10–0
Out-degree distribution [0 : 1 : 2 : 3]	3 : 3 : 2 : 1	1–6 : 1–6 : 1–6 : 1–6
Level distribution [W : N : S]	1 : 1 : 1	1–4 : 1–4 : 1–4
Percentage of popular objects	20%	10–50%
Replication frequency	2	1–10

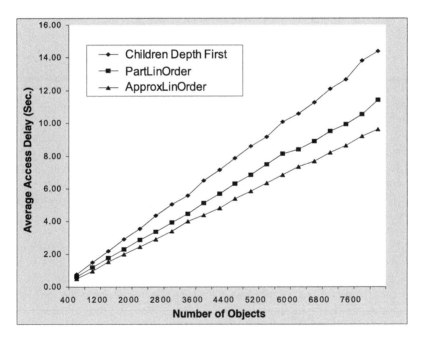

FIG. 14. Average access delay vs. number of requested objects.

goal of both algorithms is to cluster semantically related objects close to one another, adding extra objects has only a minimal effect on the distance separating semantically related objects. The ApproximateLinearOrder algorithm outperformed the Par-

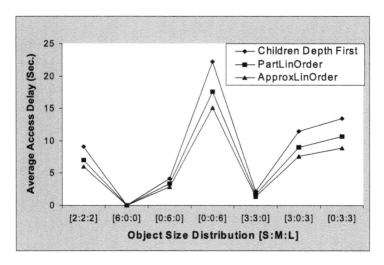

FIG. 15. Average access delay vs. objects size distribution.

tiallyLinearOrder algorithm since, the latter attempts to cluster strongly connected objects closer to one another than loosely connected ones and, hence, compromises the linearity property for the loosely connected objects.

4.3.2.2   Size Distribution.   Figure 15 shows the effects of varying the distribution of the object size among small, medium, and large. As expected, the smallest average access delay took place when the air channel contained smaller objects (point [6 : 0 : 0]). However, as the population of objects shifted towards the larger objects, the average access delay increased (point [0 : 0 : 6]).

4.3.2.3   Next Node Ratio.   During the course of a query, objects are either accessed along the semantic links or in a random fashion—a C : R ratio of 10 : 1 means that for all accesses between two objects, 10 are based on the semantic links and 1 on a random basis. Figure 16 depicts the effect of varying the ratio of the next-node access type. At one extreme (C : R = 10 : 0), when all objects were accessed along the semantic links, the average access delay was minimum. The delay, however, increased for randomly accessed objects. Finally, where all the accesses are on a random basis, clustering (and linearity) does not improve the performance, and all mapping algorithms perform equally.

4.3.2.4   Out Degree Distribution.   This parameter indicates the number of children of a node within the graph—an out-degree of 0 indicates a sink node.

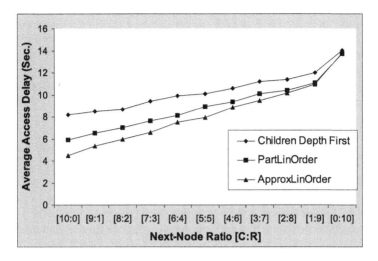

FIG. 16. Access delay vs. next-node ratio.

The simulation results showed that in general, the average access delay is reduced as more connectivity is injected in the access graph.

In separate simulation runs, the simulator also measured the effect of varying the percentage of popular objects and the replication frequency. As one can note, these two parameters have the same effect on the total number of objects on the air channel, though from the access pattern perspective, the semantic of the accesses are different. In both cases, the average access delay increased as either parameter increased. The average access delay for different degrees of connectivity among objects was also observed and measured. The average access delay for objects connected through strong connections was about 4.3 seconds, whereas it was 7.3 and 7.6 seconds for normal and weakly connected objects, respectively. As would be expected, these results show that the improvement is considerable for the objects connected by a strong connection but for a normal connection the performance was close to that of the weak-connection case since the algorithm performs its best optimization for strongly connected objects.

4.4   Section Conclusion

In this section two heuristically-based mapping algorithms were discussed, simulated, and analyzed. Performing the mapping in polynomial time was one of the major issues of concern while satisfying linearity, locality, and replication of popular objects. The ApproximateLinearOrder algorithm is a greedy-based approximation algorithm that guarantees the linearity property and provides a solution in polynomial time. The PartiallyLinearOrder algorithm guarantees the linearity property for the strongest related objects and relaxes the linearity requirement for objects connected through looser links. Finally, it was shown that the proposed algorithms offer higher performance than the traditional children-depth first algorithm.

5.   Parallel Channels Object Organization

Section 4 addressed the methods by which objects should be placed on a single air channel. However, as noted before, reducing the broadcast length is one way to provide timely access to information, i.e., broadcasting objects along parallel air channels. Realizing the similarity between this goal and scheduling tasks in a multiprocessor environment, two heuristic-based static scheduling algorithms are discussed and analyzed in this section [31].

5.1   Largest Object First (LOF)

This algorithm relies on a simple and localized heuristic by giving priority to larger objects. Consider a 2-channel allocation and three objects A, B, and C. Further assume the following relationships among the sizes of the objects $A > B > C$ (Fig. 17). Figure 17(a) shows a random allocation, whereas, Fig. 17(b) shows the allocation based on the aforementioned heuristic. As can be seen, this heuristic has the advantage of achieving better load balancing. The algorithm follows the following procedure: Recursively, the largest node with in degree of zero is chosen (initially the root) and assigned to the least loaded channel. The assigned node along with all of its out-edges are eliminated from the object DAG.

5.2   Clustering Critical-Path (CCP)

A critical path is defined as the longest sequence of dependent objects that are accessed serially. Traditionally, a critical path is defined based on the weights as-

FIG. 17.   Load balancing using Largest-Object First heuristic.

signed to each node. A simple approach would set the weight proportional to the size of an object and the size of its largest descendant node. However, such a scheme fails to consider parameters such as the total size and number of children and the degree of connectivity among related nodes. Therefore, a critical-path algorithm that uses a more sophisticated set of heuristics in determining the weight of the node is represented here.

Definition 4. A critical node is a node that has a child with an in-degree greater than 1.

5.2.1 Load Balancing

5.2.1.1 Critical Node Effect.
Allocate a critical node with the highest number of children with in-degree > 1 first. Consider the subDAG shown in Fig. 18—A, B, and C are all critical nodes. However, A has priority over B and C (it has precedence over two nodes whereas B and C have precedence over one node each). Assume that there are two parallel channels. As can be seen from the figure, regardless of the sizes of A, B, and C, allocating A first results in a better load balancing.

5.2.1.2 Number of Children with In-Degree 1.
Allocate nodes with the highest number of children with in-degree 1 first. This could free up more nodes to be allocated in parallel. Consider the allocation shown in Fig. 19, and the alloca-

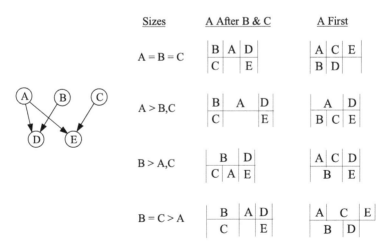

FIG. 18. Critical-node effect.

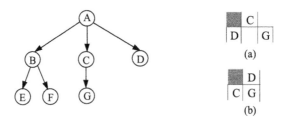

FIG. 19. Multiple children with in-degree 1.

tion of the two children *C* and *D*. Assume that at the starting point only one channel is available. As can be seen allocating *C* first produces better load balancing.

5.2.2 Related Objects Clustering

The weight of a node should be made a function of the weights of the incoming and outgoing edges. Based on the aforementioned discussion, the weight of each node is calculated based on the: (i) size of the node, (ii) the maximum weight of its children, (iii) the number of children with in-degree 1 and in-degree > 1, and (iv) the degree of connectivity among objects [31].

The critical-path clustering algorithm (CCP) takes a DAG as its input and calls the AssignWeights Algorithm.

CCP(*DAG*) Algorithm

1) AssignWeights(*DAG*)
2) **repeat** until all the nodes have been processed
3) Select the free node *N* with the largest weight
4) **if** all parents of *N* are fully allocated on the channels
5)   place it on the currently least-loaded channel
6) **else**
7)   fill up the least-loaded channel(s) with nulls up to the end of the last allocated parent of *N* then place *N* on it.

The **repeat** loop starting on line 2 implements the critical path heuristics by selecting the free node with the largest weight and placing it on the least-loaded channel, after all its parents have been fully allocated. The running time of the CCP algorithm is equal to the running time of AssignWeights plus the running time of the **repeat** loop. The loop has to be repeated *n* times and line 4 can be done in $O(n)$. Therefore, the overall running time of the CCP algorithm is $O(n^2)$.

5.3   Performance Evaluation

To evaluate the performance of the proposed algorithms, the scope of the simulator discussed in Section 4 was extended to measure the average response time per object retrieval. To measure the effectiveness of the algorithms across a more unbiased testbed, the degree of connectivity among the objects in the DAG was randomly varied, and 100 different DAGs were generated. In every DAG, the out-degrees of the nodes were determined within the range between 0 and 3. The weight of each node was categorized as strong, normal, and weak.

5.3.1   Number of Air Channels

Figure 20 shows the effect of varying the number of air channels on the average response time per object. As anticipated, increasing the number of channels resulted in a better response time for both the LOF and CCP. However, this improvement flattened as the number of channels increased above a certain threshold, because additional parallelism provided by the additional number of channels did not match the number of free nodes available to be allocated, simultaneously. In addition, the CCP method outperformed the LOF method—the CCP heuristics attempt to smooth the distribution of the objects among the air channels while clustering the related objects.

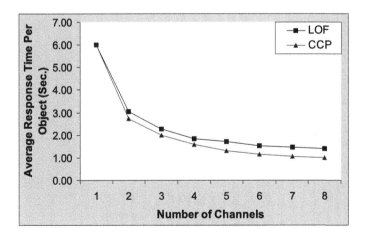

FIG. 20. Average response time vs. number of channels.

5.3.2 Out-Degree Distribution

Figure 21 depicts the effect of modifying the distribution of the out-degrees of the nodes on the average response time per object. The distribution of the out-degrees is shown in terms of a distribution vector composed of four entries. Each entry corresponds to the relative number of nodes with a certain out-degree. For example, a vector [1 : 3 : 1 : 1] represents the fact that within a DAG, 15% of nodes have no out-degrees, 45% have out-degrees of 1, 15% have out-degree of 2, and 15% have out-degree of 3. In general, the CCP method outperformed the LOF method. As can be seen, when the out-degree distribution is biased to include nodes with larger out-degrees (i.e., making the DAG denser), the LOF performance degrades at a much faster rate than the CCP method. This is due to the fact that such bias introduces more critical nodes and a larger number of children per node. The CCP method is implicitly capable of handling such cases.

5.4   Section Conclusion

In the pursuit of "timely access" to public information, this section concentrated on the proper mapping of database objects on multiple parallel air channels. The goal was to find the most appropriate allocation scheme that would (i) preserve the connectivity among the objects, (ii) provide the minimum overall broadcast time

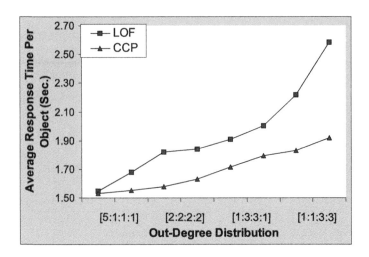

FIG. 21. Average response time vs. out-degree distribution.

(load balancing), and (iii) cluster related objects close to one another (improving the response time). Applying the largest object first heuristic showed an improvement in load balancing. However, it was proved short in solving the third aforementioned requirement. The CCP algorithm was presented in order to compensate this shortcoming. Relying on the critical path paradigm, the algorithm assumed several heuristics and showed better performance.

As noted before, introducing methods that can reduce the overall response time at the MH was the main objective of this chapter. Naturally, such reduction could also minimize the amount of power consumption at the MH. In spite of such minimization, the MH has to scan the air channel(s) to locate its desired data. In an effort to reduce such scanning time, providing an index for the objects on the broadcast channel(s) could be proved to be beneficial in minimizing power consumption. In addition, application of parallel air channels could result in conflicts and consequently, would effect both response time and power consumption. These two issues are the subjects of discussion in the next two sections.

6.   Energy Efficient Indexing

Due to the power limitation of the mobile host, in retrieving objects from the air channel, one has to minimize the amount of power consumption. In general, in the presence of an indexing mechanism one could use the following protocol to retrieve data objects from the air channel(s):

(1) *Initial probe*: The client tunes into the broadcast channel to determine when the next index tree is broadcast.
(2) *Search*: The client accesses the index and determines the offset for the requested objects.
(3) *Retrieve*: The client tunes into the channel and downloads all the required data objects.

In the initial probe, the mobile unit must be in active operational mode. As soon as the mobile unit retrieves the offset of the next index, its operational mode could change to doze mode. To perform the *Search* step, the mobile unit must be in active mode, and when the unit gets the offset of the required data items, it could switch to doze mode. Finally, when the requested data items are being broadcast (*Retrieve* step), the mobile unit changes its operational mode to active mode and tunes into the channel to download the requested data. When the data is retrieved, the unit changes to doze mode again.

Object-oriented indexing is normally implemented via a multi-level tree. We can classify the possible implementation techniques into two general schemes: single-class indexing and hierarchical indexing [15]. In the single-class scheme, multiple multi-level trees are constructed, each representing one class. In this case, the leaf nodes of each tree point to objects belonging only to the class indexed by that tree. A query requesting all objects with a certain *id* has to navigate all these trees. On the other hand, the hierarchical-based scheme constructs one multi-level tree representing an index for all classes. The same query has to only navigate the common tree.

6.1   Indexing on Single Broadcast Channel

Similar to a disk medium, an *"air-channel page"* can be assumed as the storage granule on the air channel. Due to the sequential nature of the air channel, the allocation of the nodes of a multi-level tree has to follow the navigational path used to traverse the tree, starting at the root. Therefore, an ordering scheme should be used to sequentially map the nodes on the air channel. Similarly, data objects are allocated onto air channel pages following their index. Note that in either case, it is possible to interleave and distribute the index pages and associated data pages in a variety of methods (e.g., 1–*m*- or *distributed* indexing as suggested in [38] for a file indexed by a B-tree).

6.1.1   Hierarchical Method

In this scheme, whether the domain of the query covers one class or all classes along the hierarchy, the same index structure has to be traversed. Any request has to probe the channel first, read one page, and get an offset to the first page of the index. The modules of the mobile unit can then go into doze mode. Once the index is reached, the modules are brought back into active mode. A number of index pages are read and offsets to the required objects are obtained. The offsets are followed and the required objects are retrieved. In the interim between the retrieval of objects, the modules are brought into doze mode. The protocol is shown below.

Hierarchical Protocol
1) Probe onto channel and get offset to the next index   *active*
2) Reach the index   *doze*
3) Retrieve the required index pages   *active*
4) Reach the required data pages   *doze*
5) Retrieve required data pages   *active*

6.1.2   Single-Class Method

In this scheme, we assume that the first page of every index contains information indicating the location of each index class. This structure can be implemented by including a vector of pairs [*class_id, offset*]. Assuming that the size of the *offset* and the *class_id* is size 4 bytes each, the size of this structure would be 8*c*, where *c* is the number of class indexes on the broadcast. The protocol below consists of accessing the first page of an index to get the offset to all the required indexes. The indices and their corresponding data pages are accessed sequentially, as in the previous scheme.

Single-Class Protocol

1) Probe onto channel and get offset to the next index   *active*
2) Reach the index   *doze*
3) Retrieve offsets to the indexes of required classes   *active*
4) for every required class
5)   Reach the index   *doze*
6)   Retrieve the required index pages   *active*
7)   Reach the required data   *doze*
8)   Retrieve required data pages   *active*

6.1.3   Performance Evaluation

The simulator reported in Section 5 was extended to study both the response time and energy consumption for the aforementioned allocation schemes. The overall structure of the schema graph determines the navigational paths among the classes within the graph. The relationships of the navigational paths within the graph influence the number and structure of indexes to be used. Realizing this fact, we take a closer look at the effects of the inheritance and aggregation relationships.

- *Inheritance relationship*: Within an inheritance hierarchy, classes at the lower level of the hierarchy inherit attributes of the classes at the upper level. Therefore, objects belonging to the lower-level classes tend to be larger than those within the upper levels. The distribution of the number of objects is application dependent. In our analysis, without loss of generality, we assumed the objects to be equally distributed among the classes of the hierarchy.

- *Aggregation relationship*: In an aggregation hierarchy, objects belonging to lower classes are considered "part of" objects and those at the higher ends are the "collection" of such parts. In other words, objects at the upper classes are composed of objects of the lower ends. Therefore, objects belonging to higher classes are generally larger than those belonging to the lower ones. In addition, the cardinality (number of objects per class) of a class at the upper end is smaller than a class at the lower end. This is because, generally, one complex (collection) object utilizes multiple "part" objects (that could be from the same or different classes).

As a result, the organization of classes within the schema graph has its influence on the distribution of both the number and size of objects among the classes of the database. To reflect this notion statistically, every hierarchy was divided into four quarters (starting with the lowest quarter) and assigned a varying percentage of the number of objects of various sizes to the classes of that quarter. Therefore, a percentage distribution takes the form of a vector with 4 entries ([low quarter, mid_low quarter, mid_high quarter, high quarter]). The simulator assumed an average of eight classes for each hierarchy and categorized the sizes of objects as small, medium, large and very large—a percentage distribution of object sizes of [VL, L, M, S] means that the lowest quarter of classes along the hierarchy contains very large objects, whereas the highest quarter contains small objects. Similarly a percentage distribution of the cardinality of classes that equals [34,25,18,9] means that 40% of the objects within the database are found within the lowest quarter classes, 30% in the higher hierarchy and so on. A small object is a textual-based security price of size 16 bytes. A very large (non-complex) object can be a (2×3)-inch graph that contains 16 colors. Such an object would require 6K bytes. Finally, the size of the index structure is dependent on the number of distinct keys for the objects within a class. It was assumed that 60% of the objects have distinct keys and that the value of any attribute is uniformly distributed among the objects containing such attribute. Table IV shows a list of all the input parameters assumed for this case.

For these simulation runs, the information along the broadcast channel is organized in four different fashions: the hierarchical and single-class methods for the inheritance and aggregation relationships. Note that it is the number of objects (not data pages) that controls the number of index blocks. For example, the number of data pages of the inheritance case is about 2.5 times more than that of the aggregation case. However, the number of the index blocks is equivalent since the number of the objects in both cases is the same. Within each indexing scheme, for each query, the simulator simulates the process of probing the air channel, getting the required index pages, and retrieving the required data pages. In each query, on average, two objects from each class are retrieved. The simulation measures the response time and amount of energy consumed.

6.1.3.1 *Response Time.*

Placing an index along the air channel contributes to extra storage overhead and thus longer response time. Therefore, the best response time is achieved when no index is placed on the broadcast, and the entire

TABLE IV
INPUT PARAMETERS

Parameter	Value (default/range)
Number of objects on broadcast	5,120
Average number of classes along hierarchy	8
Percentage distribution of number of object in inheritance hierarchy	25, 25, 25, 25%
Percentage distribution of number of objects in aggregation hierarchy	40, 30, 20, 10%
Distribution of object size [S, M, L, VL]	16, 512, 3K, 6K bytes
Distribution of the object sizes in inheritance hierarchy	VL, L, M, S
Distribution of the object sizes in aggregation hierarchy	S, M, L, VL
Percentage of classes to be retrieved (default/range)	70% / [10–100%]
Average number of objects to retrieve per class	2
Fan-out in index tree	5
Average number of objects with distinct key attribute per class	60% of objects per class
Size of air-channel page	512 bytes
Broadcast data rate	1 M bits/sec
Power consumption active mode	130 mW
Power consumption doze mode	6.6 mW
Power consumption (switching channels)	13 mW

broadcast is searched. Table V shows the degradation factor of the average response time due to the inclusion of an index in the broadcast. The factor is proportional to the ratio of the size of the index blocks to that of the entire broadcast. However, this degradation comes at the expense of drastic improvement in the energy consumption. As can be seen there is a great deal of benefit, ranging from a factor of 17.5 to 19, in including an index.

The simulator generated the response time for different broadcast organizations (Fig. 22). From the figure, one could conclude that for both the inheritance and aggregation cases, the response time of the hierarchical organization remained almost constant. This is due to the fact that regardless of the number of classes and the location of the initial probe all accesses have to be directed to the beginning of the index (at the beginning of the broadcast). The slight increase is attributed

TABLE V
RESPONSE TIME DEGRADATION AND ENERGY IMPROVEMENT DUE TO INDEXING

	Aggregation/ Hierarchical	Aggregation/ Single	Inheritance/ Hierarchical	Inheritance/ Single
Response time degradation	1.17	1.05	1.1	1.02
Energy improvement	17.5	18.9	18.4	19

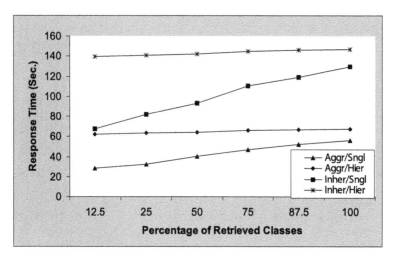

FIG. 22. Response time vs. number of retrieved classes.

to the increase in the total number of objects to be retrieved assuming that the objects to be retrieved are distributed uniformly along the broadcast. In addition, the single-class method offers a better response time than the hierarchical case, and the response time for the single-class method increases as the number of retrieved classes increase. The first observation is because of the fact that in the single-class method accesses do not have to be directed to the beginning of the broadcast. When a probe takes place, the first class belonging to the set of classes to be retrieved can be accessed directly. Other required classes are accessed in sequence. The second observation is due to the fact that an increase in the number of classes to be retrieved directly increases the number of index and data pages to be accessed. Finally, indexing based on the aggregation relationship offers lower response time than indexing based on the inheritance relationship, since the distribution of the number of objects in the inheritance relationship is more concentrated on the larger objects. Having larger objects results in a longer broadcast, and hence, longer time to retrieve the objects.

6.1.3.2 *Energy Consumption.* For each query, the amount of energy consumed is the sum of the consumed energy while the unit is in both active and doze modes. In the case where no index is provided, the mobile unit is in active mode during the entire probe. However, in the case where an index is provided, the active time is proportional to the number of index and data pages to be retrieved. As expected, the active time of each case increases as the number of retrieved classes

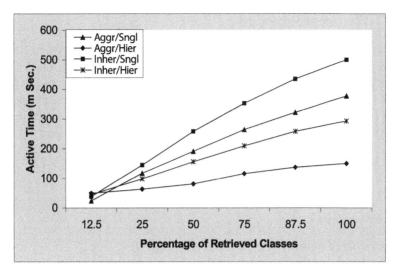

FIG. 23. Active time vs. number of the retrieved classes.

increases (Fig. 23). In general, the hierarchical method requires less active time than the single-class method. The hierarchical method searches only one large index tree, whereas the single-class method searches through multiple smaller index trees. The number of pages retrieved per index tree is proportional to the height of the tree. For a query spanning a single class, the single-class method produces a better active time than the hierarchical method. As the number of classes to be retrieved increases, the hierarchical tree is still traversed only once. However, more single-class trees have to be traversed, and hence, resulting in an increase in the active time.

In both the single-class and the hierarchical methods, the aggregation case requires lower active time than the inheritance case. This is simply due to the fact that the inheritance case has larger objects and thus, requires the retrieval of more pages.

6.2 Indexing on Parallel Air Channels

Retrieval of data from an air channel at the mobile host (MH) is somewhat limited by the MH's power supply. In an effort to reduce power consumption and response time, this section investigates the application of indexing, the organization, and the distribution of objects along the parallel air channels [9]:

6.2.1   Retrieval Protocols

In case of parallel air channels, one has to account for switching between channels when analyzing access time and power consumption. The switching time between two different frequencies is assumed to be in the range of microseconds [51]. During the switching time, the pages that are being broadcast on different channels can not be accessed by the mobile unit. In addition, the mobile unit, at each moment of time can tune into one channel. Finally, we assumed that the power consumption for switching between two channels is 10% of the power consumed in active mode.

6.2.1.1   Hierarchical Method.   The following protocol shows the sequence of operations.

Hierarchical Protocol

1) Probe onto channel and retrieve offset to the next index		*active*
2) Do {Reach the next index		*doze*
3) Retrieve the required index pages		*active*
4) Do {Reach the next possible required data page		*doze*
5) Retrieve the next possible required data page		*active*
6) } while every possible required data page is retrieved from the current broadcast		
7) } while there are un-accessed objects because of overlapped page range		

6.2.1.2   Single-Class Indexing Scheme.   Similar to the single air channel environment, we assume that the first page of every index contains information indicating the location of each index class. The protocol below shows the sequence of steps:

Single-Class Protocol

1) Probe onto channel and retrieve offset to the next index		*active*
2) do {Reach the next index		*doze*
3) Retrieve offsets to the indexes of required classes		*active*
4) Reach the next possible index		*doze*
5) Retrieve the next possible required index page		*active*
6) do {Reach the next possible index or data page		*doze*
7) Retrieve the next possible index or data page		*active*
8) } while not (all indexes and data of required classes are scanned)		

9) } while there are some data pages which are not retrieved because of overlapped page range

6.2.2   Performance Evaluation

Once again, the scope of simulator reported in Section 5 was extended to study the response time and energy consumption of the single-class and hierarchical indexing schemes in parallel air channels based on the input parameters presented in Table IV.

6.2.2.1   Response Time.   Figure 24 shows the response time of broadcast data in parallel air channel without and with indexing. From this figure, it can be concluded that:

- In the case of no indexing, the response time was constant and independent of the number of channels in that without any indexing mechanism in place, the mobile unit has to scan every data page in sequence until all required data pages are acquired. Nevertheless, for a single channel environment, the response time without an indexing scheme is less than with any indexing scheme. Moreover, when indexing schemes are in force, the response time lessens as the number of channels increases.

- For inheritance and aggregation cases the response time decreases as the number of channels increases—as the number of channels increases, the length of the broadcast decreases. The shorter the information in each channel, the lesser the response time. However, the higher the number of channels, the higher the probability of conflicts in accessing data residing on the different channels. As a result, doubling the number of channels will not decrease the response time by half.

- For inheritance and aggregation indexing schemes, the single-class method offers a better response time than the hierarchical method. The single-class method accesses do not have to be started at the beginning of the broadcast. When a probe takes place, the first class belonging to the set of classes to be retrieved can be accessed directly. Other required classes are accessed in sequence. For the hierarchical method, on the other hand, any access has to be started from the beginning of the broadcast, which makes the response time of the hierarchical method longer.

- Indexing based on the aggregation relationship offers a lower response time than that of the inheritance relationship. Since the distribution of objects in the inher-

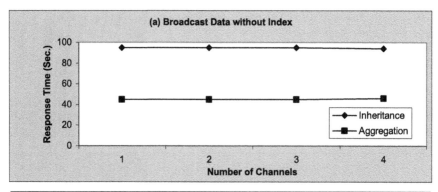

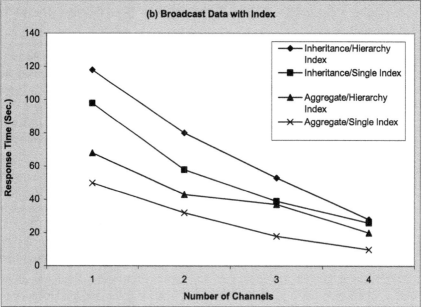

FIG. 24. Response time vs. number of channels.

itance relationship is more concentrated on the larger objects. Having larger objects results in a longer broadcast, and hence, more time to retrieve the objects.

6.2.2.2   Energy.
The active time is proportional to the number of index and data pages to be retrieved. The active time for broadcast data without and with index for all four indexing schemes is shown in Fig. 25:

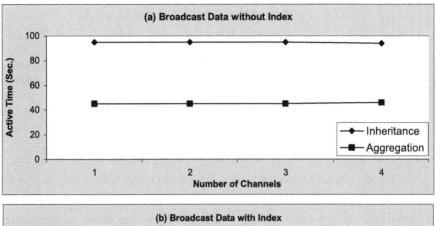

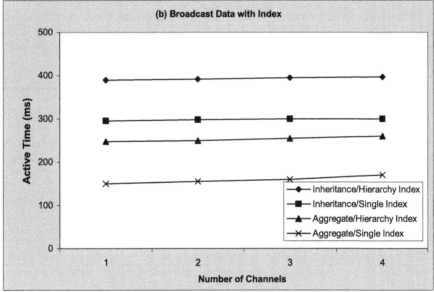

FIG. 25. Active time vs. number of channels.

- For broadcast data without an index, the mobile unit has to be active all the time in order to scan data in parallel air channels until all required data is accessed. This simply means that the active time is the same as the response time. In addition, for all four indexing schemes, the active time remains almost constant and independent of the number of air channels. This is because the active

time is proportional to the number of index and data pages to be retrieved, and
this number is a function of the query and independent of the number of air
channels.

- In general, the hierarchical method requires less active time than the single-class
  method. The hierarchical method searches only one large index tree, whereas
  the single-class method searches through multiple smaller index trees and the
  number of pages to be retrieved per index tree is proportional to the height of
  the tree.

- In both the single-class and the hierarchical methods, the indexing based on an
  aggregation relationship requires lower active time than the inheritance method.
  This is simply due to the fact that the inheritance relationship resulted in larger
  objects, thus requiring the retrieval of more pages.

The simulator also measured the total energy consumption. It was concluded that
the total energy consumption of broadcasting without any indexing schemes is much
higher than that of broadcasting supported by indexing, and the energy consumption of the single class method is lower than that of the hierarchical method. This
is very similar to the results obtained for the response time. When indexing was
supported, energy consumption, on the average, decreased about 15 to 17 times
in the case of the aggregation relationship and the inheritance relationship, respectively. In addition, broadcasting over parallel air channels also reduced the power
consumption in comparison to the power consumption of the single air channel. Finally, the mobile unit's power consumption decreased as the number of channels
increased.

6.3 Section Conclusion

This section investigated an energy-efficient solution by the means of applying indexing schemes to object-oriented data broadcast over single and parallel air
channel(s). Two methods, namely the hierarchical and single-class methods were ex-
plored. Timing analysis and simulation were conducted to compare and contrast the
performance of different indexing schemes against each other. It was shown that including an index moderately degrades the response time; however, such degradation
is greatly offset by the improvement in energy consumption. For a single air channel,
broadcasting with supported indexing schemes increased the response time when
compared with broadcasting without indexing support. However, the response time
is reduced by broadcasting data with an index along the parallel air channels. Moreover, the response time decreased as the number of air channels is increased. Relative
to non-indexed broadcasting, the mobile unit's energy consumption decreased rather
sharply when indexing is supported. For a set of queries retrieving objects along the

air channel(s), the single-class indexing method resulted in a faster response time and lower energy consumption than the hierarchical method.

7. Conflict Resolution and Generation of Access Patterns—Heuristic Solution

Broadcasting information over the parallel air channels reduces the access time and power consumption at the expense of conflicts between accessing objects on different channels. As a result of conflicts, the retrieval protocol requires several passes over the air channels in order to pull the requested information. Conflicts will directly influence the access latency and hence, the overall execution time.

7.1 Retrieving Objects from Parallel Broadcast Air Channels in the Presence of Conflicts

The problem of scheduling the retrieval order of the requested objects can be modeled as a Travel Salesman Problem (TSP). Making the transformation from a broadcast to the TSP requires the creation of a complete weighted directed graph G with K nodes, where each node represents a requested object. The weight w of each edge (i, j) is either 0 or 1. A weight of 0 indicates that the object j is after object i in the broadcast and that objects i and j are not in conflict. A weight of 1 indicates that object j is either before or in conflict with objects i. An example of this conversion is shown in Fig. 26.

The nature of the problem dictates that G is asymmetric; that is, the weight of edge (i, j) is not necessarily equal to the weight of edge (j, i). Thus, in solving this problem we can apply those techniques that are applicable to the Asymmetric TSP.

7.1.1 Performance Evaluation

A simulator was developed to randomly generate broadcasts and determine how many passes were required to retrieve a varying number of requested objects. Several algorithms for ordering the retrieval of objects from the broadcast, both TSP-related and non-TSP-related, were analyzed. In addition, issues such as the optimal number of broadcast channels to use, optimal broadcast length, and the effectiveness of splitting large requests into smaller ones were also studied [40,41].

7.1.2 Simulation Model

In this simulation model, a broadcast is represented as an $N \times M$ two-dimensional matrix, where N represents the number of objects in each channel of a broad-

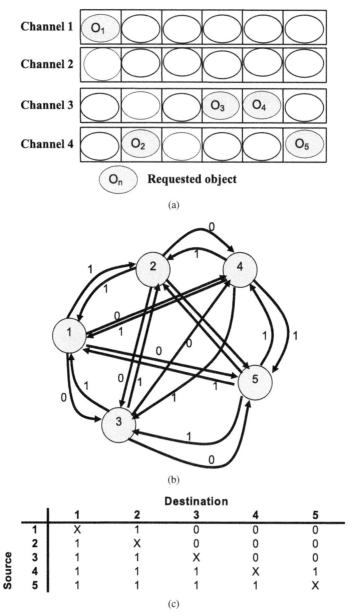

FIG. 26. Representation of a broadcast as a traveling salesman problem. (a) Broadcast representation; (b) Graph representation; (c) Matrix representation.

cast and M represents the number of parallel channels. For *K-object request*, $1 \leqslant K \leqslant NM$, the simulator randomly generates 1000 patterns representing the uniform distribution of K objects among the broadcast channels. The K objects from each randomly generated pattern are retrieved using various retrieval algorithms. The number of passes is recorded and compared. To prevent the randomness of the broadcasts from affecting the comparison of the algorithms, the same broadcast is used for each algorithm in a particular trial and the mean value is reported for each value of K.

7.1.3 Object Retrieval Algorithms

Several algorithms were used to retrieve the objects from the broadcast. This includes both exact and approximate TSP solution finders. In addition, we studied two heuristic based methods as well.

7.1.3.1 TSP Methods.
An exact TSP algorithm was used to provide a basis for comparison with the other algorithms. These algorithms are simply too slow and too resource-intensive to use at a mobile unit. For example, some TSP problems with only 14 nodes took several minutes of CPU time in this experiment. While a better implementation of the algorithm may somewhat reduce the cost, it cannot change the fact that finding the exact solution will require exponential time for some inputs. Knowing the exact solution to a given TSP does, however, allow us to evaluate the quality of a heuristic approach. A TSP heuristic based on the assignment problem relaxation is also included. This heuristic requires far less CPU time and memory than the optimal tour finders, so it is suitable for use on a mobile unit. A publicly available TSP solving package named TspSolve was used for all TSP algorithm implementations.

7.1.3.2 Next Object Access.
This is a heuristic based algorithm. The strategy is a simple greedy heuristic that always retrieves the next available object in a broadcast. It is also similar to the Nearest Neighbor approach to solving TSP problems.

7.1.3.3 Row Scan.
This algorithm simply reads all the objects from one channel in each pass. Naturally, if a channel does not have any objects in it, it is skipped. The upper bound execution time is proportion to the number of air channels. The benefit of this algorithm is that it does not require any time to decide on an ordering for objects. In addition, it does not require any channel switching during a broadcast pass. It can thus begin retrieving objects from a broadcast immediately.

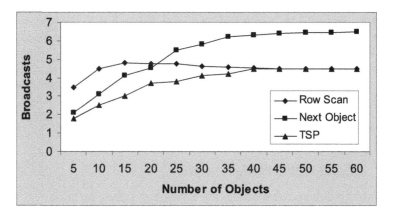

FIG. 27. Comparison of several algorithms for retrieving objects from parallel channels.

This is especially important when a large percentage of the objects in a broadcast are requested.

7.1.4 Simulation Results

As expected, the TSP methods provide much better results than both the Next Object and Row Scan heuristics. Simulation results showed that the TSP heuristic performed almost exactly as well as the optimal TSP algorithm. This is a very interesting observation, because it means that one can use a fast heuristic, rather than a slow but exact algorithm, to schedule retrievals of objects from the broadcast without any performance degradation.

Figure 27 used 5 parallel channels and 20 pages per channel. It is also interesting to note that the straightforward row scan nearly matches the performance of the TSP-based algorithm when more than about 45% of the total number of objects is requested. In this case, there are so many conflicts that it is virtually impossible to avoid having to make as many passes as there are parallel channels. When this occurs, it is better to do the straightforward row scan than to spend time and resources running a TSP heuristic.

7.1.5 Number of Broadcast Channels

One of the important questions that must be answered in designing a broadcasting system is how many parallel channels to use for broadcasting information. More channels means shorter broadcast length and more potential for conflicts. Figure 28 shows the number of pages of data that must be broadcast, on average, to retrieve *K*

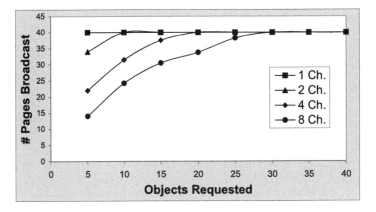

FIG. 28. Optimal number of broadcast channels.

objects from four different broadcasting schemes. The 4 broadcasting schemes have 1, 2, 4, and 8 parallel channels. This test was performed with up to 40 pages in each broadcast. The results show that it is always advantageous to use more broadcast channels, especially when relatively a few objects are requested. While there will be more conflicts between objects, this does not quite counteract the shorter broadcast length of the many-channel broadcasts. This is especially evident when only a few objects in a broadcast are being accessed.

7.2   Ordered Access List

Based on the results reported in Sections 7.1 and 3.6, in order to balance and to compromise between the access time and power consumption, the general access protocol for an indexed broadcast parallel channel configuration should be modified [48,49,53,61]. The goal was to use heuristics that generates an ordered access list of requested objects that reduces:

• The number of passes over the air channels, and

• The number of channel switches.

With reference to the discussion in Section 7, during the search step, the index is accessed to determine the offset and the channels of the requested objects. With this information available a sequence of access patterns to pull objects from the air channels during each broadcast cycle is generated (see Section 3.6). Finally the retrieval step is performed following the generated access patterns. The extended protocol is as follows:

Extended Retrieval Protocol
  1) Probe the channel and retrieve the offset to the next index.
  2) Access the next index
  3) Do {Search the index for the requested object
  4)   Calculate the offset of the object
  5)   Get the channel on which the object will be broadcast
  6) } while there is an unprocessed requested object
  7) Generate access patterns for the requested objects (using retrieval scheme)
  8) Do {Wait for the next broadcast cycle
  9)   Do {Reach the first object as indicated by the access pattern
10)   Retrieve the object
11)   } while there is an un-retrieved object in the access pattern
12) } while there is an unprocessed access pattern

7.2.1 Performance Evaluation

To validate the feasibility of this approach, to compare and contrast them against each other, and to show the trade-off between access latency and computational complexity the scope of the simulator reported in Section 6 was extended. The extended simulator emulates the process of accessing data from a hierarchical indexing scheme for both the bottom up and the top down approaches discussed in Sections 3.6.1 and 3.6.2, respectively, in addition, it analyzes the effect of conflicts on the average access time and power consumption.

The index structure can be transmitted in different fashions including:

- A complete index is transmitted at the beginning of each broadcast in the first channel before the data;
- Index is distributed among the data elements;
- Index is replicated and interleaved with the data elements; or
- A dedicated channel is used to exclusively and continuously transmit the index in a cyclic manner.

The experimental results indicated that repeated transmission of the index on a separate channel provides the best response time. Hence, the following discussion is limited to the employment of dedicated channel to broadcast the index structure.

User requests were randomly generated representing a collection of K objects in the broadcast. In various simulations runs, the value of K was varied from one to $N \times M$—in a typical user query of public data, K is much less than $N \times M$. Finally, to take future technological advances into account, parameters such as transmission rate and power consumption in different modes of operation were fed to the simulator as variable entities.

The simulator generates the average time spent on each of the three steps of the retrieval process (see Section 6). For each step, the unit switches to active mode to perform the action, and then returns to doze mode. Hence, the simulator calculates the average active time when the mobile unit is in active mode accessing data and the average idle time when the unit is in doze mode. It also estimates the average query response time. Along with the average times reported, the simulator determines the average number of broadcast passes required to retrieve objects, as well as the number of channel switches performed by the mobile unit while retrieving data. Finally, the simulator uses the collected information to determine the energy consumption of the retrieval process. As a note, the size of the index was 13.52% of the size of the data objects (not including the index) and the number of data channels varied from 1 to 16.

7.2.2   Simulation Model

For each simulation run, a request of K objects was randomly generated. A set of input parameters including the number of parallel air channels, the broadcast transmission rate, and the power consumption in different modes of operation was passed to the simulator. The simulator was run 1000 times and the average of the designated performance metrics was calculated.

7.2.3   Simulation Results

The retrieval protocols, discussed in Section 3.6, are intended to reduce the number of passes over parallel channels by scheduling data retrieval. This by default should reduce the average response time. To show this fact, in a configuration composed of 2, 4, 8, and 16 channels, the *bottom up retrieval scheme* (see Section 3.6.1) and the *Row Scan* algorithm were simulated when the number of requested data elements was varied between 5 and 50, out of 5,464 securities within the NASDAQ exchange database, which is a reasonable range of objects requested by a query. The simulation results showed that, regardless of the number of parallel air channels, the *bottom up retrieval scheme* reduces both the number of passes and the response time compared to the *Row Scan* algorithm. Moreover, the energy consumption was also reduced, but only when the number of data elements retrieved was approximately 15 or less. For example, in an environment composed of 16 parallel air channels when requesting 10 data elements (see Table VI), the *bottom up retrieval scheme* performed the retrieval with:

- 72% fewer passes,
- 41% reduced response time, and
- 3% less energy

than that of the *Row Scan* algorithm.

TABLE VI
IMPROVEMENT OF THE BOTTOM UP RETRIEVAL SCHEME VS. THE
ROW SCAN (10 OBJECTS REQUESTED)

# of channels	# of passes	Response time	Energy
2	48.0%	28.0%	2.7%
4	68.0%	43.6%	3.1%
8	72.3%	46.5%	3.3%
16	71.8%	40.8%	3.4%

However, relative to the *Row Scan* algorithm, one should also consider the expected overhead of the proposed retrieval schemes. The simulation results showed that in the worst case, the overhead of *retrieval scheme1* was slightly less than the time required to transmit one data page.

7.2.3.1   *Response Time.*   The simulation results showed that, regardless of the underlying retrieval protocol, the response time decreases as the number of channels increases. In addition, the response time increases as the number of requested data elements increases. Finally, for all cases, *top down retrieval scheme* (see Section 3.6.2), relative to the *bottom up retrieval scheme* compromises the response time (Fig. 29)—the additional time requirement can be associated to the goal of reducing channel switches during the retrieval, thus incurring more broadcast passes that inherently increase the access latency. From Fig. 29 it can be observed that the least-cost path technique is more efficient in generating the access patterns than the technique used in the *bottom up retrieval scheme.*

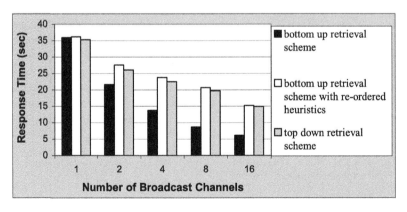

FIG. 29. Response times comparison for different retrieval protocols.

The retrieval protocols proposed in Section 3.6 attempt primarily to reduce the conflicts in each broadcast pass; however, when the number of potential conflicts increases considerably, some conflicts become unavoidable causing an increase in the number of passes and hence an increase in the response time. The increase in the number of passes makes the retrieval scheme inadequate when the percentage of requested data elements is large. The simulation results also showed that when the percentage of requested data elements approaches 100%, the response time reduces. This shows the validity of the proposed scheduling protocols since, when a relatively large number of data elements are requested, they generate the same retrieval sequence as the *Row Scan* method would.

7.2.3.2 *Channel Switching Frequency.*

In general, with respect to the *bottom up retrieval scheme* as the number of requested data elements increases, up to a threshold value, one should observe more frequent channel switches. This is due to the increase in the number of conflicts. As the number of conflicts increases, the *bottom up retrieval scheme* attempts to reduce their effect on the response time through the use of channel switches. The number of channel switches reaches a maximum and begins to decrease when retrieving more than 50% of the broadcast. This decrease occurs because of the heuristic rule employed that attempts "to maximize the number of data elements retrieved during each broadcast cycle." As the density of requested objects increases, the *bottom up retrieval scheme* does not have to switch channels as often to retrieve the maximum number of requests (Fig. 30).

The *Top down retrieval scheme* compromises the response time to minimize the number of channel switches. Figure 31 depicts the channel switching frequency

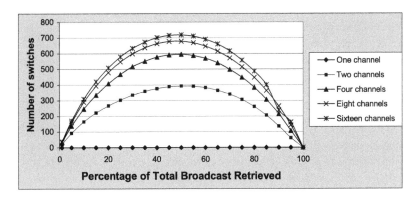

FIG. 30. Channel switching frequency (*Bottom Up Retrieval Scheme*).

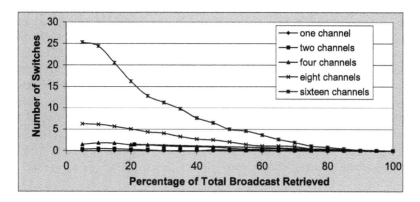

FIG. 31. Channel switching frequency (*Top Down Retrieval Scheme*).

when the *top down retrieval scheme* is employed. The maximum number of channel switches is reached for when size of a user query is less than 5%. At this point, the number of broadcast passes approaches the number of channels, thus mimicking the access pattern of the *Row Scan* Method. In short, the *top down retrieval scheme* does not allow the number of broadcast passes to exceed the number of channels, and thus as the number of requested data elements increases, the number of channel switches decreases.

7.2.3.3   Energy Consumption.

In general, the energy consumption follows the same pattern as the channel switching frequency. For the *bottom up retrieval scheme*, the energy consumption is dominated by the number of channel switches. As a result, the energy consumption increases as the number of channels increases. In addition, the energy consumption increases, up to a threshold point, as the number of requested data elements increases, and then it decreases as the number of requested data elements continues to increases (Fig. 32).

Figure 33 depicts the energy consumption of the *top down retrieval scheme*. The figure illustrates that the energy consumption increases as the number of data elements being retrieved increases. The increase in energy consumption follows a linear trend that is directly related to the increase of data elements requested. This is because the retrieval of a data element implies the active operational mode. In addition, the *top down retrieval scheme* attempts to minimize the channel switching frequency. As a result, the energy consumption is dominated by the number of requested data elements.

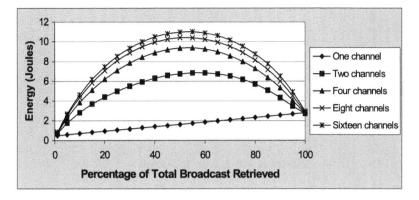

FIG. 32. Energy consumption (*Bottom Up Retrieval Scheme*).

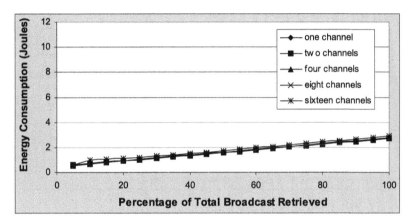

FIG. 33. Energy consumption (*Top Down Retrieval Scheme*).

7.2.3.4 *Number of Passes.*

The number of passes directly relates to the number of conflicts. As a result, as the number of requested data elements and/or the number of channels increases, one should expect to observe more passes over the parallel air channels. This by default implies higher access latency. An increase in the number of channels implies an increase in the number of conflicts, and hence a higher possibility of unavoidable conflicts, which in turn results in an increase in the number of passes. Figure 34 demonstrates these facts. Interestingly, when the number of requested data elements is large, the number of passes exceeds the number of channels available. This is due to the priority order of the heuristics used in the *bottom up retrieval scheme*—the proposed method tries to reduce the amount of

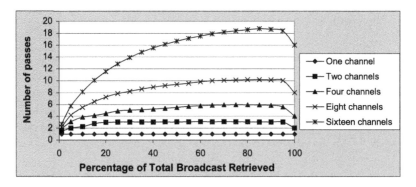

FIG. 34. Number of passes (*Bottom Up Retrieval Scheme*).

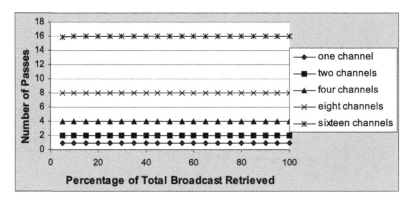

FIG. 35. Number of broadcast passes (*Top Down Retrieval Scheme*).

conflicts first. However, it is not likely that a query of public data would involve a substantial percentage of the total data available, hence it can be concluded that in general, the *bottom up retrieval scheme* reduces the number of passes.

The *Top down Retrieval scheme* sacrifices the response time and the number of passes, for lower power consumption. Experiences showed that the number of passes increases greatly for a small number of requests and reaches a maximum where the number of passes equals the number of channels. This is mainly due to the intelligence of the least-cost path method that only expands the path that has the smallest number of channel switches. As the number of user requests increases, the algorithm generates the access patterns according to the *Row Scan* method (Fig. 35).

7.3 Section Conclusion

One of the problems associated with broadcasting information on parallel air channels is the possibility of conflicts between accessing objects on different channels. Since the mobile unit can tune into only one channel at a time, conflicting objects have to be retrieved on a subsequent broadcast. In addition, switching between channels imposes an extra cost. During the channel switch time, the mobile unit is unable to retrieve any data from the broadcast. Conflicts will directly influence the access latency and hence, the overall execution time. The issue of conflicts was introduced in Section 3.5. In an attempt to reduce the access time and power consumption, as noted in Section 3.6 heuristics were used to develop a scheduling access patterns that reduces the number of passes over the parallel air channels. Analysis and effectiveness of such a policy was also the subject of this section.

8. Conflict Resolution and Generation of Access Patterns Beyond Heuristics

Our discussion in Section 7 mainly focused on problem-specific heuristics. *Next Object* is a heuristic algorithm that always retrieves the next available object on a broadcast. *Row Scan* simply reads all the objects from one channel in each pass. The so called *bottom up*, and *top down tree-based algorithms* generates an access forest and uses a set of heuristics to choose the "most suitable access pattern" with the goals to reduce the number of passes. It should be noted that the heuristic solutions, in general, offer a "good" solution, not always. For example the protocols discussed in Section 7, in some instances could require unnecessary number of passes and/or channel switches. The following two examples are intended to motivate this issue.

Assume retrieval of eight objects from a three-channel configuration (Fig. 36). The application of the *bottom up retrieval approach* requires four passes (objects 3,

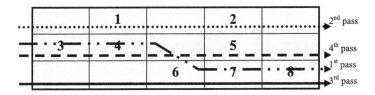

FIG. 36. Generation of unnecessary passes by the *Bottom Up Retrieval Approach.*

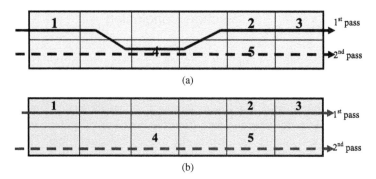

FIG. 37. Generation of unnecessary number of channel switches by the *Top Down Retrieval Approach.* (a) Generation of access patterns when top down retrieval approach is employed. (b) Generation of access patterns when row scan heuristic is employed.

4, 7, and 8 are scheduled in the first pass, objects 1 and 2 are scheduled in the second pass, object 6 is scheduled in the third pass, and finally, object 5 is scheduled in the forth pass), however, a simple row scan algorithm will retrieve these objects in three passes.

Figure 37 shows an example where the *top down retrieval algorithm* requires unnecessary number of channel switches.

The next section will introduce two new scheduling algorithms that can find the minimum number of passes and the corresponding minimum number of switches with reasonable costs [61]. Similar to our earlier discussion in Section 8, a two-dimensional array of $N \times M$ is used to represent a parallel broadcast. In this array, each cell $C_{i,j}$, $1 \leqslant i \leqslant N$, $1 \leqslant j \leqslant M$, represents a page. Without loss of generality, we assume objects are not fragmented across adjacent pages, and if we request any object in a page, we will retrieve the whole page. A row of cells represents a channel on the broadcast, while a column of cells represents pages transmitted at the same time on parallel channels. For a query requesting a set of objects S, if the cell $C_{i,j}$ has a requested object then $C_{i,j} \in S$. Finally, a query requests K objects O_k, $1 \leqslant k \leqslant K$. Based on the aforementioned assumptions we have the following definitions with respect to a given query (Figs. 38 and 39 are intended to clarify these definitions).

Definition 5 (*Empty columns*). A column without any requested objects occurring in it is empty.

Definition 6 (*Sparse columns*). A column containing requested objects without any conflicts with others is sparse.

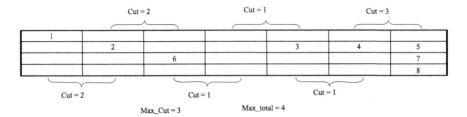

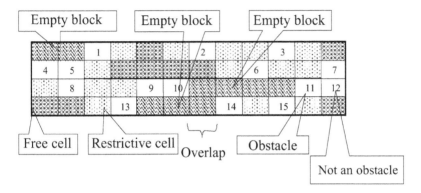

FIG. 38. cut, MAX_cut and MAX_total.

FIG. 39. Free cells, restrictive cells, overlapped empty blocks, and obstacles.

Definition 7 (*Dense columns*). A column that is neither *Empty* nor *Sparse* is *Dense*. With respect to a user request, the minimum required number of passes depends on dense columns.

R_j is defined to be the set of rows we need to scan in column j based on objects in columns j through $j + OPR - 1$. This naturally leads to the definition of the cut at column j.

Definition 8. Let $R_j = \{i \mid \exists j', \; j \leqslant j' \leqslant j + OPR - 1$, such that $C_{ij'} \in S\}$. Consequently, the *cut* at column j is $|R_j|$.

Definition 9. The *maximum cut*, *MAX_cut*, is $max\{cut_j \mid 1 \leqslant j \leqslant N\}$.

Definition 10. The *total requested channels*, *MAX_total*, is $|\{i \mid j$ such that $C_{i,j} \in S\}|$.

We can conclude that *MAX_cut* $\leqslant$ *minimum number of passes* $\leqslant$ *MAX_total*.

Definition 11. The set of *empty cells*, E, is $\{C_{i,j} \mid C_{i,j} \notin S\}$.

Definition 12. The set of *restrictive cells*, R, is $\{C_{i,j} \mid C_{i,j} \notin S \wedge (C_{i,j+1} \in S \vee C_{i,j-1} \in S)\}$.

Definition 13. The set of *free cells*, F, is $\{C_{i,j} \mid C_{i,j} \in E \wedge C_{i,j} \notin R\}$.

An important concept in our algorithms is the empty block which is a contiguous sequence of empty cells in one row.

Definition 14. An *empty block*, $B_{i,j}$, is the largest set of contiguous empty cells in row i starting in column j.

Given a set of empty blocks all starting in the same column, a *rightmost empty block* is a block in the set that is not smaller than any other block in the set, i.e., no other empty block extends farther to the right of it.

Definition 15 (*Overlapped empty blocks*). Two empty blocks B and B' overlap each other, iff they each contain a cell from some column, i.e., $\exists j$, such that $C_{i,j} \in B \wedge C_{i',j} \in B' \wedge i \neq i'$.

Definition 16. The set of *obstacles*, O, is $\{C_{i,j} \mid C_{i,j} \in S \wedge C_{i,j-1} \in E \wedge C_{i,j-2} \in E\}$.

8.1   Parallel Object Scan

In this presentation, graphically, lines (access lines) are used to represent the access patterns in different passes. Parallel Object Scan (POS) uses *MAX_cut* passes to scan all requested objects on a broadcast. Starting from the leftmost column to the right, POS in parallel constructs *MAX_cut* lines, column by column. It attempts to use access lines to visit all the requested objects in the next column with the fewest number of switches from the previous column. POS observes which cell $C_{i,j}$ with an access line has a less chance to have a requested object in the future on the same channel and uses this line to make a channel switch when necessary. This strategy minimizes the number of switches.

Definition 17 (*Access line*). A vector of length M representing one pass through the matrix. The value $l[j]$ is the channel (row #) that the line reads at time (column) j.

We define *freeright*(i, j) to be the rightmost column of the *Empty block*.

Definition 18. Let *freeright*(i, j) be the largest j' such that for all k, $j \leqslant k \leqslant j'$, $C_{ik} \in E$.

We define *next*(j, L) to be the line in L that reads from the channel with the rightmost empty block in column j.

Definition 19. Let *next*(j, L) be a line $l \in L$ such that *freeright*$(l[j], j) = max\{freeright(l'[j], j) \mid l' \in L\}$.

We define *First*(i) to be the column in which a requested object first appears in row i.

Definition 20. Let *First*(i) be the smallest j such that for all j', $1 \leqslant j' < j$, $C_{ij'} \notin S$.

Let *Start*(m) be rows $\{i_1, \ldots, i_m\}$ such that for any row $i' \notin \{i_1, \ldots, i_m\}$ *First*$(i) \leqslant$ *First*(i') for all $i \in \{i_1, \ldots, i_m\}$. In other words, *Start*(m) are rows that contain objects before any other rows. These rows will be the starting point for our *MAX_cut* lines, as we obviously do not want to switch a line before it has read any objects on a channel (Fig. 40(a)).

POS Algorithm

```
1.  if (MAX_total = MAX_cut)
2.      use Row Scan;
3.  else
4.      Let m = MAX_cut
5.      Create m lines, l₁, . . . , lₘ
6.      Lines = {l₁, . . . , lₘ}          /* Set containing all the lines */
7.      l₁[1], . . . , lₘ[1] = Start(m)      /* Initialize lines */
8.      for j = 2 to M do {
9.          L = Lines    /* All the lines */
10.         A = Rⱼ       /* Required Rows: |A| ⩽ |L| */
11.         foreach l ∈ L    /* check for no switch, line reads an object */
12.             if l[j] ∈ A then l[j] = l[j − 1]; A = A − {l[j]}; L = L − {l}
13.         foreach i ∈ A    /* remaining objects, inside switch */
14.             l = next(j, L)
15.             l[j] = i
16.             L = L − {l}
17.         foreach l ∈ L    /* no object to read, no switch */
18.             l[j] = l[j − 1]}
```

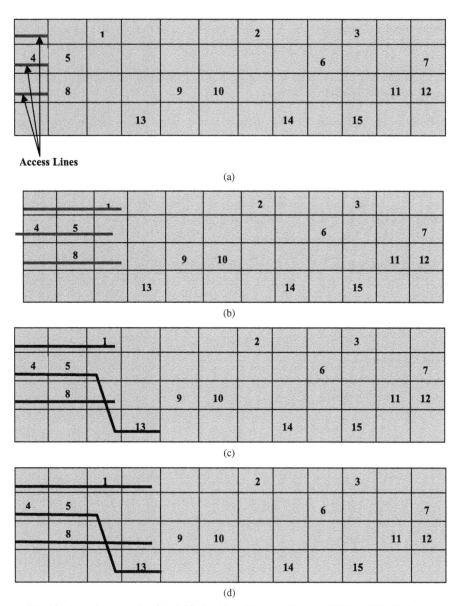

FIG. 40. A running example of the POS algorithm. (a) Access lines are initialized (7). (b) Extending the access lines without channel switching (11–12, 17–18). (c) Moving to the right and an inside switch (13–16). (d) Advancing the access lines without any inside switch (17–18). (e) Generation of the final access lines.

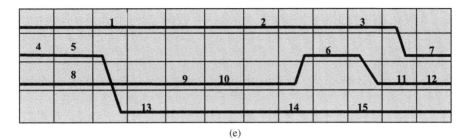

(e)

FIG. 40. Continued.

The POS algorithm runs in $O(N^2 M)$ time—all of the required sets and functions except *next* (e.g., R_j, E, *freeright*, *First*, *Start*) can be computed in $O(NM)$ time. If we pre-compute these once, then any use of them during the algorithm requires just constant time. The function *next* takes $O(N)$ time since the size of L (the number of access lines) will be at most N. The algorithm consists of an outer loop iterated $M - 1$ times. The algorithm contains three inner loops each iterated at most N times (since the sizes of L and A are bounded by N). The first and third inner loop bodies take constant time while the second inner loop body takes $O(N)$ time due to the call to *next*.

Figure 40 is a running example that shows the behavior of the POS algorithm in finding the optimal number of the access lines for the requested objects (numbers in the captions refer to the line number in the POS algorithm) when applied to the request shown in Fig. 36. In this request, refer to Definitions 9 and 10, *MAX_cut* is 3, *MAX_total* is 4 and at least 3 passes with at least 4 channel switches are required to retrieve the requested objects.

As a result, three passes are required to retrieve the requested objects. In one pass, objects 1, 2, 3, and 7 are retrieved. In the second pass, objects 4, 5, 13, 14, and 15 are retrieved. Finally, in the third pass, objects 8, 9, 10, 6, 11, and 12 are retrieved.

8.2 Serial Empty Scan

The Serial Empty Scan (SES) which examines empty blocks. The basic idea behind the algorithm is as follows. We construct $(MAX\_total - MAX\_cut)$ paths that scan only empty blocks (empty paths). As we do this we also compress the requested objects into *MAX_cut* channels. Each of these resulting "logical" channels describes the sequence of requested objects that an access line reads. The action of compressing (copying objects from one channel to another) simulates a switch during a scan.

The SES algorithm is serial since it finds the ($MAX\_total - MAX\_cut$) empty paths one by one. The SES algorithm constructs an empty path by starting with the rightmost empty block $B_{i',1}$ in some row i'. The path starts in row i' at column 1 and continues to column k, where k is the length of $B_{i',1}$. Next it finds a rightmost overlapping empty block $B_{i'',k}$. The path continues on row i'' for the length of this empty block and so forth. Additionally, the SES algorithm begins to create a logical channel by moving all requested objects $C_{i'',a}$, to $C_{i',a}$, for $1 \leqslant a < k$. Finally it marks the empty cell $C_{i',lk}$ as *no obstacle*, indicating a physical switch occurs at this point in the logical channel. This end marker is used during the construction of subsequent empty paths. By convention, we also define that $\forall i'$, $C_{i',M} = $ *no obstacle*, iff $C_{i',M} \in E \wedge C_{i',M-1} \in E$. The SES algorithm repeats this construction of an empty path until it reaches the right end. During subsequent scans, when choosing an overlapping empty block, the SES algorithm chooses the rightmost block ending with the *no obstacle* marker, if one exists. If no such empty block exists, the algorithm simply chooses the rightmost empty block. After every scan, MAX_total is decremented by 1. The algorithm will terminate when $MAX\_total = MAX\_cut$, and all the requested objects have been moved into MAX_cut logical channels, on each of which the order of the requested objects gives the access pattern during each broadcast.

Since choosing the next empty block is a fundamental step in the SES algorithm, we define it first. Given a set of row indices *Rows* and a column j, *nextblock(Rows, j)* returns the appropriate row i to add to the empty path being constructed. To define this function we also define *rightmost(Rows, j)* which returns the row index of the rightmost free block in among B_{ij} for $i \in Rows$.

Definition 21. *rightmost(Rows, j)* $= i$ such that $i \in Rows$ & *freeright(i, j)* $=$ *max(freeright(i', j)* $| i' \in Rows)$.

Definition 22.   *nextblock(Rows, j)* $=$
    let EBs $= \{i \mid i \in Rows$ & $C_{ij} \in E\}$ /* Empty Blocks */
    let OBs $= \{i \mid i \in$ EBs & $k = $ *freeright(i, j)* & $C_{ik} = $ *no obstacle*$\}$
     if OBs $\neq \{\}$ then return(*rightmost*(OBs, j))
      else return(*rightmost*(EBs, j))

In the SES algorithm, an obstacle on a broadcast may result in an inside switch if the empty block on the left of it is scanned. Those obstacles whose empty blocks on the left are not chosen to scan will not result in a switch. Cells that are not obstacles will not generate inside switches. It should be noted that if the algorithm moves requested objects from channel A to channel B, a switch is indicated, but if they are subsequently moved from channel B to channel C, it is equal to moving from channel A to channel C, and still only one switch occurs. Thus, the strategy of choosing blocks marked no obstacle (in the function *nextblock*) minimizes the number of in-side switches. Choosing the rightmost empty block, at each step also contributes to minimizing the number of inside switches of a scan.

The SES algorithm has complexity $O(N^2M)$. The functions *rightmost* and *nextblock* are both bounded by the number of rows, hence they are both $O(N)$. The SES algorithm's outer loop iterates at most N times and its inner loop iterates at most M times. Finally, the body of the inner loop takes $O(N)$ times due to the call to *nextblock*. Consequently, the inner loop has complexity $O(NM)$ and so does the body of the outer loop.

Figure 41 depicts the snap shots of a running example of SES algorithm to re-trieve fourteen objects from a five-parallel channel configuration. For this request, *MAX_cut* is 3, *MAX_total* is 5 and at least 3 passes with at least 7 switches are re-quired to retrieve the requested objects (numbers in the captions represent the line number in SES algorithm).

SES Algorithm
1. if $(MAX\_total = MAX\_cut)$
2.   use Row Scan;
3. else
4. $Rows = \{1, \dots, N\}$ /* Rows we can compress */
5.   repeat until $(MAX\_total = MAX\_cut)$ {
6. $j = 1$;
7. $i = nextblock(Rows, j)$
8. $k = freeright(i, j)$ /* free block is C_{ij} to C_{ik} */
9.   repeat until $k = M$ {
10. $i' = nextblock(Rows, k)$
11. $k = freeright(i', j)$
12. $C_{ia} = C_{i'a}$ for $1 \leqslant a < k$ /* compress channels */
13. $C_{i'k} = no\ obstacle$ /* indicate a switch occurs */
14. $i = i'$
15. $j = k$
16.   }
17. $MAX\_total = MAX\_total - 1$
18. $Rows = Rows - \{i\}$ /* delete the empty row */
19.   }

An Empty block without an obstacle (Definition 14) represents a channel switch.

As one can conclude, in the first pass, objects 1, 3, 5, and 3 are retrieved. During the second pass, objects 4, 7, 8, 9, and 10 are fetched. Finally, during the third pass, objects 11, 13, 12, 14, and 6 are retrieved.

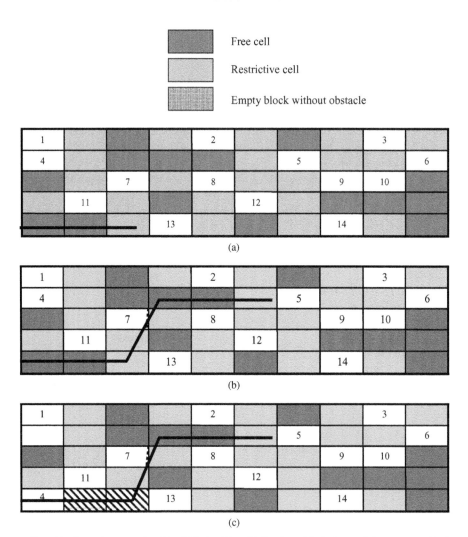

FIG. 41. A running example of the SES algorithm. (a) Starting with the largest leftmost empty block with an obstacle (Definition 18 and 6–8). (b) Find an overlapped empty block (Definition 13, 10–11) and switch. (c) Logical rearrangement of object 4 and advancing the empty block (12). Repeated operational flow as of (a), (b) and (c), and generation of an empty channel (9–16). (e) Starting with the largest leftmost empty block with an obstacle (6–8). (f) Find an overlapped empty block and switch (10–11). (g) Find an overlapped empty block and switch (12). (h) Logical rearrangement of object 4 and advancing the empty block (10–11). (i) Find an overlapped empty block and switch (10–11, 12–13). (j) Logical rearrangement of objects 11 and 13, switch, and advancing the empty block (10–11, 12–13). (k) Generation of second empty channel. (l) The Final access patterns.

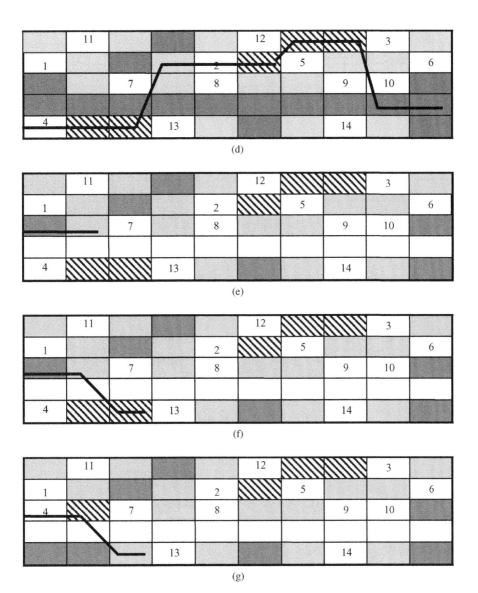

FIG. 41. Continued.

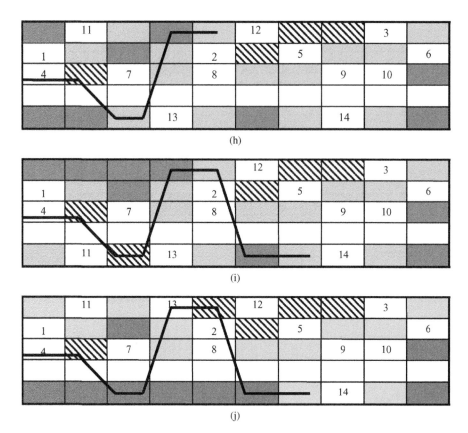

FIG. 41. Continued.

9. Conclusion and Future Research Directions

Broadcasting has been proposed as a viable solution to allow anytime, anywhere access to the public data. Within the constraints of mobile devices and wireless communication, this chapter was aimed to address the application and effectiveness of data broadcasting from two viewpoints: energy and response time. Indexing schemes are essential to exploit different operational modes of mobile devices in order to conserve energy at the expense of additional overheads. Broadcasting over the parallel air channels is essential to reduce the broadcast length and hence, to reduce the access latency. Our results showed that the use of parallel air channels not only is successful in reducing the access latencies, as compared to a single air channel, but also decreases the power consumption of the mobile device, significantly. Moreover,

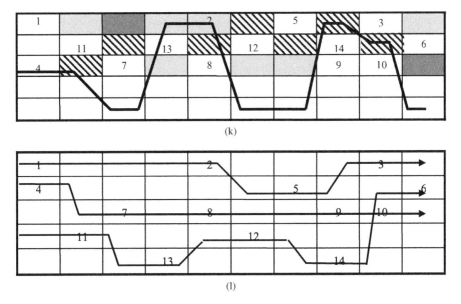

FIG. 41. Continued.

the results revealed that the index allocation in the broadcast channels has an effect in terms of both response time and energy consumption. It should be noted that an increase in the number of channels increases both the amount of energy expended in switching from one channel to another and conflicts in accessing data across the parallel channels.

In order to address these issues, we developed and implemented different data retrieval algorithms for parallel broadcast channels. In particular, we found that existing solutions for TSP problem were applicable to our problem. The results from our study showed that when a small (less than about 45%) percentage of the objects in a broadcast are requested, a TSP heuristic should be used to determine the access order in which the broadcast objects should be retrieved. However, when a larger percentage of the objects is requested, the Row Scan method should be used to avoid the delay associated with switching between channels.

The retrieval scheme proposed reduces the number of passes over the broadcast channels as the number of channels increases; however, this increases the number of conflicts and consequently, an increase in the switching frequency among channels. This results in an increase in the energy consumption. In an attempt to balance energy consumption and access latency, the scope of our research was extended by developing a set of heuristics that generates an ordered access patterns, i.e., the bottom up and top down retrieval schemes. We simulated and analyzed the effectiveness of these heuristic based retrieval methods. However, as expected, in some instances, these heuristic based schemes would generate access patterns that require extra passes over the air channels and/or extra channel switches. Finally, two algorithms were proposed that always generate minimum number of the access patterns with minimum number of channel switches.

The scope of this research can be extended in many directions:

- Within the scope of the Mobile Data Access System, our research studied the allocation and retrieval methods based on tree-based indexing techniques. However, tree-based indexing methods have some shortcomings in retrieving objects based on multiple attributes. It may be possible to develop a new method that combines the strengths of a tree-based indexing method with the strengths of signature-based methods to overcome this shortcoming.

- This work assumed that the resolution of queries happens on an individual basis at the mobile unit. It may be possible to reduce computation by utilizing a buffer and bundling several queries together and processing them as a whole.

ACKNOWLEDGEMENTS

This work would have not been made possible without the sincere effort of many students who participated in the development of conceptual foundation as well as simulation results. We would like to thank them. In addition, this work in part has been supported by the Office of the Naval Research and the National Science Foundation under the contracts N00014-02-1-0282, IIS-0324835, and STI-0129682, respectively.

REFERENCES

[1] Acharya S., Franklin M., Zdonik S., "Dissemination-based data delivery using broadcast links", *IEEE Personal Commun.* **2** (6) (1995).
[2] Acharya S., Alonso R., Franklin M., Zdonik S., "Broadcast disks: Data management for asymmetric communication environments", in: *Proceedings ACM SIGMOD International Conference on the Management of Data*, 1995, pp. 199–210.
[3] Acharya S., Franklin M., Zdonik S., "Balancing push and pull for data broadcast", in: *Proceedings ACM SIGMOD International Conference on the Management of Data*, 1997, pp. 183–194.
[4] Alonso R., Ganguly S., "Energy efficient query optimization", Technical Report MITL-TR-33-92, Matsushita Information Technology Laboratory, Princeton, NJ, 1992.

[5] Alonso R., Korth H.F., "Database system issues in nomadic computing", in: *Proceedings ACM SIGMOD Conference on Management of Data*, 1993, pp. 388–392.

[6] Atkinson M., Bancilhon F., DeWitt D., Dittrich K., Maier D., Zdonik S., in: *Proceedings of the Conference on Deductive and Object-Oriented Databases*, 1989, pp. 40–57.

[7] Banerjee J., Kim W., Kim S.-J., Garza J.F., "Clustering a DAG for CAD databases", *IEEE Trans. Software Engrg.* **14** (11) (1988) 1684–1699.

[8] Bhide M., Deolasee P., Katkar A., Panchbudhe A., Ramamritham K., Shenoy P., "Adaptive push-pull: Disseminating dynamic web data", *IEEE Trans. Comput.* **51** (6) (2002) 652–668.

[9] Boonsiriwattanakul S., Hurson A.R., Vijaykrishnan N., Chehadeh C., "Energy-efficient indexing on parallel air channels in a mobile database access system", in: *3rd World Multiconference on Systemics, Cybernetics and Informatics (SCI'99) and 5th International Conference on Information Systems Analysis and Synthesis (ISAS'99)*, 1999, pp. IV 30–38.

[10] Bright M.W., Hurson A.R., Pakzad S., "A taxonomy and current issues in multidatabase systems", *IEEE Comput.* **25** (3) (1992) 50–60.

[11] Bright M.W., Hurson A.R., Pakzad S., "Automated resolution of semantic heterogeneity in multidatabases", *ACM Trans. Database Systems* **19** (2) (1994) 212–253.

[12] Cetintemel U., Franklin M., Giles L., "Self-adaptive user profiles for large-scale data delivery", in: *Proceedings of ICDE*, 2000, pp. 622–633.

[13] Chang E.E., Katz R.H., "Exploiting inheritance and structure semantics for effective clustering and buffering in an object-oriented DBMS", in: *Proceedings ACM SIGMOD Conference on Management of Data*, 1989, pp. 348–357.

[14] Chehadeh C.Y., Hurson A.R., Tavangarian D., "Object organization on single and parallel broadcast channel", in: *High Performance Computing*, 2001, pp. 163–169.

[15] Chehadeh C.Y., Hurson A.R., Miller L.L., "Energy-efficient indexing on a broadcast channel in a mobile database access system", in: *IEEE Conference on Information Technology*, 2000, pp. 368–374.

[16] Chehadeh C.Y., Hurson A.R., Kavehrad M., "Object organization on a single broadcast channel in the mobile computing environment", Special issue on mobile computing environments for multimedia systems, *Multimedia Tools Appl. J.* **9** (1999) 69–94.

[17] Chehadeh C.Y., Hurson A.R., Miller L.L., Pakzad S., Jamoussi B.N., "Application of parallel disks for efficient handling of object-oriented databases", in: *Proceedings Fifth IEEE Symposium on Parallel and Distributed Processing*, 1993, pp. 184–191.

[18] Chen M.-S., Wu K.-L., Yu P.S., "Optimizing index allocation for sequential data broadcasting in wireless mobile computing", *IEEE Trans. Knowledge and Data Engrg.* **15** (1) (2003) 161–173.

[19] Cheng J.-B.R., Hurson A.R., "Effective clustering of complex objects in object-oriented databases", in: *Proceedings of ACM SIGMOD Conference on Management of Data*, 1991, pp. 22–27.

[20] Cheng J.-B.R., Hurson A.R., "On the performance issues of object-based buffering", in: *Proceedings International Conference on Parallel and Distributed Information Systems*, 1991, pp. 30–37.

[21] Chlamtac I., Lin Y.-B., "Mobile computing: When mobility meets computation", *IEEE Trans. Comput.* **46** (3) (1997) 257–259.

[22] Demers A., Pertersen K., Spreitzer M., Terry D., Theier M., Welch B., "The Bayou architecture: Support for data sharing among mobile users", in: *IEEE Proceedings of the Workshop on Mobile Computing Systems and Applications*, 1994.

[23] Fong E., Kent W., Moore K., Thompson C., "Object Oriented Databases Task Group (OODBTG) Final Report", OODBTG of the Database Systems Study Group (DBSSG) of the Accredited Standards Committee X3 (ASC/X3) of the Standards Planning and Requirements Committee (SPARC), under the American National Standard Institute (ANSI), 1991.

[24] Gifford D., "Polychannel systems for mass digital communications", *Commun. ACM* **33** (2) (1990) 141–151.

[25] Fox A., Gribble S.D., Brewer E.A., Amir E., "Adapting to network and client variability via on-demand dynamic distillation", in: *Proceedings of ASPLOS-VII, Boston, MA*, 1996.

[26] Honeyman P., Huston L., Rees J., Bachmann D., "The LITTLE WORK Project", in: *Proceedings of the Third IEEE Workshop on Workstation Operating Systems*, 1992.

[27] Hu Q.L., Lee W.-C., Lee D.L., "Conserving and access efficient indexes for wireless computing", in: *Proceedings of the 16th International Conference on Data Engineering*, 2000.

[28] Hu Q.L., Lee D.L., "Power conservative multi-attribute queries on data broadcast", in: *Proceedings of IEEE International Conference on Data Engineering*, 2000, pp. 157–166.

[29] Hu Q.L., Lee D.L., "Power conserving and access efficient indexes for wireless computing", in: Tanaka K., Ghandeharizadeh S., Kambayashi Y. (Eds.), *Information Organization and Databases*, Kluwer Academic Publications, Boston, MA, 2000, pp. 249–264.

[30] Hu Q.L., Lee D.L., "A hybrid index technique for power efficient data broadcast", *Distributed and Parallel Databases J.* **9** (2) (2001) 151–177.

[31] Hurson A.R., Chehadeh C.Y., Hannan J., "Object organization on parallel broadcast channels in a global information sharing environment", in: *IEEE Conference on Performance, Computing, and Communications*, 2000, pp. 347–353.

[32] Hurson A.R., Pakzad S., Cheng J.-B.R., "Object-oriented database management systems", *IEEE Comput.* **26** (2) (1993) 48–60.

[33] Hurson A.R., Bright M.W., "Multidatabase systems: An advanced concept in handling distributed data", in: *Advances in Computers*, vol. 32, 1991, pp. 149–200.

[34] Imielinski T., Viswanathan S., Badrinath B.R., "Energy efficient indexing on air", in: *Proceedings ACM SIGMOD Conference on Management of Data*, 1994, pp. 25–36.

[35] Imielinski T., Badrinath B.R., "Mobile wireless computing: Challenges in data management", *Commun. ACM* **37** (10) (1994) 18–28.

[36] Imielinski T., Badrinath B.R., "Adaptive wireless information systems", in: *Proceedings of SIGDBS Conf., Tokyo, Japan*, 1994.

[37] Imielinski T., Korth H.F., "Introduction to mobile computing", in: Imielinski T., Korth H.F. (Eds.), *Mobile Computing*, Kluwer Academic Publishers, Dordrecht/Norwell, MA, 1996, pp. 1–43.

[38] Imielinski T., Viswanathan S., Badrinath B.R., "Data on air: Organization and access", *IEEE Trans. Knowledge and Data Engrg.* **9** (3) (1997) 353–372.

[39] Joseph A.D., Tauber J.A., Kaashoek M.F., "Mobile computing with the Rover toolkit", Special Issue on Mobile Computing, *IEEE Trans. Comput.* **46** (3) (1997) 337–352.

[40] Juran J., Hurson A.R., Vijaykrishnan N., "Data organization and retrieval on parallel air channels: Performance and energy issues", *ACM J. WINET* **10** (2) (2004) 183–195.

[41] Juran J., Hurson A.R., Vijaykrishnan N., Boonsiriwattanakul S., "Data organization on parallel air channel", in: *International Conference on High Performance Computing*, 2000, pp. 501–510.

[42] Kaashoek M.F., Pinckney T., Tauber J.A., "Dynamic documents: Mobile wireless access to the WWW", in: *Proceedings of the IEEE Workshop on Mobile Computing Systems and Applications*, 1995.

[43] Kim W., *Introduction to Object-Oriented Databases*, MIT Press, Cambridge, MA, 1990.

[44] Lai S.J., Zaslavsky A.Z., Martin G.P., Yeo L.H., "Cost efficient adaptive protocol with buffering for advanced mobile database applications", in: *Proceedings of the Fourth International Conference on Database Systems for Advanced Applications*, 1995.

[45] Lim J.B., Hurson A.R., Miller L.L., Chehadeh C.Y., "A dynamic clustering scheme for distributed object-oriented databases", *Math. Modeling Sci. Comput.* **8** (1997).

[46] Lim J.B., Hurson A.R., "Transaction processing in mobile, heterogeneous database systems", *IEEE Trans. Knowledge and Data Engrg.* **14** (6) (2002) 1330–1346.

[47] Lim J.B., Hurson A.R., "Heterogenous data access in a mobile environment—issues and solutions", in: *Advances in Computers*, vol. 48, 1999, pp. 119–178.

[48] Munoz-Avila A., Hurson A.R., "Energy-efficient objects retrieval on indexed broadcast parallel channels", in: *International Conference on Information Resource Management*, 2003, pp. 190–194.

[49] Munoz-Avila A., Hurson A.R., "Energy-aware retrieval from indexed broadcast parallel channels", in: *Advanced Simulation Technology Conference (High Performance Computing)*, 2003, pp. 3–8.

[50] "NASDAQ World Wide Web Home Page", 2002, http://www.nasdaq.com.

[51] Nemzow M., *Implementing Wireless Network*, McGraw Hill, New York, 1995.

[52] Oh J., Hua K., Prabhakara K., "A new broadcasting technique for an adaptive hybrid data delivery in wireless mobile network environment", in: *IEEE Conference on Performance, Computing, and Communications*, 2000, pp. 361–367.

[53] Orchowski N., Hurson A.R., "Energy-aware object retrieval from parallel broadcast channels", in: *Proceedings of the International Database Engineering and Applications Symposium*, 2004, pp. 37–46.

[54] Peng W.-C., Chen M.-S., "Dynamic generation of data broadcasting programs for a broadcast disk array in a mobile computing environment", in: *ACM International Conference on Information and Knowledge Management*, 2000, pp. 38–45.

[55] Peng W.-C., Haung J.-L., Chen M.-S., "Dynamic leveling: Adaptive data broadcasting in a mobile computing environment", in: *Mobile Networks and Applications*, 2003, pp. 355–364.

[56] Rusinkiewics M., Czejdo B., "Query transformation in heterogeneous distributed data base systems", in: *Proceedings of Fifth International Conference on Distributed Computing Systems*, 1985, pp. 300–307.

[57] Satyanarayanan M., Noble B., Kumar P., Price M., "Application-aware adaptation for mobile computing", in: *Proceedings of the 6th ACM SIGOPS European Workshop*, 1994.

[58] Satyanarayanan M., Kistler J.J., Mummert L.B., "Experience with disconnected operation in a mobile computing environment", in: *Proceedings of USENIX Symposium on Mobile and Location-Independent Computing*, 1993.

[59] Shivakumar N., Venkatasubramanian S., "Efficient indexing for broadcast based wireless systems", *ACM–Baltzer Journal of Mobile Networks and Nomadic Applications* **1** (1996) 433–446.

[60] Stathatos K., Roussopoulos N., Baras J., "Adaptive data broadcast in hybrid networks", in: *Proceedings of VLDB*, 1997.

[61] Sun B., Hurson A.R., Hannan J., "Energy-efficient scheduling algorithms of object retrieval on indexed parallel broadcast channels", in: *International Conference on Parallel Processing*, 2004, pp. 440–447.

[62] Vaidya N., Harneed S., "Scheduling data broadcast in asymmetric communication environments", *Wireless Networks* **5** (1999) 171–182.

[63] Wong J., Dykeman H.D., "Architecture and performance of large scale information delivery networks", in: *12th International Teletraffic Congress, Torino, Italy*, 1988.

[64] Zdonik S., Alonso R., Franklin M., Acharya S., "Are disks in the air just pie in the sky?", in: *Proceedings Workshop on Mobile Computing Systems and Applications*, 1994, pp. 1–8.

[65] Weiser M., "Some computer science issues in ubiquitous computing", *Commun. ACM* **36** (7) (1993) 75–84.

Programming Models and Synchronization Techniques for Disconnected Business Applications

AVRAHAM LEFF AND JAMES T. RAYFIELD

IBM T.J. Watson Research Center
P.O. Box 704
Yorktown Heights, NY 10598
USA
avraham@us.ibm.com
jtray@us.ibm.com

Abstract

Programming models usefully structure the way that programmers approach problems and develop applications. Business applications need properties such as persistence, data sharing, transactions, and security, and various programming models exist—for connected environments—that facilitate the development of applications with these properties. Recently, it has become possible to consider running business applications on disconnected devices. Developers thus confront two areas of concern. The first is to solve the pragmatic problems of how to implement the properties required by business applications in a disconnected environment. The second is to determine whether programming models for disconnected environments exist (as they do for connected environments) that facilitate the development of business applications.

This chapter discusses these two areas of concern. We explain why business applications are particularly hard to "project" to disconnected devices. We then introduce some of the approaches used to solve these problems (focusing especially on *data replication* and *method replay* techniques), and the programming models that exist for the disconnected environment. Finally, we analyze whether connected programming models for business applications can be usefully projected to disconnected environments. We compare the data replication and method replay approaches, discuss the features of each, and show that a connected programming model is useful even in a disconnected environment.

1. Introduction

1.1 Programming Models for Business Applications

A *business application* is characterized by the fact that the application (1) updates
state that is shared by multiple users; (2) must perform these updates transactionally
[15] to a shared database; and (3) must operate securely. Business applications therefore have requirements that other applications do not: chiefly, to access persistent
shared datastores securely and transactionally. Programming models can ease the
difficulty of developing complex business logic that meets these requirements. This
is typically done by abstracting business application requirements as generic services
or middleware that the developer can access in as unobtrusive a manner as possible.
Good programming models enable a "separation of concerns" through which the
application developer can concentrate on the application-specific logic, and assume

that the deployed application will meet the business application requirements. Well-known examples of such programming models include CORBA [4], DCOM [6], and Enterprise JavaBeans (EJBs) [10].

1.2   Business Applications on Disconnected Devices

Business applications have traditionally been deployed in *connected* environments in which the shared database can always be accessed by the application. In contrast, when applications are deployed to mobile devices such as personal digital assistants (PDAs), hand-held computers, and laptop computers, these devices are only inter-mittently able to interact with the shared database. (In a client/server environment, the shared database resides on the server.) Historically, resource constraints (e.g., memory and CPU) have precluded disconnected devices from running business applications. Ongoing technology trends, however, imply that such resource constraints are disappearing. For example, DB2 Everyplace [7] (a relational database) and Web-Sphere MQ Everyplace [29] (a secure and dependable messaging system) run on a wide variety of platforms such as PocketPC™, PalmOS™, QNX™, and Linux; they are also compatible with J2ME [22] configurations/profiles such as CDC and Foundation. It seems likely that mobile devices will even be able to host middleware such as an Enterprise JavaBeans container. As a result, business applications that previously required the resources of an "always connected" desktop computer can potentially run on a disconnected device.

Of course, there are non-business applications which do not have these require-ments, but we argue that this set is declining in size and importance. For example, even simple mobile applications typically support synchronization of updates back to the user's personal PC. Since the PC copy of the database may be updated by both the synchronization agent and other PC-based applications (e.g., calendaring), the database is, in fact, shared. Also, users will probably be very disappointed to discover that synchronization of updates did not occur transactionally (e.g., if con-current updates to the same record were not detected and resolved in some way). Finally, security of PDA databases is certainly a concern nowadays.

However, other issues, besides resource constraints, have precluded deployment of business applications on disconnected devices. Fundamental algorithmic and in-frastructure problems must also be solved. The algorithmic problems stem from the fact that the application executes while disconnected from the server, but the work performed must later be propagated to the server. To see why this is a problem, consider the fact that business applications, by our definition, are structured as ap-plication logic that reads from, and writes to, a transactional database that can be concurrently accessed by other applications. Connected business applications have taken for granted that the transactional database can always be accessed by the application. Even if they are structured so as to access locally cached data for "read" operations, state changes ("updates") must still applied to the shared, master database [12,25] at the completion of each user operation. Obviously, the shared-database assumption does not hold when business applications are disconnected: they are then forced to read from, and write to, a database that is *not* shared by other applications and users. Also, almost inevitably, the disconnected application will execute against data that is out-of-date with respect to the server's version of the data. How can work performed on the disconnected device be merged into the shared database in a manner that preserves the transactional behavior of both disconnected and connected clients? The lock-based concurrency control mechanisms used in connected environments to prevent concurrent updates and other transaction serializability violations are not suitable for disconnectable applications because they unacceptably reduce database availability. Also, lock-based concurrency control is simply not dynamic enough; it is typically impossible to know what needs to be locked before the device disconnects from the server.

Infrastructure must also be developed to deal with the life-cycle of an application deployed to a disconnected device. Data must first be "checked out" (copied) from the shared database; the data are then used by the application; and the committed work must be merged into the server database when the device reconnects. Without middleware that provides replication (from the server to the device) and synchronization (from the device to the server) functions, each application must provide its own implementation of these features. A programming model is therefore needed to facilitate development of business applications for disconnected devices. The programming model must provide constructs that address these algorithmic issues, and must integrate with middleware that provides the services described above.

1.3   Programming Models for Disconnected Business Applications

Comparing programming models is very difficult, because reasonable people can disagree about (1) the correct set of evaluation criteria and (2) how well a given programming model performs with respect to a set of evaluation criteria. Thus, even in environments with which people have much experience, such as connected business applications, discussing the superiority of EJBs versus CORBA versus DCOM can produce much more heat than light. This difficulty is compounded for emerging areas such as disconnected business applications. In addition, programming models may have features that are interesting in their own right, independently of whether applications execute in a connected or disconnected environment.

In this chapter, we shall adopt the following approach. Our chief evaluation criterion is whether, and to what degree, a disconnected programming model is a *projection* of a connected programming model onto disconnected devices. By "projection," we acknowledge explicitly that developers will always have to take the disconnected environment into account. The goal, however, is for the programming model to enable application semantics that are identical, or similar, to a connected application. The algorithmic issues discussed above should be solved in a way that is transparent to the developer, who does not have to write more (or different) code than she does for the connected environment. However, we are also interested in what the code "looks like," and the features that are exposed to developers independently of connection-specific issues. Our criteria here will be more subjective since one person's "feature" is another person's "needless complexity." The chapter will use snippets of code to give a concrete sense of the programming model.

Much work has been done in the area of transactionally synchronizing work performed on a disconnected client to the server. The implications of disconnection for transactional applications are well known (see [39] for a recent survey of the area of "mobile transactions"). The presentation in this chapter differs in that we focus on whether, and how, a mature programming model can be projected to disconnected devices in a way that takes advantage of such prior algorithmic work. The ability to project existing connected programming models is important because it can reduce an application's development and maintenance costs. Development costs are reduced because developers can use their existing programming model experience to develop disconnected applications. Maintenance costs are reduced because differences between the connected and disconnected versions of an application are minimized.

We shall also refer to a prototype that demonstrates that the Enterprise JavaBeans [10] programming model can be projected onto disconnected devices. Useful work can be performed on the disconnected device (i.e., few constraints are imposed), while the likelihood of synchronization problems is minimized. The prototype is interesting because it shows how middleware can concretely realize the connected programming model on disconnected devices.

1.4   Related Work

Our chapter focuses on how a connected programming model can be projected to disconnected devices. This part of our work is closely related to the area of mobile transactions [39]. However, we believe that a simpler programming model and synchronization algorithm than many proposed in the mobile transactions literature is adequate to project business applications to disconnected devices. We assert that this simpler approach is sufficient for several reasons.

First, we address a programming model for environments that are more robust than is typically assumed for mobile transactions. Much mobile transactions research, for example, assumes that these transactions execute in resource constrained environments. They must therefore address issues related to limited bandwidth capacity, communication costs, and energy consumption. In contrast, we assume that business applications are deployed to (the increasingly more powerful) devices that can locally execute business applications against a transactional database.

Second, we assume that transactions are able to execute *entirely* on the disconnected device, without assistance from a server. This allows considerable simplification compared to the mobile transactions work designed to support transaction processing in which a client may initiate transactions on servers or may distribute transactions among the mobile client device and servers. Such environments require that transaction processing be supported while the mobile device moves from one networked cell to another or drops its network connections. Mobile transaction models such as *Kangaroo Transactions* [9] are explicitly designed to operate in such complex environments, whereas the synchronization techniques discussed here can use traditional transaction semantics. Similarly, the synchronization techniques discussed here do not deal with distributed transactions (between the mobile device and the network), nor do they deal with heterogeneous multi-database systems. Our focus, instead, is to jump-start deployment of business applications to disconnected devices in well-controlled environments.

Finally, we *do* disagree with the assumption made by some research that optimistic (non-locking) concurrency control mechanisms must perform badly for the long disconnect durations typical of mobile transactions. Such research assumes that the classic optimistic algorithms [15] perform well only for short disconnections, and will experience unacceptable abort ratios for long disconnections. Non-traditional transaction models such as *pre-write operations* [27] and *dynamic object clustering* replication schemes [32] are designed to increase concurrency by avoiding such aborts. In our experience, however, business processes greatly reduce the actual occurrence of such aborts by implicitly partitioning data among application users. Furthermore, the transform-based approach used by method replay synchronization (Section 3.2) is designed to reduce the size of a transactional footprint, and thus reduces the probability of aborts during synchronization.

Finally, note that method replay synchronization and the synchronization middleware discussed later (Section 4.5) build on earlier work using log-replay in support of long-running transactions [30]. These ideas are similar to the approach taken by the IceCube [17] system, although IceCube does not focus on transactional applications.

1.5   Chapter Structure

The chapter is structured as follows. Section 2 explains one of the main challenges faced by disconnected programming models, namely the need to support the life-cycle of a generic disconnected application. Section 3 introduces two classes of synchronization techniques: data replication and method replay. Section 4 discusses two business application programming models. In one (Enterprise JavaBeans), the programming model was intended for connected environments. In the other (Service Data Objects), the programming model is intended to be used in both connected and disconnected environments. We discuss interesting features of both programming models, and show some of their implication with respect to building business applications. We close, in Section 5 by evaluating various programming models for disconnected applications.

1.6   Motivating Application

The chapter will use the following "order entry" application to help motivate the discussion. *Order Entry* enables agents to record customer orders using a stock catalog consisting of line-items and in-stock quantities. If a customer has not previously placed orders, the agent enters information about the new customer into the system.

Figure 1 shows the top-level entities used in the application.

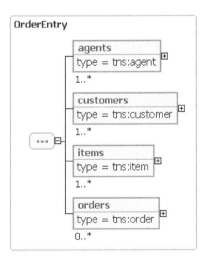

Fig. 1. Order entry sample application.

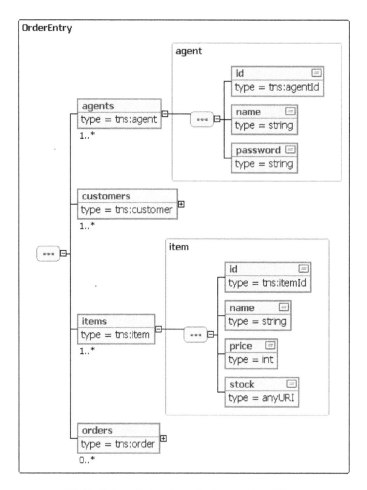

FIG. 2. Order entry sample application: agents and items.

Figure 2 shows the internal structure of an agent and line-item, and Fig. 3 shows the internal structure of the customer entity.

Figure 4 shows how an order has references to both the agent who placed the order, and to the customer for whom the order was placed.

As we shall show, the relative lack of complexity in *order entry* does not detract from its ability to illustrate some of the key issues in building disconnected business applications.

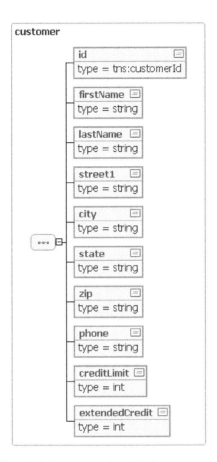

FIG. 3. Order entry sample application: customers.

2. Life-Cycle of a Disconnected Business Application

In order to be successful, a programming model for disconnected devices must be compatible with the life-cycle of a disconnected application.

Deployment of a disconnectable business application requires that an administrator perform a one-time setup (life-cycle stage **0**) of the mobile device's database(s). The key challenge in stage **0** is to replicate sufficient data (from the server to the device) such that the application can execute correctly. This can be a difficult task when an application can potentially access a data set that is too large to fit on the device. In such cases, application administrators must determine the subset of data

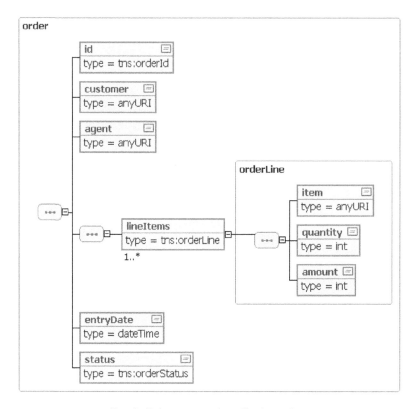

FIG. 4. Order entry sample application: orders.

that will actually be used by the application, and replicate that subset to the device. This is often done through ad hoc, but effective, business rules. For example, a salesman may not need to have the entire set of customer data replicated; only the set of customers in her district is typically needed.

After this initial setup is performed, the mobile device repeatedly executes the following life-cycle:

Stage 1 (Propagate server updates): Before disconnecting, the server's updates are propagated to the device.

Stage 2 (Execution): User executes one or more business applications on the disconnected device.

Stage 3 (Propagate client updates): Device reconnects to server, and propagates its updates to the server-side database.

Stages **0** and **1** benefit from middleware that allows devices to define the subset of relevant data that needs to be copied to the device. The subset is typically expressed as a query or set of queries applied to the server database.

Stage **1** ensures that the device's database is as up-to-date as possible before beginning disconnected execution. It greatly benefits from middleware that:

- *Subscribes* to relevant changes on the server (i.e., those changes which fall within the defined subset of relevant data).

- *Propagates* server changes to the client device database, with the result that the device's data is now up-to-date with respect to the server.

Standardized protocols such as SyncML [40] can be used to pass data between the device and the server—across wireless and wired networks and over multiple transport protocols—using the standard representation format defined in the SyncML *Representation* protocol. The SyncML Synchronization protocol efficiently replicates server-side data to the device, by doing either a "one-way sync from server only" or a "Refresh sync from server only." In the former, the device gets all data modifications that have been committed on the server; in the latter, the server exports all of its data to the device, which then replaces its current set of data.

Assuming that the correct set of data has been replicated to the device, stage **2** simply involves the execution of the disconnected application against the local database.

For example, enabling the *order entry* application to run on a disconnected device requires, during stage **0**, that a system administrator replicate the stock catalog consisting of items, in-stock quantities, agents, customers, and prior orders, if any. Before disconnection, the device's database is brought up-to-date (stage **1**), so that the recorded stock levels match the server's values. The agent is then able to take new orders (stage **2**) while disconnected from the server database. We assume that the agents prefer to work while out in the field, where connectivity may be unavailable or sporadic.

In order for work performed on the disconnected device to become visible to other applications, the device must transactionally propagate its updates (or "change set") to the server-side database that maintains the master version of the data seen by other applications and users (stage **3**). While propagating the change set from the client to the server, stage **3** must deal with the following issues:

- *Conflict detection*, in which the application or middleware detects whether the change set conflicts with the current state of the server-side database.

  One important issue is how the notion of a "conflict" is defined. Connected business applications typically define conflicts as non-serializable transaction schedules [15]. Can this definition be used for disconnectable business applications as well? Efficiency is also a consideration: for example, does a detected conflict require only that one transaction be aborted, or must the entire set of work performed on the device be aborted?

- *Conflict resolution*, in which (if conflicts were detected), the application or middleware attempts to determine a new server-side state which eliminates the conflict. If no resolution is possible, the synchronization must be (partially or completely) aborted (i.e., the device's state cannot be automatically propagated to the server), and the failure logged and reported to the user. If some resolution is possible, it is performed, and the update is propagated to the server-side database.

  A key challenge here is whether general purpose conflict resolution algorithms can be devised or whether application-specific resolution is required.

- *Transactional merge*, during which the change set, possibly modified by conflict resolution, is merged with the server-side database. As a result, work performed on the disconnected device is now visible to other applications and users—without violating the transactional guarantees made by the application.

Note that update propagation between the client and server is asymmetric: updates performed on the server may invalidate transactions performed on the client, but client updates cannot invalidate previously-committed server-side transactions (because the server-side transactions were previously visible to all users and applications).

The programming model discussed in this chapter is orthogonal to stage **1**: middleware such as DB2 Everyplace [7] shows that efficient subscription and replication techniques can propagate server updates to the client. The programming model's task is to ensure that the application's execution behavior during stage **2** conforms as closely as possible to its behavior in a connected environment. The difficulty is that the programming model must deal with, and be supported with middleware for, the stage **3** synchronization process, during which the client's updates are propagated to the server. Broadly speaking, two synchronization approaches exist: *data replication* and *method replay*.

3. Synchronization Techniques

3.1   Data Replication

The data replication synchronization technique represents a change set as a log of data modifications that were performed on the disconnected device. (The term "modifications" denotes data creation and deletion as well as data changes.) Data replication is used by both DB2e [7] and Lotus Notes [26]. It also underlies the notion of cached RowSets [33] in which the reference implementation uses optimistic concurrency-control. The synchronization process begins by transmitting the data modification log to the server.

- *Conflict detection*: the server must track the data it has replicated to individual clients and determine whether activity by a given client—as represented by the data modification log—conflicts with changes that were previously committed by other clients or server-side applications. The standard algorithm is to detect a conflict if the synchronizing client has modified a datum that was concurrently modified on the server while the synchronizing client was disconnected. The server copy may have been modified by a server-based application or the synchronization of another client.

  Note that this algorithm, though commonly used in data replication, does not guarantee detection of all non-serializable conflicts. For example, if client 1 executes A = A + B, and client 2 executes B = B + A, this algorithm does not detect a problem, because the write-sets do not intersect. However, such cases do not seem to arise in practice.

- *Conflict resolution*: the conflict resolution algorithm used in commercial systems places the burden on the user or system administrator. This is not due to laziness, but reflects the fact that (1) synchronization conflicts at the data level are difficult to resolve automatically, and (2) the cost of a mishandled conflict resolution being merged into the shared database may be very high. This implies that the application itself must specify how conflicts should be resolved.

  In some applications, the cost of a mishandled conflict is not as serious, and/or the probability of an incorrect automatic resolution is not that high. For example, Lotus Notes can be configured to resolve conflicts between document records automatically, either by merging all the modified columns together or by taking the last-modified version of the document. This is adequate for some applications. Also, the resolved documents are typically viewed by users rather than by programs, and the users will tend to see most merge problems. Finally, if an automatic resolution fails, a new "conflict document" is created, which again will typically be seen by users.

  For general databases and applications, though, this is not acceptable. Many applications databases are accessed directly by programs, and those programs will not know how to deal with conflict documents or "funny looking" data. For example, many databases are accessed via a JDBC [21] interface. There is no provision in JDBC for calling "user exit" code to resolve conflicts, or for providing a view of conflict records to applications.

- *Transactional merge*: data deleted on the device must be deleted on the server; data created on the device must be created on the server; and updates performed on the device's data must also be performed to the server's data. For example, in

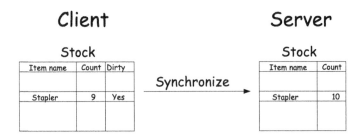

FIG. 5. Data replication synchronization.

the case of DB2 Everyplace, the server transactionally performs the appropriate sequence of SQL DELETE, INSERT and UPDATE operations. In the case of Lotus Notes, the client's version of the NSF (Notes Storage Facility File) records are copied over the master copy.

If data replication is used to implement the *order entry* example, as orders are placed on the disconnected device, the stock levels are correspondingly modified. During synchronization, those stock table rows that were modified (by reducing the stock level) are transmitted to the server. Figure 5 sketches what happens during a successful data replication synchronization. The synchronization middleware detects (through the "dirty" bit value) that the client decremented the stock of staplers, and that only nine staplers are currently in stock. Because the corresponding column value was not concurrently modified in the server-side database, the middleware changes the server-side value to match the client's value, resulting in a successful synchronization.

3.2   Method Replay

The method replay synchronization technique represents a change set as a log of the method invocations performed on the disconnected device. Each log entry constrains the information needed to replay a single method: e.g., the method name, the method's signature, and the method's parameter values. In can thus be seen as the "dual" of the data replication approach which logs the data modifications. A version of log replay is used in the "Field Calls" in IMS Fast Path [19], earlier work on long-running transactions [30], and IceCube [17] (see also [18]). The synchronization process begins by transmitting the method log to the server.

- *Conflict detection*: the method invocations are replayed, in sequence, against the server's current state. This simultaneously propagates the device's updates to the server (if the method replay is successful) and detects a conflict (if the

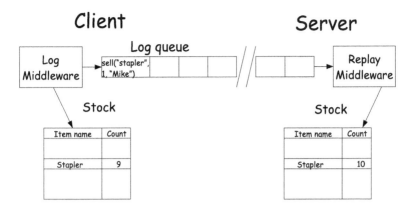

FIG. 6. Method replay synchronization.

method replay is unsuccessful). Whether a method replay is successful depends *solely* on the application's business logic: i.e., on whether the method throws an exception when invoked on the server.

- *Conflict resolution*: the exception that caused the method to fail, when replayed on the server, is logged and the user is informed of the error. The conflict must be resolved manually.

- *Transactional merge*: the disconnected work is transparently applied to the server through successful method replay.

Figure 6 sketches what happens during a successful method replay synchronization for the disconnectable *order entry* application. In contrast to the process shown in Fig. 5, only the method call that decremented the stock of staplers is logged. That method – which does not include the resulting stock level—is replayed on the server, and results in similarly decrementing the server-side stock of staplers. This figure corresponds to the scenario in which sufficient stock is shown in both the client-side database (during disconnected execution) and the server-side database (during synchronization) to fulfill the customer's order. In contrast to the data replication approach, the fact that three staplers were shown in the client-side database, but only two in the server-side database, is irrelevant: the order will be successfully committed to the server so long as the customer ordered fewer than the two staplers that are available on the server. The "order" business logic simply checks (on both the client and the server) that sufficient stock exists to fulfill the order, and does not verify that the stock levels of the client-side database match that of the server-side database. Consider, however, the scenario in which sufficient stock is shown in the client-side database (during disconnected execution) but the server-side database (during synchronization) shows *insufficient* stock to fulfill the customer's order. The method-replay approach will detect—as it should—a "conflict," in the sense that the method's business logic should only place an order if sufficient stock exists to fulfill the order. Thus, although the order was committed on the disconnected device, it will *not* commit on the server.

Broadly speaking, two approaches exist to handle such "insufficient stock" scenarios for method replay. In the first, the method's business logic throws an exception (e.g., `OutOfStockException`) instead of following the typical code path that fulfils the order. While this approach makes life simpler for application developers, and is arguably appropriate for connected applications, it will result in a synchronization error for disconnected applications that may be hard to recover from. In contrast to connected applications, here the client concluded their session thinking that work had successfully committed (because sufficient stock was available). The client may be very confused when a mysterious exception is logged when she synchronizes several days later. (Note that conflicts detected using the data replication approach have the same problem.) We therefore favor the second approach, in which a business's work-flow is integrated with, and becomes part of, a method's business logic. Thus, when stock is available, the order is added to the "fulfilled order" queue; when insufficient stock is available, the order is either added to the "back-order" queue or to the "customer issue" queue. With this approach, the order will be committed on the disconnected client as before. However, if insufficient stock exists when synchronizing with the server, the order will continue to be processed exactly as if it was a connected application. The programming model is thus transparent with respect to the disconnected execution environment.

4. Disconnected Programming Models: Service Data Objects and Enterprise JavaBeans

A programming model can be viewed as a contract between a computing environment and developers who write programs that execute in that environment. On the one hand, the contract specifies "services" that the computing environment must provide to developers. On the other hand, the contract imposes "constraints" on the type of programs that developers may write. A programming language is thus associated with a programming model. For example, the Java programming model specifies that the Java Virtual Machine will automatically "garbage collect" an object's memory when that object is no longer referenced by other objects. Java programs, for their part, must do *lexical* scoping because the programming model simply forbids any other type of scoping, such as *dynamic* scoping.

Specialized frameworks such as those for *business* (enterprise) components [4,6, 10] are associated with more specialized programming models. The computing environment (often called a *container*) provides more services to developers, but also imposes more constraints on developers. Typically, the more sophisticated the services provided (e.g., transactions or persistence), the greater the constraints imposed on developers, and the less they can simply "do their own thing" [24].

Business components are usually comprised of an *interface* (used by the application's clients) and an *implementation* (provided by developers). In such cases we must therefore distinguish between a *client* and *developer* programming model. The developer programming model requires developers to deal with an architected component life-cycle. The life-cycle dictates a state transition diagram that will be followed as components are created, activated, and destroyed. As the component makes transitions from one state to another, the container invokes specific methods on the component: developers must ensure that their implementation of the component's interface provides the appropriate semantics. The client programming model specifies the way that clients must access the container in order to create, locate, update, or delete components.

In this section we discuss two programming models for disconnected business applications, focusing on how the programming models reduce (for both developers and clients) the effort required to deal with "disconnection" (i.e., the issues discussed in Section 3).

4.1   Service Data Objects: Concepts

We begin our discussion with Service Data Objects (SDOs). A paper [35] describing the motivation for, and providing context about, SDOs was released in 2003, along with version 1.0 of the specification. Version 2.0 of the SDO specification was released in 2005 [36]. In general we will refer to SDO 2.0 in this chapter.

Although SDOs were initially presented as a joint proposal from IBM and BEA, they are also under development as a Java Specification Request (#235) [37]. Reference [34] provides an overview of the SDO specifications; and IBM's reference implementation can be downloaded from the Eclipse site [38].

A *Data Access Service* (*DAS*) is the SDO "container" construct. As shown in Fig. 7, a data access service mediates between persistent datastores and applications by materializing and managing *data graph* instances. Data graphs are comprised of *DataObjects*, the "DO" of the SDO specification. Note, that although the DAS is a key concept of the SDO architecture, it is not currently covered by the SDO 2.0 specification. The various sample mediators which have been constructed [2,41] appear to have DataStore-specific APIs.

A DAS provides the following function to applications:

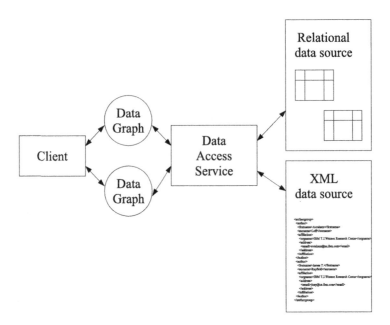

FIG. 7. Top-level SDO concepts.

- It populates a data graph using state from a datastore.
- It propagates a modified data graph (i.e., after an application's interactions) back to the datastore.

The DAS ideally provides uniform data access to different datastores (e.g., relational and XML).

Data graphs thus provide applications with a *transient* copy of data that has a consistent API regardless of the underlying source of the data. As denoted by its name, it presents a graph API to applications, where each node of the graph is a DataObject. The following data graph features are especially relevant to understanding how SDOs support disconnected applications:

- Changes made by an application are (optionally) automatically captured in a "change log" history. The change log indicates which DataObjects were created and deleted, and contains the old values of any properties that have been modified.
- Data graphs are serialized as XML, using a well-defined format, and thus ease communication between clients and servers.

A DataObject has a relatively simple structure. It consists only of a set of properties (properties are either "primitives" or references to other DataObjects in the data graph). The properties are exposed through "getters" and "setters." Applications can access DataObjects by navigating through the data graph or by using accessors with an XPath syntax [44].

Data graphs may include an XML schema [43] that describes the structure of its DataObjects. Depending on whether or not the schema was known to the application developers, applications can access DataObjects in one of two styles: "static" (known schema) and "dynamic" (unknown schema). The static style allows tools to generate typed interfaces to the DataObjects and can potentially improve performance since the DAS can optimize access for a known type. The dynamic style further decouples application developers from the data used in the application, but at the expense of a generic interface to the DataObjects.

We implemented a subset of *order entry* using SDOs in order to illustrate the current state of SDO programming. This sample was built and tested using Eclipse 3.02, and SDO EMF Tools version 2.0.1 [38].

Since the current Eclipse SDO support does not provide any DAS implementations, we create the OrderEntry data graph manually using EMF-specific APIs (Sample 1). The remainder of the example uses only the APIs of the SDO 1.0 specification [36].

OrderEntry is the "root" DataObject for *order entry*. If a *DataGraph* API were used, OrderEntry would be returned by `DataGraph.getRootObject()`. All the "entity" DataObjects from *order entry* are created as contained DataObjects under OrderEntry.

Sample 2 shows the creation of a Agent DataObject contained within OrderEntry. Note that currently no Java interface is generated which extends both DataObject and

```
OrderentryFactoryImpl oeFactory = new OrderentryFactoryImpl();
OrderEntry orderEntry = oeFactory.createOrderEntry();
```

SAMPLE 1. Create root DataObject OrderEntry.

```
DataObject orderEntryDO = (DataObject) orderEntry;
DataObject agentAsDO = orderEntryDO.createDataObject("agents");
```

SAMPLE 2. Create Agent DataObject.

```
Agent agentAsAgent = (Agent) agentAsDO;
agentAsAgent.setId("123"); // static API

agentAsDO.setString("name", "Tom"); // dynamic API

System.out.println("agent = " + agentAsDO);
```

SAMPLE 3. Updating Agent properties.

```
agent = com.ibm.watson.oats.orderentry.impl.AgentImpl@5a50a67a (id:
123, name: Tom, password: null)
```

SAMPLE 4. Output from print Agent.

```
DataObject agentDOViaXPath =
    orderEntryDO.getDataObject("/agents.0");

DataObject agentDOViaXPath2 = (DataObject) orderEntryDO
    .get("agents[name='Tom']");
```

SAMPLE 5. Retrieving an Agent.

OrderEntry; we must therefore cast OrderEntry to DataObject to access the DataObject methods.

DataObject properties may be updated using static, Agent-specific, methods such as setId, but this requires the application to first cast the *DO* to an Agent. Alternatively, the application can use the dynamic (generic) DataObject methods such as setString() (see Sample 3). The output from printing the Agent DataObject is shown in Sample 4.

Sample 5 shows the usage of XPath queries to retrieve Agents. If the Agent is known to be the first one contained within OrderEntry, the query "/agents.0" will retrieve it. If the value of one of the Agent properties is known (e.g., "name"), the property can be specified in the XPath query, as in the second example.

XPath queries may also be used to navigate within DataObjects, or from one DataObject to another. Sample 6 shows an XPath query which navigates from the Agent to its "name" property.

```
Object agentName = agentDOViaXPath2.get("name");
```

SAMPLE 6. Navigating from Agent to property.

```
agentAsDO.delete();
```

SAMPLE 7. Deleting an Agent.

Finally, a DataObject may be deleted by invoking the `DataObject.delete()` method, as shown in Sample 7.

4.2 Enterprise JavaBeans: Concepts

EJBs are a component model for enterprise applications written in Java. In contrast to SDOs, EJBs are a relatively mature technology: version 1.0 [11] was released in 1998, version 2.0 in 2001, and a draft version 3.0 is currently (in 2005) under review. We offer a brief overview of the EJB programming model here; in addition to the specifications [10] themselves, thorough coverage is presented in [28].

Three types of EJBs exist:

(1) *entity* beans, components that are shareable and transactionally recoverable, and whose state is typically persistent in a datastore (e.g., an account in a banking system);

(2) *session* beans, transient business process components that can participate in a transaction without being transactionally recoverable themselves (e.g., a funds transfer between two accounts). Session beans can maintain client state across method invocations (*stateful* session beans), or they may maintain no client state between method boundaries (*stateless* session beans);

(3) *message-driven* beans, asynchronous components that are invoked by JMS [16] messages. Message-driven beans play an application role that is similar to session beans, and differ chiefly in that (1) they are asynchronous and (2) do not have an API that is driven by clients.

In the client EJB programming model, life-cycle operations (e.g., creation and query) are performed on an EJB *Home*. Homes are thus "factories" that produce and aggregate EJBs of a specific interface type. If an EJB exists, and the client has obtained a reference to it from its Home, the client can then directly invoke the EJB's interface methods.

In contrast with the client EJB programming model which is concerned with Home and EJB *interfaces*, the developer EJB programming model is concerned with integrating EJB *implementations* into an EJB container. A stateless session bean method implementation is analogous to a procedure call implementation. An entity bean method implementation manipulates an *abstract persistence schema* to implement the component's API. The notion of an abstract persistence schema is important because it allows developers to delegate the management of a bean's state to the container. Developers are concerned only with virtual persistence fields and relationships, so that container-supplied tools are free to implement this state independently of the developer. EJB *containers* automatically provide EJBs with common requirements of business applications such as persistence, concurrency, transactional integrity, and security. Standardized life-cycle methods such as `ejbCreate`, `ejbActivate`, and `ejbStore`, are "hooks" for developers to interact with the hosting container in well-defined ways. The distinction between "local" and "remote" interfaces is another architected interaction between developers and a container. Using a local interface allows beans that are deployed within a single container to communicate efficiently by eliminating the overhead associated with a RMI call (because the beans are instantiated in the same address space). The remote interface is required only when remote (i.e., resident in a different address-space) clients interact with the EJB. Bean developers can thus focus on the business logic of the application; when deployed to an EJB container, the components are embedded in an infrastructure that automatically supplies the business component requirements.

We implemented *order entry* using EJBs to facilitate a comparison to the SDO client-side programming model.

Sample 8 shows how an Agent is created from its Home. In contrast to SDOs, agent instances are not contained within an encapsulating "OrderEntry" graph, but rather are contained within their own Home. Also, entity EJBs are required to define a primary key, because it is needed in order to support single-level store (see Section 4.3). For Agent, there is a UUID [42] defined by the abstract persistence schema for use as the primary key. The UUID must be provided at entity creation time, and is immutable. In contrast, although the Agent SDO defines an Id (see Sample 3), it

```
final javax.naming.Context context = new javax.naming.InitialContext();
final AgentHome agentHome = (AgentHome) context.lookup("Agent Home");
final String    uuid = UUID.generate();
final Agent     agent = agentHome.create(uuid);
```

SAMPLE 8. Creating an Agent EJB.

```
agent.setName("Tom");
agent.setPwd("***");
System.out.println ("agent = "+agent);
```

SAMPLE 9. Updating an Agent.

```
agent = [EJB class = com.ibm.oats.test.disco.order.OATSBMPAgentJDBC,
  key = fad895da00000103000000012a571211779bd88c, contents = AgentBean
=[name=Tom, pwd=***]
```

SAMPLE 10. Printing the State of an Agent EJB.

```
final Agent      agentByPK = agentHome.findByPrimaryKey(uuid);
```

SAMPLE 11. Retrieving an Agent via its Primary Key.

```
final Collection agentCollection = agentHome.findAll();
final Iterator  agentIterator = agentCollection.iterator();
while (agentIterator.hasNext()) {
  System.err.println ("agent="+agentIterator.next());
}
```

SAMPLE 12. Retrieving a Collection of Agents

is not immutable, and does not even have to be set to a value, since it is not used for identity mapping.

EJBs are updated via the component interface. Sample 9 shows how clients update the Agent state. The output from printing the Agent EJB is shown in Sample 10. Unlike SDOs (see Sample 3), there is no dynamic get/set API for EJBs, other than the standard Java Reflection API.

An EJB can always be retrieved via its *primary key* since an EJB is required to have a unique identity with respect to its Home. In addition, EJBs can also be retrieved via "custom queries" that may be optionally declared on the EJB's Home. Such queries can either return a single EJB instance or multiple EJB instances that match the query predicate. Sample 11 shows how a single Agent is retrieved via its primary key.

Sample 12 shows how multiple Agent instances are retrieved through a custom query that specifies "all Agents."

Finally, Sample 13 shows two ways to delete an Agent EJB.

```
agent.remove();
// or: agentHome.remove(uuid);
```

SAMPLE 13. Deleting an Agent.

4.3   Comparison of SDO and EJB Application Programming Models

The SDO architecture uses a *two-level* store approach to database-state management. That is, an explicit distinction is made between the DataObject(s) that are resident in memory (the first-level store) and the persistent data resident in the database (the second-level) [24]. Operations must be explicitly invoked on the DAS in order to copy state between the two levels.

With respect to entity beans, in contrast to the two-level store approach used by SDOs, EJBs use a *single-level* store approach [5]. That is, no distinction is made between the instantiated (in-memory) (entity bean) component and the persistent copy. Essentially, whenever the in-memory component is modified, the persistent copy is automatically updated (although the changes are not committed until the transaction is committed). This has a number of advantages over two-level store: first, since a maximum of one copy of each component is memory-resident, the application does not have to worry about aliasing problems, in which the application accidentally obtains multiple copies of the component, and their states become different. Second, the application does not have to remember to propagate updates from the in-memory copy to the persistent copy. This is handled automatically at commit time.

In order to implement single-level store, each component must be assigned a unique identity. This allows the middleware to maintain an association with its location in persistent storage. In addition, it allows the middleware to detect references to components already in memory, and thus avoid duplicate copies (aliasing). For EJBs, the EJB container is responsible for maintaining the mapping between a component and its persistent state, obviating the need for explicit state-transfer methods. The mapping consists of two parts: the abstract persistence schema and the component identity definition. The abstract persistence schema specifies the mapping between portions of the database record and the bean's corresponding `getter` and `setter` methods. The component identity definition defines the subset of the database record used to uniquely identify the component: this is always "read-only" state, since changing this state causes the object's identity to change as well.

For an example of the potential problems of aliasing, suppose that the application retrieves a data graph DG1 from the DAS, and then retrieves a second data graph DG2 from the DAS. DataObjects in DG1 and DG2 which represent the same logical data (e.g., Agent 86) may have different values in memory. In contrast, EJB Entity Beans returned by different calls to the EJB server will always have the same value within the same transaction.

Although it may be possible to change the SDO architecture into a single-level store architecture, this will require defining identity for the entity DataObjects. In addition, runtime middleware would be needed to manage the DataObjects. The middleware would need to track DataObjects by identity, and force returned DataObject references to point to in-memory copies if they exist.

EJBs and SDOs both use a similar meta-model, sometimes called a Navigational Database [31]. The database consists of entities (discrete "things"), with pointers and paths which can be used to navigate between entities. Both EJBs and SDOs have a notion of a special "containment" relationship, as contrasted with a "reference" relationship: entities must be contained within exactly one other entity. Entity EJBs are always contained within an EJB Home specific to that entity, whereas SDOs have a more general containment structure (DataObjects must be contained by a DataGraph). Reference relationships are largely unrestricted in both EJBs and SDOs.

Since EJBs are objects, they may have (significant) business logic embedded in them. For example, an entity EJB which contains a "birthdate" property as part of the abstract persistence schema may have a `getAge()` method. The business logic which implements `getAge()` is embedded in the EJB, and calculates the age based on the current date. Stateless session EJBs also have business logic, but do not have an abstract persistence schema. In contrast, SDOs only have properties (`getXXX()` and `setXXX()` methods or equivalent), and lifecycle methods (create and remove DataObjects and/or properties). The developer may not specify the implementation of these methods, nor may they add non-property methods. An SDO-based application must push such application logic into higher-levels of the application, since it cannot be packaged with the appropriate component.

Both EJB and SDO attempt to hide the details of the persistent datastore from the client application. For EJBs, the EJB Specification [10] specifies Home and EJB component (EJBObject) APIs which are independent of the underlying datastore. For SDOs, the Data Access Service provides the API to the underlying datastore, ideally in a way which is independent of the datastore.

SDOs are intended to work with meta-data describing the DataObjects that populate the data graph. The meta-data itself could be populated from various model frameworks, including XML schema, Eclipse Modeling Framework (EMF), and augmented relational schema [37]. In examining the code produced by [38] and other SDO samples, however, we noted that applications were certainly not required to supply this meta-data, nor took advantage of its potential. EJBs use meta-data derived both from invoking the Java Reflection API on the component interfaces and bean implementation, and from the deployment descriptor itself. The EJB version 3 specification is placing an even greater emphasis on the use of meta-data.

As compared to EJBs, SDOs are much better suited for transmission between address spaces. SDOs, in fact, are a type of Data Transfer Object (DTO [8]). As such, SDOs are useful because they allow data graphs to be passed between address spaces in a well-architected fashion. EJBs, in contrast, are explicitly restricted to serialize "by reference" rather than "by value," and are thus much more closely tied to a given address space. Although EJBs can be transmitted between address spaces through an approach that applies Java Serialization [20] to an entity bean's *state* [25], SDOs are an improvement in this regard because serialization can have difficulty when serializing objects between different Java versions.

4.4   Suitability of SDOs & EJBs for Disconnected Applications

The SDO Whitepaper [35] discusses the suitability of the SDO programming model for disconnected applications:

> *Support for disconnected programming models.* Many applications naturally have a disconnected usage pattern of data access: an application reads a set of data, retains it locally for a short period of time, manipulates the data, and then applies the changes back to the data source. For example, this is a very common pattern in Web-based applications: a Web client requests to view a form, a Servlet or JSP requests data in a local read transaction and renders the data in an HTML form, the Web client submits updates to a form, and the Servlet or JSP uses a new transaction to update the data. Best practice typically dictates that optimistic concurrency semantics be used for this scenario, which provides for high levels of concurrency with the appropriate business-level semantic.

However, it is important to note that this usage of "disconnected" is very different from our usage. Our discussion of disconnected applications is with respect to enabling the successful execution of applications on devices which do not have connectivity to the master database server, including replication of the database subset to the client, disconnected execution of the application, and propagation of the client updates to the server upon reconnection (see Section 2). In contrast, the usage of "disconnected" in the SDO documentation is very similar to the meaning of "pseudo-conversational" transactions in the literature [3]. Pseudo-conversational transactions are a design pattern for supporting optimistic concurrency-control on top of database managers that do not directly support optimistic concurrency-control. In pseudo-conversational transactions, the database transaction is closed (committed) while a user-interaction takes place. This prevents the application from holding locks during user think-times. After the user interaction is completed, the transaction context is reopened, and any updates specified by the user are then made to the database.

The updates are made using optimistic concurrency control, so that incompatible database changes made during the user interaction (e.g., by other users and/or applications) will be detected, and the transaction will be aborted.

A close reading of the SDO literature shows that the use-cases rely on continuous connectivity between the application, the DAS, and the database. If the DAS is collocated with the application, it cannot access the database during disconnected operation. Conversely, if the DAS is collocated with the database, it cannot be accessed by the disconnected application.

One possible way in which disconnected applications could be implemented on the current SDO architecture would be to have the application avoid making calls to the DAS while disconnected. In this scenario, the application would make a call to the DAS before disconnection, and the DAS would return the database subset of interest to the client. The first difficulty with this approach, is that the application almost certainly already has most of the database subset (from the previous disconnection). There is no mechanism within the current SDO architecture to conveniently retrieve only the incremental changes to a data graph, and automatically merge them with the outdated (but mostly correct) version of the data graph.

Another difficulty is that, upon reconnection, the application would need to pass the entire database subset (as a data graph) to the DAS. Thus, the unmodified portions of the data graph would also need to be communicated to the DAS. Within the current SDO architecture, there is no way to serialize only the change log and updated values of the datagraph.

Thus, although the DataGraph and DataObject APIs support a good client programming model, these difficulties suggest that a reasonable approach to supporting disconnected applications with the SDO architecture would require placing additional middleware between the application and the existing DAS. Since the DAS interface is currently undefined, we propose that the new client-side middleware be architected as a DAS which provides disconnected client support (see Fig. 8). The server-side DAS is used only by the client-side DAS, and provides whatever API is needed by the client-side DAS.

Since multiple (disconnected) client-side transactions would now need to be propagated to the server, presumably, the SDO architecture would be enhanced with an API or annotations to specify how changes to the data graph are interleaved with transactional behavior. A possible approach would to simply incorporate technologies such as the Java Transaction API (JTA [23]) "by reference." This would require developers to explicitly control transaction activity through `begin`, `commit`, and `rollback` commands. It would harder for the programming model to supply declarative transactions in the way that EJBs do (to seamlessly integrate session and entity transactional activity) since SDOs do not include business logic (Section 4.3).

SDO Application

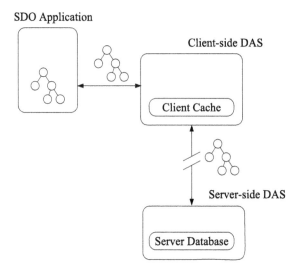

FIG. 8. Proposed client-side data access service.

More fundamentally, such a client-side DAS would have to address the need to support conflict resolution when conflicts *do* occur, which is one of the main features of a disconnected programming model (Section 3). This is a difficult problem because conflict resolution appears to require detailed knowledge of application semantics, and cannot therefore be easily done by middleware. Unfortunately, there is no "silver bullet" for this challenge. Relative to technologies such as DB2e [7] or cached RowSets [33], SDOs provide synchronization middleware with an API to a DataObject's change history. The SDO ChangeSummary API, however, assumes that synchronization is done using data replication rather than method replay (Section 3). New ideas for change management, such as method replay, do not easily fit into the architected change summaries.

Can EJBs be used as a disconnected programming model? The claim by the SDO whitepaper that EJBs are not suitable for "disconnected" environments is really a claim that EJBs use pessimistic concurrency control and lock data. As shown by work in EJB caching [25], EJBs (like SDOs), certainly *can* use optimistic concurrency control mechanisms. Granted that the EJB specification *assumes* a connected environment, we do not see why the EJB programming model cannot be projected to disconnected environments as well. As discussed in Section 2, the chief challenge introduced by disconnection is client synchronization with the server. Although EJBs do not provide a change history API, EJB containers can transparently provide this information in a straightforward fashion, and can thus transparently provide developers with synchronization between the client and server. In fact, unlike SDOs, EJB containers can provide the information needed to implement *either* the data-replication or method-replay approaches.

Thus, an evaluation of the suitability of SDOs or EJBs for disconnected applications should realize that the differences between the EJB and SDO programming models (Section 4.3) are orthogonal to the problems of replication, synchronization, and conflict resolution. What matters is whether the programming model precludes deployed components from interacting with synchronization middleware in a way that provides transparent synchronization function. From this perspective, EJBs are at least as suitable as SDOs for developing disconnected applications.

Recall that the EJB programming model is explicitly concerned with identifying and facilitating the distinct roles that are required to develop and deploy an application. The programming model specifies contracts that separate, for example, the bean-provider role (provider of the application's business logic) from the container-provider role (provider of the deployment tooling and runtime that supply deployed EJBs with functions such as transaction and security management). Stage **3** synchronization function can be similarly abstracted as a container-provided function that bean providers can take for granted, and that is transparently provided by the middleware. The EJB programming model is thus well suited for projection to disconnected devices: the existing role separation enables us to enhance existing containers without changing the API and semantics used in connected EJB applications.

We validated this hypothesis by building *EJBSync*—prototype middleware that projects the EJB programming model to disconnected devices using the method-replay approach. Because an EJB's state is backed by a datastore (typically a relational database), data replication can also be used to synchronize an EJB application that executed on a disconnected device to the server. As the EJBs are modified, they modify the backing datastore, and that datastore can be synchronized with existing middleware such as DB2e. However, for the reasons presented in Section 5, synchronization based on method-replay enables a more successful programming model projection than one based on data-replication.

4.5 *EJBSync*: Middleware for Disconnected EJBs

EJBSync (see Fig. 9) is middleware that is both application-independent and application-transparent. That is, an EJB business application developed for a connected environment can be deployed to a disconnected environment with no (or few) changes.

As discussed in Section 4.2, EJB methods are specified in an interface definition that is invoked by clients. *EJBSync* extends the tooling that deploys EJBs to a connected container in the following way. Whenever the deployed component (i.e., the

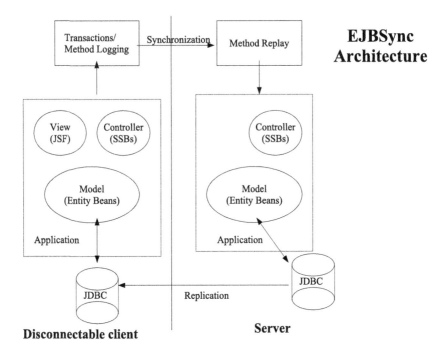

FIG. 9. *EJBSync*: method replay infrastructure.

class that implements *EJBObject*) delegates a client invocation to the bean implementation (i.e., the class that implements *SessionBean* or *EntityBean*), a *top-level* method invocation is logged by creating a LogRecord EJB. For example, if an application invokes the SSB newOrder method, and that method, in turn, invokes the OrderHome.createOrder and a series of Order.addLineItem methods, only newOrder (and its arguments) are logged. *EJBSync* is responsible for tracking the dynamic method depth at which a given method executes. Note that only remoteable EJBs support method logging using the *EJBSync* middleware. Local-only EJBs do not have Handles that allow references to them to be saved persistently, and their parameters are not restricted to serializable datatypes.

Sample 14 shows the signature of the newOrder method as specified in the *ManageOrder* SSB. The bean developer implements this method to validate the input parameters, and iterate over the set of line items in the order so as to interact with the OrderHome, OrderLineHome, StockHome, and CustomerHome and place the order. ManageOrder and its implementation are specified independently of any container implementation or environment, and can be deployed to any EJB container.

```
public String newOrder
  (final String agentID, final String customerID, final Set orderSet)
  throws RemoteException, PlaceOrderException;
```

SAMPLE 14. Signature of newOrder.

```
public String newOrder (String p0, String p1, Set p2)
throws RemoteException, PlaceOrderException
{
  PVCSSBContext context = null;
  final TxMethodToken token = preInvoke(TransactionAttribute.REQUIRED);
  retVal = null;
  try {
    context = getHome().getPooledSessionContext();
    retVal = getBean(context).newOrder(p0, p1, p2); // business logic
  }
  catch (PlaceOrderException e) {
    postInvoke(TransactionAttribute.REQUIRED, token);
    throw e;
  }
  catch (Throwable e) {
    postInvoke(TransactionAttribute.REQUIRED, token, e);
  }
  finally {
    getHome().replaceContext(context);
  }

  // no exception -- commit if necessary
  postInvoke(TransactionAttribute.REQUIRED, token);
  return (retVal);
}
```

SAMPLE 15. newOrder for connected container.

When deployed in a connected environment, the container's tooling generates an implementation that interacts with the container to provide container services to the component. Such tooling is obviously container-specific, and the code shown in Sample 15 is only meant to show how the deployed bean delegates business logic to the original bean implementation.

Sample 16 shows how the ManageOrder SSB is deployed to a disconnected container. As the deployed component executes, it has exactly the same semantics as the connected version of the application. This is because the container does not modify

```
  public String newOrder (String p0, String p1, Set p2)
    throws RemoteException, PlaceOrderException
    {
      PVCSSBContext context = null;
      final DiscoMethodToken token =
      discoPreInvoke (TransactionAttribute.REQUIRED);
      String retVal = null;
      try {
        context = getHome().getPooledSessionContext();
retVal = getBean(context).newOrder(p0, p1, p2);
if (token.shouldLog()) {
  final Class[]             formalParameterTypes = new Class [3];
  formalParameterTypes[0] = String.class;
  formalParameterTypes[1] = String.class;
  formalParameterTypes[2] = Set.class;
  final Object[]            args = new Object[3];
  args[0] = p0;
  args[1] = p1;
  args[2] = p2;
  discoLogMethod("newOrder", retVal, formalParameterTypes, args);
}
      }
      catch (PlaceOrderException e) {
discoPostInvoke(TransactionAttribute.REQUIRED, token);
throw e;
      }
      catch (Throwable e) {
discoPostInvoke(TransactionAttribute.REQUIRED, token, e);
      }
      finally {
getHome().replaceContext(context);
      }

      discoPostInvoke(TransactionAttribute.REQUIRED, token);
      return (retVal);
    }
```

SAMPLE 16. newOrder for disconnected container.

the business logic provided by the bean developer in any way. (This is the approach used by connected EJB containers in which the deployed component delegates all business logic to the original bean, and only adds additional, container-specific, function.) Rather, the deployed component "calls out" to the logging function after a top-level transaction completes successfully, in a manner that resembles—from the bean-provider's viewpoint—"aspect-oriented" programming [1]. The only difference between the connected and disconnected versions of the application are that disconnected execution dynamically constructs a log that can be used to do synchronization based on the method-replay approach.

Because it has access to the container's transaction mechanisms, *EJBSync* respects the transaction structure that is dynamically created as the application executes. Thus, LogRecords are scoped with respect to a given transaction; within a transaction, they are ordered in the sequence that the methods were invoked. This allows all methods invoked in a given transaction to be atomically replayed on the server.

As outlined in the EJB specification, remoteable EJBs are passed by reference between address spaces. This implies that, when they are serialized, the serialized form contains only the EJB reference, not the state. This presents some difficulty for LogRecords, because LogRecords are implemented as Entity EJBs in our middleware. The middleware must transfer the saved state of the LogRecords from the client to the server during synchronization. In order that Entity EJB states may be serialized, we introduce the *EJB Memento* [13] construct. EJB Mementos contain all the values of the abstract persistence schema [10], and implement the `java.io.Serializable` interface. Entity EJBs are passed by value by extracting their EJB Mementos and serializing them instead. *EJBSync* tooling provides automatic generation of EJB Mementos, as well as Home methods for creating EJBs from their deserialized EJB Mementos.

When logging EJB method calls, the EJB references are saved, rather than the values. This is because the replay should be invoked against the current state of the EJBs, not the state at the time the method calls were logged. Normally EJB references contain information about the address-space in which the EJB exists. Since we need to replay against a different address space (the server rather than the client), our middleware changes the serialization to remove the address-space information, so that EJB references are deserialized as references to server EJBs with the same primary key, residing in a server-located Home with the same JNDI name. (Normally these references would deserialize into remote proxy objects.) This information, together with Java's reflection mechanisms, enables server-side reconstruction of the EJB on which the method was invoked as well as the method's parameters. A method is replayed by executing `invoke` on the corresponding `Method`.

This approach enables an application-independent synchronization protocol.

(1) The synchronizing client invokes the client-side *EJBSync* middleware when it wishes to synchronize with the server. All LogRecords created since the last synchronization are transmitted to the server, in addition to the client's id and current synchronization-session id.

(2) The server-side Replicator SSB iterates over the set of LogRecords, batching the LogRecords of a given transaction together, and ordering the transactions

as they were originally invoked on the client. Each batch is invoked in a separate server-side transaction and replayed atomically. The failure (as indicated through an exception thrown by a replayed method) of one transaction, automatically causes the failure of all subsequent transactions. Finally, the server returns a *SyncToken* to the client which can be used to query the status of the synchronization.

5. Evaluating Disconnected Programming Models

This chapter contends that a connected programming model for business applications *can* be projected to disconnected devices such that:

- the semantics of the programming model are (almost) unchanged regardless of whether the application executes in a connected or disconnected environment;
- the need to synchronize the device's work to the server is hidden from developers by a combination of the programming model and middleware;
- applications developed with this approach can be usefully deployed to disconnected devices because work performed on the device will be committed successfully to the server.

This programming model consists of:

- A transaction model using detection-based algorithms to perform concurrency control [12].
- Synchronization based on method-replay algorithms.
- A component model that delegates transactions, persistence, and security to container middleware rather than requiring developers to supply this function.

As short-hand, we shall refer to this programming model as *EJBSync* (Section 4.5) because *EJBSync* is a prototype realization of the programming model. A quantitative evaluation of this contention requires considerable experience with deployed applications over a long period of time. In the absence of such experience, we will validate our claim by comparing our approach to some popular alternatives.

5.1   Exotic Transaction Models

Several more complicated programming models have been introduced to address the problems of mobile disconnected business applications [9,27,32]). These attempt to reduce conflicts and/or operate in resource-constrained environments. As discussed in Section 1.4, business applications (at least in the medium term) will be deployed to sufficiently robust environments that the use of non-standard transaction models is not needed to reduce synchronization conflicts. Also, it seems likely that many of the resource constraints of disconnected clients will be reduced or eliminated in the future. Thus is seems preferable to use a programming model which is familiar to developers of connected applications.

5.2   Message-Based Programming Model

The *message-based* programming model is a common approach to building disconnectable applications. Business applications are explicitly partitioned into two portions: one is explicitly coded to execute on the disconnected device, and the other is explicitly coded to execute on the server when the device reconnects to the server. The programming model is "message-based" because, on a per-application basis, developers devise a suite of messages that are transmitted by the device to the server during the stage **3** synchronization process. Upon receiving these messages, the server invokes programs that propagate the change-set to the server's database.

In our *order entry* example, the portion of the application that runs on a disconnected device is responsible for saving enough of the new order information to allow the server to update its database as if the order had been placed by a server-side application program. This might include the name of the agent executing the order, the customer for whom the order is executed, and the set of items in the order. During synchronization, this state is transmitted to the server; a server-side program then executes the order on the server using the state that was previously saved on the disconnected device.

Figure 10 sketches message-based synchronization to implement *order entry*. It shows the client portion of the application as having decremented the stock level of staplers because one was sold to Mike; it also shows the subsequent message to the server, instructing the server to decrement its stock level so as to process the customer's order on the server.

In terms of our evaluation criteria, the message-based programming model is less useful than *EJBSync* because it requires two distinct application implementations (for connected and disconnected applications), and it forces developers to be explicitly aware of the synchronization process. On the other hand, because developers can completely customize the message suite and message contents, developers can potentially "tune" the application so as to commit the maximum amount of the device's work to the server. Similarly, message-based synchronization can potentially minimize bandwidth because only the minimum number of methods and the minimum amount of state needed to invoke the server-side program has to be recorded on the client and transmitted to the server.

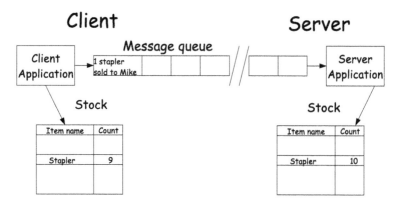

FIG. 10. Message-based programming model.

We consider the disadvantages of the message-based programming (compared to *EJBSync*) to be considerable. Developers must "hand-craft" a two-part solution (client and server) on a per-application basis. The application itself is responsible for transactionally constructing and transmitting the message from the device to the server, processing the message on the server, invoking the program that executes the order on the server, and returning the results to the reconnected device. *EJBSync* is a step forward in the way it pushes more function into generic middleware. *EJBSync* also provides a productivity improvement, in that developers can focus their efforts on the application-specific logic, rather than the infrastructure. From the standpoint of productivity, as well, businesses would prefer to develop only one version of an application, and deploy that application to both connected and disconnected environments. The message-based approach usually requires that two versions of an application must be developed: the *partitioned* version of the application, described above, and a *connected* version, for machines which are always connected to the server. Thus the partitioned version requires additional development, test, and maintenance effort beyond that required for the standard connected version. The message-based approach also requires extra programming to enable the disconnected device to see locally-applied state changes—that is, state changes made by the application to the cached database. This is because the straightforward implementation of the messaging approach does not actually make changes to the local database; instead, the actions are saved for eventual transmission to the server. Applying the changes locally complicates the implementation because the changes must be transactionally merged with the updated server state after the server has executed the application messages.

Interestingly, *EJBSync* can be seen as a middleware-based version of the message-based programming model. As with the message-based approach, *EJBSync* tracks the key business activities that have occurred during the disconnected application's execution. Unlike the message-based approach, middleware is responsible for tracking these business activities; the application itself is unmodified, and remains unaware that log activity is occurring. As with other comparisons between hand-crafted and automated solutions, the message-based programming model may well (at least initially) provide a more optimal solution than *EJBSync*. The usual tradeoff applies, however: development and maintenance costs are considerably cheaper with an automated approach, and automated solutions are typically improved over time.

5.3   Data Replication versus Method Replay

As mentioned in Section 3, the techniques used by *EJBSync* can be used to "hide" data-replication synchronization in the same way that method-replay is hidden. Based only on our first two evaluation criteria, these approaches are equally good since middleware is used to capture the device's change set and propagate it to the server. Both approaches facilitate the deployment of disconnected applications since the development, test, and maintenance costs have already been incurred when building the connected version of the application. In fact, DB2 Everyplace provides precisely this synchronization technique together with integrated middleware in a commercial product. The key differentiator between these approaches relates to our third criterion: the way in which the programming model supports *successful* propagation of work from the client to the server. Specifically, method replay has the following advantages compared to data replication:

- Method replay creates a smaller "footprint," in that it is less likely to cause conflicts during the synchronization process.

- Method replay projects a more consistent connected programming model to the disconnected device because of the way conflict resolution logic is specified.

- With method replay, the device's work executes against current data (during synchronization) rather than an out-of-date version of the data.

We discuss these advantages in more detail below, and then discuss their implications for building disconnectable applications.

5.3.1   Smaller Conflict Footprint

The more that the device's database state differs from the server's database, the more likely that synchronization will fail. While we definitely do not want to ignore a "true" conflict, we also want to minimize detection of "false" conflicts since those will cause useful work performed on the device to be discarded, or will require manual intervention to fix. Because data replication performs synchronization in terms of low-level data (where it is difficult to introduce higher-level semantics or application logic), it is more likely to create such false conflicts than method replay.

To see why this is so, consider the *order entry* example, and note that two clients may concurrently decrement the stock level for the same item. Data replication synchronization sees these actions as conflicting: different clients have modified the same row of the database. The middleware *must* flag this as a conflict, because this will lead to a transaction serializability violation (one of the clients' updates will be a *lost write* [15]). From the perspective of the application, however, the desired semantics are merely that sufficient stock exists during synchronization to satisfy the order. The precise stock level value for a given item is irrelevant. These semantics are easily expressed by a connected version of the application. They are also easily expressed for a disconnected version that uses method replay. In fact, only one version of the application need exist, since the identical `purchaseOrder` method executes for both connected and disconnected environments, decrementing the stock levels appropriately, and validating only that (0 != `stockLevel`). The same method—with the same validating business logic—that executed and was logged on the device, is replayed on the server during synchronization. Disconnected versions of the application that use data replication synchronization must use different semantics: stock levels during synchronization must be identical to their levels during disconnected execution. Because application-independent data replication middleware does not have enough semantic information about the application to resolve this automatically, synchronization will fail.

5.3.2 Consistent PM Projection

Advocates of data replication may counter that the previous argument is naive. The sort of false conflicts described above can be easily avoided by adding business logic as necessary to the synchronization engine. The middleware makes application-specific synchronization "hooks" available to developers in order to explicitly compensate for (and resolve) such false conflicts. The synchronization hooks could (reasonably) assume that applications only increment and decrement stock levels, and thus could determine the stock level that would result from the synchronization of multiple transactions.

However, this starts the synchronization middleware down the path of understanding the application semantics. Maintaining business logic in both the application and synchronization middleware is problematic, to say the least. The synchronization business logic is placed in the position of trying to reverse-engineer the changes made by the application logic, so that it can reconcile the data. More importantly, however, the more that such special-purpose logic must be added by *developers*—rather than being performed automatically by middleware—the more the programming model's consistent projection is compromised. While making the application disconnectable, it forces developers to explicitly "code around" the issue of disconnected operation. More pragmatically, rather than maintaining a single version of the application that can be deployed to both connected and disconnected environments, the business must now maintain two (or one and a half) versions of the application.

5.3.3 Execution Against Current Data

Because business applications must behave transactionally, a transaction model is part of any programming model for business applications. At a high-level, both data replication and method replay offer the same transaction semantics. In terms of the taxonomy presented in [12], both use a detection-based algorithm, with deferred validity checking, and invalidation when notified by the server about an update. (This approach is sometimes termed "optimistic," in contrast to pessimistic, lock-based, concurrency control mechanisms.) This enables high server-side availability—despite long periods of disconnection or even device failures—because the server is not forced to avoid potential conflicts.

Similarly, both approaches enable the connected transaction model to be projected to disconnected devices. *EJBSync*, for example, presents a disconnected device with the J2EE/EJB transaction model: sections of code can be explicitly demarcated with a `UserTransaction`, or the developer can use declarative transactions on a per-method basis. Transactions that are rolled back on the disconnected device are not replayed on the server (since the LogRecords are not committed). During synchronization, the transaction boundaries created during the client's execution are preserved on the server, as is the original transaction ordering. Data replication, as well, can project the connected transaction model to a disconnected environment. Although DB2 Everyplace sync does not maintain an application's transaction boundaries or ordering, this is a limitation of the implementation—not that of the idealized algorithm. Gold Rush, for example [14], shows that mobile transaction middleware can do data replication synchronization and preserve transaction boundaries and ordering. A similar situation holds with respect to validating "read sets"—the set of data read, but not written, by the application. Data replication implementations validate that conflicts have not occurred with respect to the application's "write set," but do not appear to check whether other users have concurrently modified the synchronizing device's read set. Although this can theoretically lead to a violation of transaction isolation [15], in practice, we find it difficult to identify a realistic scenario in which this leads to a serializability violation that was not caused by the application logic. Regardless, enhancing data replication implementations to also validate an application's read sets is relatively straightforward, and is not a fundamental limitation of the algorithm.

The key difference between the transactional models of data replication and method replay is more subtle, and involves the definition of transactional isolation. Data replication synchronization ideally attempts to ensure that the device's transactions are *conflict serializable* [15] with the transactions that were previously committed on the server. This criterion is defined in terms of read and write operations on data. Method replay attempts to ensure that *transformations* performed on the device are compatabile with transformations previously committed on the server. In effect, transactions executed on the disconnected device are *delayed* to a later point in time: namely, the time at which synchronization occurs. They are guaranteed to be serializable with the server-side transactions because, from the shared database viewpoint, they are executed *after* all the connected transactions have executed, and using any data modified by the server-side transactions as their inputs. Thus, strictly speaking, there cannot be a serializability violation. Under method replay semantics, the fact that work executed on a disconnected client is (almost) irrelevant to the transaction model. From a developer's viewpoint, therefore, the programming model is projected more consistently; from the client's viewpoint, the work executed against the most current version of the data.

The only caveat to the method replay transaction model is that any "human input" into the disconnected client transactions may not be replayed accurately, because the human thought processes are not captured in the method implementations. For example, the user may have looked at her checking balance on the disconnected client, seen a balance of $1000, and decided to withdraw $100. When the disconnected transactions are replayed on the server, the balance may have been $101. The replayed method will withdraw $100, leaving $1, but had the user known she only had $101 she may have decided to withdraw $50, or nothing. Also, she thinks her new balance is $900, which does not represent the balance at any time in the shared database. Typically, however, business logic will prevent a withdrawal of an amount greater than the available funds at synchronization time, unless overdrafts are permitted. Thus the synchronization process will not result in database consistency violations, unless the application is flawed. Note also that these "human serializability violation" scenarios occur with data replication as well. Data replication algorithms typically do not verify that data which was read but not modified by the disconnected client is unchanged on the server at synchronization time (in fact we are not aware of *any* data replication system which does this verification).

5.4   Useful Disconnectable Business Applications

We conclude by arguing that only approaches similar to *EJBSync* enable development of useful disconnectable applications, because of the inevitable issues that arise as server-side function is moved to the client. A continuum exists with respect to the degree to which server-side function is moved to the client. Browser-based applications exist at one extreme, in which almost all of the application resides on the server. This "thin-client" approach has certain advantages, but the application cannot execute on a disconnected device. To enable disconnectable applications, more of the data and more of the application logic must reside on the client. At the other extreme of the continuum, *all* of the application executes on the device. This may not always be practical, but can be done for certain types of applications (e.g., for the *order entry* example used in this chapter). However, as we have shown, this approach causes the maximum amount of data changes to take place on the device (e.g., stock level changes). As more changes are made to the device's database, it becomes more likely that false conflicts will be detected by data replication middleware (false in the sense that human intervention could easily resolve them). Relatively speaking, method replay will cause fewer false conflicts to occur, because the replays happen against up-to-date server data.

Consider the middle of this continuum, in which some application logic is moved to the disconnected device, but some remains on the server. For example, take the usage of a customer's "available credit" balance in validating an order. The credit balance could be replicated to the client, and orders placed only if the customer has sufficient credit. If the balance is sufficient, the credit balance would be decremented by the value of the order. Obviously this requires that *more* data be replicated to the client. For data replication, this also raises a problem similar to the stock-level problem discussed above. Because a customer's credit balance is modified by each placed order, orders placed for the same customer by different clients will always result in a (usually false) conflict during the synchronization of the second client. This conflict is usually false because only the exhaustion of the customer's credit balance is actually a problem. Two debits to the credit balance that do not exhaust the customer's credit could be combined arithmetically during synchronization.

In order to eliminate this false conflict for data replication, the credit-balance check could be eliminated from the disconnected client version of the application. Since the *business* still requires that the balance be checked and updated before fulfillment of the order, a separate server-side process, triggered by synchronization, must be put in place to do the credit-balance check and update. The code itself is not the problem. The problem is that this code is separate from the disconnected and connected versions of the application. It is not embedded in the original order-entry application flow, and it is not necessarily easy to fit it into the post-synchronization

work-flow. In this scenario, in fact, data replication synchronization begins to resemble the message-based synchronization (with all of its disadvantages) discussed
above.

In contrast, with method replay, the `purchaseOrder` method is modified to
conditionally perform the credit check and modify the existing balance only when
connected (and thus during synchronization as well). This additional application
logic is ignored when executing on the disconnected device. All that this approach
requires is the ability to determine whether a method is executing in a connected
or disconnected environment. The connected version performs the required credit-
check; the disconnected version branches around that code (placing the order without
the credit-check); and, during method replay, the credit-check will be transparently
performed before placing the order.

It seems therefore that the following tension exists with respect to deploying business applications to disconnected devices. If you wish to use a single programming
model so as to develop and maintain a single version of the application, the application will modify much transactional state. During synchronization, data replication
then is more likely than method replay to abort the work performed on the device because of false conflicts. This problem can be reduced, but only by creating connected
and disconnected versions of the application. Here too, method replay is more useful
than data replication because the branch logic is more easily packaged within a single
method or business process than as extraneous processes that must be hooked into
the business work-flow during synchronization. Executing the bulk of the application
on the server, with only a minimal application executing on the client, mitigates this
problem but only by drastically limiting the usefulness of disconnecting the application in the first place.

The use of method-replay synchronization does constrain the application to take
extra care when accessing data that is outside the shared datastore. If such data becomes part of the client-side datastore, it may not be used correctly during replay
because the external value may have changed since the original disconnected execution. For example, if an application sets fields based on the current time (e.g.,
timestamps) or using unique identifiers [42], the replayed application will use the
current values of the external data (e.g., the current time), not the values that were
originally used on the device. This may or may not be a problem. If the UUID is
used to set an EJB's primary key, and that EJB is referenced (and logged) by the
application, method replay synchronization will fail because that EJB's identity on
the server will be based on a new UUID value.

Data replication experiences a similar issue when dealing with unique identifiers.
Because the locally unique identifier (LUID) client ID may be different from the
globally unique identifier (GUID) server ID, the server must maintain an ID mapping
table for all items exchanged between itself and the client. Otherwise, the client's

datastore that references a set of LUIDs cannot be translated (or identified as referring to the data on the server by a different name) by the server. SyncML [40], for example, uses a *Map* operation to send the LUID of newly created data to the server. This allows the server to update its mapping table with the new LUID, GUID association. However, this is not sufficient to address all possible problems. If the LUID gets incorporated directly into application data, the synchronization process may not know how to modify the application data, or even detect that it should be modified during synchronization.

6. Summary and Conclusion

In the past, device resource constraints such as CPU and memory precluded even considering whether to execute business applications on disconnected devices. Now that such resource constraints are disappearing, we are forced to determine whether the algorithmic issues related to client synchronization of disconnected work preclude disconnected business applications. Similarly, the feasibility of programming models that facilitate the development of such applications becomes increasingly important.

We discussed these two areas of concern in this chapter. We explained why business applications are particularly hard to "project" to disconnected devices. We then introduced two general approaches used to perform synchronization: *data replication* and *method replay*.

We also discussed two programming models as applied to disconnected business applications. The first, Enterprise JavaBeans, was originally designed for connected environments. Due to its component-based design, we showed that it can be projected to disconnected environments as well. The second, Service DataObjects, is a new programming model which provides unified data access to heterogeneous data sources, unified support for both static and dynamic data APIs, and support for tools and frameworks. Although SDOs are targeted at "support for disconnected programming models," we show that the SDO definition of "disconnected" is significantly different from the definition that we consider in this chapter. The SDO programming model is designed to eliminate lock-holding during user think time, and is shown not to be suitable for environments where communications between client and server are interrupted, in its current incarnation.

Finally, we analyzed two different projections of the EJB programming model to disconnected environments. We compared data replication to method replay, discussed alternative disconnected programming models, and showed that a connected programming model can be usefully projected to a disconnected environment.

ACKNOWLEDGEMENTS

We thank Steve Brodsky, IBM Software Group, SDO Architect, for important feedback on an early draft of this chapter.

REFERENCES

[1] Special Issue on Aspect-Oriented Programming, *Commun. ACM* (October 2001).
[2] Brodsky S., private communication, dated 03/09/2005.
[3] Bainbridge A., Colgrave J., Colyer A., Normington G., "CICS and enterprise JavaBeans", *IBM Systems J.* **40** (1) (2001) 46–67, http://www.research.ibm.com/journal/sj/401/bainbridge.html.
[4] Siegel J., *Quick CORBA 3*, John Wiley & Sons, New York, 2001.
[5] Date C.J., "An architecture for high-level language database extensions", in: *Proc. ACM SIGMOD*, 1976, pp. 101–122. Note that the term "direct-reference" is used instead of "single-level store".
[6] Redmond F.E., *DCOM: Microsoft Distributed Component Object Model*, John Wiley & Sons, New York, 1997.
[7] "IBM DB2 Everyplace", http://www-306.ibm.com/software/data/db2/everyplace/index.html. Last verified on February 2006.
[8] "Data Transfer Object", http://www.martinfowler.com/eaaCatalog/dataTransferObject.html. Last verified on February 2006.
[9] Dunham M.H., Helal A., Balakrishnan S., "Mobile transaction model that captures both the data and movement behavior", *Mobile Networks Appl.* **2** (2) (1997) 149–162.
[10] "J2EE Enterprise JavaBeans Technology", http://java.sun.com/products/ejb/. Last verified on February 2006.
[11] "Enterprise JavaBeans Specification Version 1.0", http://java.sun.com/products/ejb/docs10.html. Last verified on February 2006.
[12] Franklin M.J., Carey M.J., Livny M., "Transactional client-server cache consistency: alternatives and performance", *ACM Trans. Database Systems (TODS)* **22** (3) (1997) 315–363.
[13] Gamma E., et al., *Design Patterns: Elements of Reusable Object-Oriented Software*, Addison–Wesley, Reading, MA, 1995.
[14] Butrico M.A., et al., "Mobile transaction middleware with Java-object replication", in: *Proc. Third USENIX Conference (COOTS)*, 1997.
[15] Gray J., Reuter A., *Transaction Processing: Concepts and Techniques*, Morgan Kaufmann, San Mateo, CA, 1993.
[16] "Java Message Service (JMS)", http://java.sun.com/products/jms/. Last verified on February 2006.
[17] Kermarrec A.-M., et al., "The IceCube approach to the reconciliation of diverging replicas", in: *Proc. 20th Annual ACM SIGACT–SIGOPS Symposium on Principles of Distributed Computing (PODC)*, August 2001.

[18] "IceCube", http://research.microsoft.com/camdis/icecube.htm. Last verified on February 2006.

[19] "IBM IMS Family", http://www-306.ibm.com/software/data/ims. Last verified on February 2006.

[20] Greanier T., "Discover the secrets of the Java serialization API", http://java.sun.com/developer/technicalArticles/Programming/serialization/.

[21] "Java Database Connectivity (JDBC)", http://java.sun.com/products/jdbc/. Last verified on February 2006.

[22] "Java 2 Platform, Micro Edition (J2ME)", http://java.sun.com/j2me/index.jsp. Last verified on February 2006.

[23] "Java Transaction API (JTA)", http://java.sun.com/products/jta/. Last verified on February 2006.

[24] Leff A., Prokopek P., Rayfield J.T., Silva-Lepe I., "Enterprise JavaBeans and Microsoft transaction server: frameworks for distributed enterprise components", in: *Advances in Computers*, vol. 54, Academic Press, San Diego, CA, 2001, pp. 99–152.

[25] Leff A., Rayfield J.T., "Enterprise JavaBeans caching in clustered environments, Part II", *Journal of Concurrency and Computation: Practice and Experience* **17** (7–8) (2005) 1027–1051.

[26] Benz B., Oliver R., *Lotus Notes and Domino 6 Programming Bible*, Wiley, New York, 2003.

[27] Madria S.K, Bhargava B., "A transaction model to improve data availability in mobile computing", *Journal of Distributed and Parallel Databases* **10** (2) (2001) 127–160.

[28] Monson-Haefel R., Burke B., Labourey S., *Enterprise JavaBeans*, fourth ed., O'Reilly, 2004.

[29] "IBM WebSphere MQ Everyplace", http://www-306.ibm.com/software/integration/wmqe/. Last verified on February 2006.

[30] Bennett B., et al., "A distributed object oriented framework to offer transactional support for long running business processes", in: *ACM Middleware 2000*, pp. 331–348.

[31] "Navigational database", http://en.wikipedia.org/wiki/Navigational_Database. Last verified on February 2006.

[32] Pitoura E., Bhargava B., "Maintaining consistency of data in mobile distributed environments", in: *15th International Conference on Distributed Computing Systems (ICDCS'95)*.

[33] "JDBC Rowset tutorial", http://java.sun.com/developer/Books/JDBCTutorial/chapter5.html. Last verified on February 2006.

[34] "Specifications: Service Data Objects, WorkManager, and Timers: IBM and BEA Joint Specifications Overview", http://www-128.ibm.com/developerworks/library/specification/j-commonj-sdowmt/index.html. Last verified on February 2006.

[35] "Next-Generation Data Programming: Service Data Objects", ftp://www6.software.ibm.com/software/developer/library/j-commonj-sdowmt/Next-Gen-Data-Programming-Whitepaper.doc, November 2003. Last verified on February 2006.

[36] "Service Data Objects: IBM Corp. and BEA Systems, Inc. Version 2.0", ftp://www6.software.ibm.com/software/developer/library/j-commonj-sdowmt/Commonj-SDO-Specification-v2.0.pdf, June 2005. Last verified on February 2006.

[37] "JSR 235: Service Data Objects", http://www.jcp.org/en/jsr/detail?id=235. Last verified on February 2006.

[38] "Service Data Objects. EMF Tools subproject", http://www.eclipse.org/emf/sdo/. Last verified on February 2006.

[39] Serrano-Alvarado P., Roncancio C., Adiba M., "A survey of mobile transactions", *Journal of Distributed and Parallel Databases* **16** (2) (2004) 193–230.

[40] Open Mobile Alliance (OMA), "SyncML", http://www.openmobilealliance.org/tech/affiliates/syncml/syncmlindex.html. Last verified on February 2006.

[41] Thirumalai S., private communication, dated 02/01/2005.

[42] "Universal Unique Identifier", http://www.opengroup.org/onlinepubs/9629399/apdxa.htm. Last verified on February 2006.

[43] "XML Schema", http://www.w3.org/XML/Schema. Last verified on February 2006.

[44] "XML Path Language (XPath)", http://www.w3.org/TR/xpath. Last verified on February 2006.

Academic Electronic Journals: Past, Present, and Future

ANAT HOVAV

Korea University
Seoul
South Korea

PAUL GRAY

Claremont Graduate University
Claremont, CA
USA

Abstract

Although the use of the Internet and the World Wide Web (WWW) in academic publishing advanced since the early 1990s, the growth of electronic journals proved neither as rapid nor as significant as was initially expected. Exploratory work by information and library scientists predicted the demise of the traditional academic publishing system. The Internet and electronic journals (e-journals) were expected to change the way academia approaches scholarship and publishing. As in many other industries, immediately after the introduction of the WWW, a large number of e-journals were established, followed by a high mortality rate. The resulting dominant design for academic publishing is a continuation of existing paper journals, many with an electronic presence. A competing design is the electronic replica of a paper journal. These e-journals rarely use the full "electronicity" afforded by the Internet and usually look and feel like a paper journal.

In this chapter, we investigate the rationale behind the slow adoption of e-journals by academia. The chapter examines the benefits and challenges introduced by e-journals vis-à-vis the objectives of academic scholarship. We conclude that all three forms of e-journals solve many of the economic and technical issues facing academic publishing such as reduced production and distribution costs, reduced time lag, increased available space and new formats. However, e-journals raise some fundamental social, political and institutional dilemmas such as the ability to control the quality of the published material, long term sustainability, institutional resistance, increased work for editors, reviewers and authors and backwards compatibility. Institutional resistance to e-journals increases in direct proportion to the level of electronicity used by these journals. These conflicts are difficult to resolve and will require a cultural change and power shift.[1]

1.   Introduction

Published academic work is used both for knowledge building and dissemination, and for the distribution of rewards, prestige and funds. The traditional form of academic publishing, based on printed journals, faces major, often reinforcing, obstacles including:

----

[1]For example, electronic journals enable the use of Internet search engines (i.e., Google Scholar) instead of traditional indexing services, thereby shifting power from the few indexing services to academicians.

- time lags,
- increasing production and distribution costs,
- shrinking markets,
- decreasing ability to publish innovative and unorthodox work,
- space limitations,
- limited accessibility,
- limited format, and
- lack of interactivity.

An alternative is the publication of academic articles in electronic form using a medium such as the Internet. As we will show in this chapter, introducing electronic publishing offers benefits such as:

- reduced costs,
- reduced cycle time,
- increased space availability,
- increased accessibility, and
- increased interactivity.

At the same time, electronic publishing introduces new challenges such as:

- protecting copyrights,
- controlling publication quality,
- maintaining long-term sustainable copies,
- maintaining backwards compatibility, and
- developing an appropriate fee structure in a seemingly "free" medium.

Although the use of the Internet and the World Wide Web (WWW) in academic publishing advanced since the early 1990s, the penetration of e-journals is not as rapid and significant as was initially predicted. Exploratory work by information and library scientists predicted the demise of the traditional academic publishing system (e.g., [38]). The Internet and electronic journals (which we will refer to as e-journals) were expected to change the way academia approaches scholarship and publishing [14]. Yet, the current trend in academic publishing differs from this prediction.

Much like startups in many other industries, immediately after the introduction of the WWW, a large number of e-journals were established, followed by a high mortality rate. The resulting dominant design for academic publishing is a continuation of existing paper journals, many with an electronic presence. This arrangement may not be the optimum design.[2] In addition, even with advanced electronicity[3] e-journals rarely use the full features afforded by the Internet; they often look and feel like paper journals.

In this chapter, we describe the development of academic publishing as a means of communication among scholars and as an instrument to measure scholarly productivity and grant rewards (Section 2). We next detail the forces that affect that development and the challenges currently facing the publishing industry (Section 3). In Section 4, we describe some of the solutions e-journals offer and the new challenges e-journals introduce. In Section 5, we discuss the economics of electronic journals. In Section 6, we describe the effect e-journals have on various stakeholders (authors, editors, academics as a community, libraries, and gatekeepers). We conclude (Section 7) with insights regarding the directions in which academic electronic publishing is heading.

2. History of Academic Publishing

Publishing is as ancient as herding and hunting. Even before people invented writing, they published their hunting expeditions on cave walls in the form of pictures and symbols. For thousands of years, manuscripts and letters were copied manually. This labor-intensive and time-consuming task made manuscripts a rare commodity. Manuscripts were only available to a selected group of people. The dissemination of knowledge through published work was slow. The quantity of the published work was limited and its distribution local. The few who owned manuscripts and were able to read them were so familiar with the work they did not need indexing or search mechanisms. Manuscripts were copied manually and modified intentionally or accidentally. Therefore, each copy of the manuscript was unique in some ways [49].

Cave writing was time consuming and not transportable, limiting the reach of the information to a local tribe. Clay tablets and other similar material were portable but impractical.[4] Paper first appeared in China around 2000 years ago. It signaled a major change in publishing and the dissemination of knowledge. The Arabs used paper by the 10th century. It was only around the 12th century that paper reached Europe. The invention of the printing press in 1450 was a subsequent technological innovation that was facilitated by the existence of paper as a delivery medium.

The printing press signaled a first major change in the dissemination of information among people. Manuscripts and books could be copied quickly and accu-

---

[2] Some argue that it may be the worst possible design.

[3] The term "electronicity" is used to define the extent to which an e-journal exploits the new content, format, and structure afforded by the Internet.

[4] Stone and clay were heavy, wood and scroll were not sustainable.

rately for a fraction of the cost. Initially, very little changed in the way manuscripts were organized. Over time, new features appeared such as alphabetic indexing, title pages, page numbering, indexing and citation [49]. Following the printing press, incremental technological innovations improved publishing. The introduction of the typewriter, for example, improved the speed and the readability of manuscripts. The introduction of word processors increased the speed and quality of writing by allowing in-place corrections and inserts, thus limiting the number of drafts required. Neither the typewriter nor the word processor changed the essence of publishing substantially.

Prior to the existence of academic journals, scientific findings were disseminated through personal letter, books, and professional meetings [49]. The first issue of an academic journal, the *Philosophical Transactions of the Royal Society* (London), was introduced in 1665. At about the same time a new academic journal appeared in Paris, the *Journal Des Scavans* [50]. Thus, although, technology and distribution channels existed much earlier, the scientific community did not see a need to change its way of disseminating its findings until the middle of the 17th century. The number of journals increased to 700 by 1800 and close to 10,000 journals by 1900 [23]. In the 18th century, academic publications assumed a new function; the registration of priority claims. Copyrights were first recorded in 1709. In the 19th century, journal publications assumed an additional role as indicators of productivity and standing [50]. Publishing is still an integral part of the academic community. Journal publishing is used to disseminate knowledge, enable communication among scholars and for the gain of rewards and recognition.

3.   Academic Scholarship

Because the core essence of academic publishing did not change in over 400 years (Section 2), academic journals today face multiple challenges in realizing their objectives.

3.1   Objectives

Schaffner [49] lists five objectives of the academic journal:

1. To build collective knowledge by adding to existing knowledge through new research results.
2. To communicate knowledge. Journals are used to communicate findings to other researchers, to students, and from time to time to practitioners, government agencies, and industry leaders.

3. To validate the quality of the knowledge published. Unlike other forms of publications (e.g., newspaper articles, personal letters), articles in academic journals are peer reviewed (although the exact review process varies by journal). This review process is designed to ensure the quality and validity of what is published.

4. To distribute rewards. Journal publication determines the advancement of scholars. Tenure, promotion to full professor, and merit pay all depend on the number and quality of the articles published by the scholar. Quality is usually measured by the rank of the journal and by the number of times an article is cited and where it is cited.

5. To build a community. Academic journals rely on the existence of a community of scholars to perform voluntary functions such as reviewing papers and editorial work. Without the support of the community, academic journals could not exist in their present form. Scholars that want to publish also need to contribute to their community by participating in these activities.

3.2   Criteria

To fulfill these roles, academic journals should be [24]

- sustainable,   • accessible,   • timely.
- reputable,   • of high quality,

For example, to build collective knowledge, academic publications should be accessible so that scholars can find out what knowledge exists. They should be sustainable to ensure that knowledge does not disappear and to allow scholars to add to the research record. To support useful communications journals need to be timely. The usefulness of the information depends on the cycle time from completing the work to its appearing in print. In rapidly changing fields such as computers and information systems, time lags can result in obsolescence as new ideas become available or new developments take place. Because space in print journals and the time for reading them are limited, readers want assurance that the journal offers high quality research results.

3.3   Unique Characteristics

Peek [44] notes that "Academic journals are, by their nature, a unique genre in the world of publishing." Some of these unique features are:

- The circulation of most journals is relatively small [40,44]. For example, three of the leading journals in information systems are Information Systems Research (ISR), Journal of Management Information Systems (JMIS) and the

MIS Quarterly (MISQ). Their data given in the government mandated annual Statement of Ownership showed that their respective circulation in 2005 was approximately 1500 (ISR), 1000 (JMIS), and 3000 (MISQ) per issue.

- Academic publishers must concern themselves with priority claims for being first to make a discovery,[5] with journal ratings, and with perceived reputation and quality [11].

- Academic publishing, while not paying authors directly, offers scholars rewards in prestige, advancement, and funding [11].

In addition, Odlyzko [40] lists four economic factors unique to academic publishing that may influence the cost, pricing, and fee structure of the scholarly publishing industry:

1. *Decreasing markets.* Not only is the circulation of most academic journals relatively small, the number of subscribers is decreasing at an estimated rate of about 4.5% a year [20], or a 50% reduction over 16 years [39] (see Fig. 1).[6] This is partially due to the decrease in individual subscribers [52]. According to Tenopir and King [53], the number of individual subscribers has halved between 1980 and 2000. To maintain marginal profitability publishers raise subscription prices at a rate higher than inflation. The estimated price increase for North American publishers is about 10.3% a year. Of the 10.3% increase, about 2.8% account for inflation and 3% emanate from page increase. The

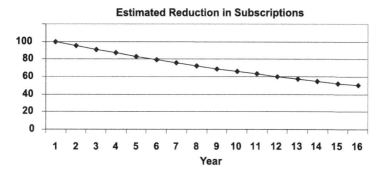

FIG. 1. Estimated reduction in journal subscriptions (based on Odlyzko [39]).

---

[5] Because journals claim to publish new work, they need to make certain that contributions are new. In effect they warrant that, to the best of their knowledge, the content is previously unpublished. Plagiarism is a major transgression.

[6] A 4.5% yearly decrease equals to a 50% decrease over 16 years [39]. This is similar to the 50% decrease over 20 years estimated by [53].

rest of the price increases cover losses of income due to reduction in subscrip-tions [52,4]. This phenomenon is also known as the "serial crisis."

2. *Conflicting stakeholder incentives.* The incentives for authors differ from the incentives for libraries. Scholars determine the journals in which they want to publish based on a journals ratings and prestige. Their choice of journal does not depend on its cost. Furthermore, scholars mandate the journals the library carry thereby creating demand. Libraries, however, are constrained by budgets that are unrelated to scholarly grants or departmental budget.

3. *Lack of price competition.* Publishers take advantage of the conflicting incen-tives of the stakeholders. Odlyzko [40] estimates the revenue, to the publisher, from a 20-page article in Mathematics or Computer Science to average $4,000. The cost to the library can range from $1,000 to $8,000.[7] These variances in charges are unrelated to the quality or prestige of the journal.

4. *Publisher's costs are minimal.* The input material is almost invariably free to the publisher. A large fraction of the work in academic publishing is done with contributed labor. Authors and reviewers are rarely paid for their work [44]. At best, editors-in-chief receive small honoraria.[8] Associate editors are not paid. Only production workers ranging from copy editors to printers to distributors are paid at going rates. Authors usually[9] do not receive royalties or payments for articles published in journals and in some cases (e.g., in the sciences) they or their institution are required to pay "page charges.[10]"

These unique characteristics introduce the challenges that academic publishing currently faces. Some of the challenges are economic and relate to the increase in cost and the reduced market share. Others are social in nature.

3.4   Current Challenges

Paper-based academic publishing suffers major deficiencies with respect to the criteria discussed in Section 3.1. Changes in the academic publishing industry are needed to alleviate some of these issues.

---

[7] Odlyzko [40] compares the cost variation to the airline industry and states that an airline charging $8000 for a ticket could not survive if its competitors charge $1000 for the same type of ticket.

[8] Based on the time they put into the journal, they are often paid less than minimum wage/hour.

[9] A few journals, such as Information Systems Management which is oriented to practitioners but publishes academic work (http://www.ism-journal.com/AuthorGuide.html#scope) give small payments to authors.

[10] Page charges refer to fees paid by the authors' institutions on a per page basis. These fees are allowable costs under government contracts and hence are usually paid for by funds from outside the University.

3.4.1 Space Limitations

The core challenge of paper-based journals is the limited space available. Space is a scarce resource that needs to be managed carefully [12]. Print journals are limited in space, due to the escalating cost of printing, copying, and distributing. Therefore, they include only the minimum information essential to understanding the work. Most articles do not include original data, long questionnaires, computer programs, or complex algorithms.[11] Graphics and photos are kept to a minimum, and color is almost never used. Authors protest when word limits are imposed that prevent rich contextual descriptions of, for example, case studies in information systems [58].

Ability of scholars to publish. Because space limits fix the number of articles quality journals can publish, authors compete for a fixed number of slots. A resulting challenge is the ability of scholars to publish. Lotka's law [33] states that "the number of authors making N contributions is about $1/N^a$ of those making one contribution, where "a" is often nearly 2. Thus, for example, if in a given field 2000 authors publish one article, then the number of authors who make $N = 10$ contributions is $2000/10^2 = 20$ authors. Thus, very few scholars publish most of the work and most scholars publish very few articles [29].

Innovation versus control. Academic publishing generally does not promote innovation and creativity [12,16,37]. The current system trades off control over quality against dissemination of knowledge and communication. To maintain high quality and stay within space limitations, gatekeepers tend to accept studies on topics that are within established paradigms [25]. New and unorthodox work is often rejected by gatekeepers [50,5]. Campanario [5] found that over 10% of the most highly cited papers of all times encountered difficulties in being published.[12] Given the limited available space, editors prefer to commit a type I error (reject a promising article) rather than commit a type II error (accept a poor article). Nord [37] suggested an increase in journal space as a solution, but increased journal space increases cost.

3.4.2 Journal Focus and Learning Curves

In addition to space limitations, authors are deterred by:

1. Most established journals have a focus, a theme and rules of acceptance. The ideology of the editorial board affects the review process. Editors choose reviewers whose ideology is similar to their own [16,25]. Therefore, new and innovative work that does not fit within the established paradigms of existing journals is hard to publish [47].

---

[11] Which of these items are published depend, to some extent, on the field and the journal.

[12] The list contains articles from various disciplines and can be found in *Citation Classics* at: http://www.garfield.library.upenn.edu/classics.html [last accessed 06/21/2005].

2. Academic publishing requires a long and tedious learning curve. Because novice writers are less familiar with the rules and norms, they are less likely to pass the initial hurdles of academic publishing. Established scholars are familiar with the system, and are often simultaneously the referees, the gatekeepers, and the enactors of direction.

3.4.3 Publication Cycle Time

Cycle time includes the time from submission to decision and the time from decision to publication and distribution (Fig. 2).

Since the early 1990s, electronic submissions of manuscripts and electronic communications among editors, reviewers and authors reduced some of the publications cycle time. For example, MIS Quarterly reduced its review time considerably by using electronic submissions and e-mail for communication [60]. Yet, some journals still take several years from submission-to-distribute. These time lags result from the cumulative effects of such legitimate functions as refereeing (often the major culprit), editing, revision (authors often let manuscripts sit for long periods of time), backlogs, space limitations, and the need to combine articles into issues. Some of the delays are due to time constraints and workload of the referees, editors and the editorial staff [60]. These are human related factors and are extraneous to the publication medium.

Paper journals tend to create a backlog because the number of accepted articles is larger than the space available in the next issue and/or due to the need to maintain a steady and consistent stream of publications. For example in their July 2004 editors' report,[13] the editors of the *Comparative Technology Transfer and Society* journal stated that "The metric here is to place the journal on a solid footing by building a *one-year backlog* of accepted articles—somewhere between 12 and 15 articles." With a fixed number of pages in an annual budget, paper journals do not vary significantly in size from one issue to the next, since a long issue results in later short issues and

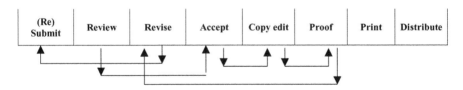

FIG. 2. The publication cycle.

[13] http://web.uccs.edu/klingner/2004%20CTTS%20Annual%20Report.doc [last accessed June 16, 2005].

vice versa. For example, Communications of ACM's backlog for accepted individual contributions in 2004 was reputed to be over two years.

3.4.4   Technical Limitations of Paper

For print journals, the medium is paper, which introduces the following technical limitations:

Format—Printed work is limited by the properties of paper. For example, a molecular biologist described the nightmare it was to publish an article with color figures. Although finally published in color, the illustrations cannot readily be reproduced for students, since the figures lose their meaning in a black and white photocopy [9].

Distribution—Distribution is costly, time consuming, and increasing in cost over time. The publication process requires maintaining a distribution list, packaging, mailing, and re-sending when necessary. Distribution cost is one factor, which leads publishers to accumulate material into issues and only publish periodically.[14]

Access—In many cases, the access to published work is geographically and temporally limited. Academicians subscribe to one or a few leading journals in their field. To access other work, they normally go to the library in their school. Scholars tend to read only the articles relevant to their area of interest and rarely read complete volumes of a given journal [3]. To broaden the range of knowledge to which they have access, academicians need access to specific parts of a variety of journals and not just subscriptions to one or two journals. These issues are discussed further in Section 5.1.2.

Interactivity—The lengthening time between when work is done and when it is published shifted the role of journal articles from providing interactive communication among researchers to providing archiving and prestige mechanisms [43]. In some disciplines, authors distribute preprints [49,19] as their primary means of communication.[15] Other disciplines use the conference paper as a tool to disseminate and communicate knowledge [13]. This issue is discussed further in Section 6.5.3.

3.4.5   The Economic Challenge

The market for academic journals is shrinking, the price of academic journals is increasing more rapidly than inflation and page counts are increasing [40,52], yet the budgets of libraries and universities are decreasing [28]. Libraries either drop subscriptions or impose a freeze on new subscriptions [28,30]. As a result, the traditional publication outlets for new fields of research are usually limited. Survey results

---

[14] Another reason is the reader's cognitive overload if articles are sent one at a time.

[15] This method is not far different from the samizdat used in the Soviet Union for distributing political knowledge among dissidents.

show that scholars view the individual subscription price of printed journals to be too high [50]. The economics of e-journals is discussed in more details in Section 5.

Some of the challenges discussed in this section were resolved with the introduction of electronic journals, particularly hybrid journals (e.g., access, format, cycle time). Other issues (e.g., ability to publish, innovation versus control) are more complex and require fundamental changes in academic views and culture.

4. Electronic Academic Journals

In this section, we describe the first decade of electronic publishing and define the various types of academic electronic journals in existence.

The use of computer networks to disseminate information was studied at least since the 1970s. King and Roderer [26] published several articles in 1978 on electronic publishing. At the New Jersey Institute of Technology Turoff [55] and later Turoff and Hiltz [56] described electronic publishing using the Electronic Information and Education Services (*EIES*), an early electronic mail and conferencing system, modified to accommodate electronic publishing. Most early attempts to publish electronically through communication networks, magnetic media (tape or CDs) or shared databases failed. Although research universities were connected to some form of a communications network since the 1970s, early forms of the Internet (such as ARPANET) were limited in their media capabilities, search facilities, and bandwidth.

By the end of the 1980s a few electronic journals started appearing. In July 1991, for example, the *Directory of Electronic Journals, Newsletters and Academic Discussion Lists* [31] published by the Association of Research Libraries (ARL) listed 27 electronic journals. The growth in the first half of the 1990s was explosive. The same directory listed 1093 electronic journals in May 1996 [32]. The ARL stopped tracking electronic journals in 1997. E-journals were no longer a novelty. As we discuss later in this section, not only did the number of e-journals increase, so did the forms that electronic journals took. Several sites list e-journals such as http://gort.ucsd.edu/newjour/toc.html, which is maintained by the University of California San Diego (UCSD). In 1999, this site listed approximately 6,000 serials. In May 2005, the number grew to 15,920.

4.1 Classification of Electronic Journals

Despite the growth in the numbers of listed e-journals, a standard for defining an e-journal does not exist.

4.1.1   Implementation and Distribution

E-journals vary in their implementation and distribution. For example, McEl-downey [35] refers to e-journals as journals accessed through communication technology. Schauder [50] considers projects like ADONIS,[16] which is implemented on CD-ROM to be an example of e-journals. Other online journals are distributed using shared databases, e-mail attachments, listserves, and FTP. Since the late 1990s, e-journals are principally distributed on the World Wide Web (WWW).

4.1.2   Forms

Articles are published in various forms such as ASCII and text, Word documents, HTML, and PDF. Some e-journals are purely electronic while many are hybrid; that is, published in both print and electronic form (Section 4.2.2). Long Standing commercial examples include Kluwer On-line (now part of SpringerLink), JSTOR, and Muse [44]. Professional Society examples are the Association for Computing Machinery (ACM), which offers its Digital Library and the Institute for Operations Research and Management Science (INFORMS). These versions are also referred to as electronic editions [22]. Among pure e-journals, a few are managed by commercial publishers (e.g., *Online of Current Clinical Trials* [44]). Other pure e-journals are managed by professional societies (e.g., *Communications of the Association for Information Systems*) or by entrepreneurial ventures (e.g., *Philosophical Foundations of Information Systems*).

Within the category of pure e-journals, some use full electronicity (capabilities of the media), offering new forms of publications while others only use the e-media as a distribution mechanism. In the latter, articles look and feel like paper but are digitized and delivered electronically.

4.1.3   Business Models

Most commercial publishers use their paper journals infrastructure to support their electronic counterparts. Some commercial publishers charge an additional 10 to 20% of the subscription for access to both paper and digital versions of the same journal. Professional societies that produce one or more electronic journals for their members, usually bundle subscription to one journal with their membership fees. Members have the option of purchasing additional subscriptions at a going rate. Finally, some e-journals are supported by entrepreneurial ventures. These ventures are often run by university research centers or by individual scholars, and are free of

---

[16] ADONIS is part of an electronic publishing initiative developed by a consortium of well-established scientific, technical, and medical publishers [50] (see http://www.rose-net.co.ir/products/PRODUCTS1/ADONIS/ejs.htm [accessed June 15th, 2005].

charge. We describe these business models further in Section 5.1.1, where we discuss the cost/benefits of electronic journals.

4.2   The Three Types of Electronic Journals

Most studies of e-journals do not differentiate among the various types of e-journals. Our discussion addresses only e-journals that are distributed via the Internet using the WWW. In this section, we describe three different forms of e-journals and how each addresses the challenges facing academic publishing.

These forms and the drivers for their adoption were initially described in Hovav and Gray [24]. Each form solves a different set of challenges but also introduces new concerns. Table I compares the three types.

4.2.1   Paper Replacement E-Journals

We term the first form of electronic publishing a "paper replacement." These e-journals have the look and feel of paper journals (p-journals). Paper replacement e-journals usually arise when financial resources or audience are limited. The need to reduce production and distribution costs leads publishers to undertake e-journals rather than p-journals. To gain the acceptance of e-journals by academicians, tenure committees and gatekeepers, paper replacement e-journals make low use of electronicity. These e-journals use the Internet only as a delivery mechanism. In paper replacement e-journals, the material remains the traditional research paper. Articles are page numbered sequentially so they can easily be printed and presented in paper form. In addition, articles are bundled into issues or volumes and delivered periodically to reduce information overload and to allow traditional referencing. Some paper replacement e-journals are broader in scope because they use the added space available to publish unorthodox material alongside traditional work.

4.2.2   Hybrid E-Journals

We term the second form a hybrid e-journal. A hybrid e-journal publishes both an e-version and a p-version. The e-version is usually identical to the p-version. However, in some cases the e-version contains more details than the p-version. For example, Information Science Research allows authors to present detailed proofs and long data sets in the e-version.

Publishers may offer hybrid journals if one or more of the following conditions occur:

- By offering an e-version, publishers increase the ease of access to the material;

TABLE I
THE CHALLENGES RESOLVED BY EACH TYPE OF E-JOURNALS

Challenge	Paper replacement	Hybrid (co-existence)	Advanced electronicity
Space	Unlimited space is available but few articles are unusually long. Allows more articles to be published than p-journals	Space is limited by paper counterpart; some journals now offer additional information (e.g., data sets, protocols, questionnaires) in the electronic version	Unlimited space is available. More articles are lengthy. Also allows more articles to be published than in p-journals
Ability to publish innovative content	Unlimited space enables inclusion of innovative content	Space limitations in the p-version limits inclusion of innovative content to what the p-journal publishes	Unlimited space enables inclusion of innovative content
Cycle time	Reduced cycle time since backlog is not needed and articles can be posted as they are ready	Limited by the number of articles per issue, leading to backlogs	Reduced cycle time. Articles can be posted as they are ready
New formats	New formats are not included to maintain a paper-like look. However, color is often used	New formats are not included with the exception of some extensions in the electronic version of articles	New formats, such as video and audio are often introduced
Interactivity	Possible but is not implemented to retain the "look and feel" of a p-article	Limited by the paper counterpart	Living scholarship is possible
Cost	Lower cost to produce and distribute the journal	Increase in cost due to the production of both a p-journal and an e-journal	Lower cost to produce and distribute the journal
Accessibility	Available anywhere at any time	Electronic version is available anywhere at any time	Available anywhere at anytime

- By posting articles on the web as they are completed, publishers reduce cycle time;
- By offering both versions, additional net revenues can be gained from the second version;
- The p-journal is the journal of record but the e-journal provides additional details that cannot be included in the p-journal because of space limitations.

The marginal cost of creating an e-version of p-journals is relatively small.[17] For example, the infrastructure needed to prepare, index and abstract articles, and market the journal are common to the p- and e-versions. Academic publishers charge an additional fee for a combined paper and online access (for example, in 2004, Kluwer charged 20% extra for combined access to Information Systems Frontiers) and require subscription to the paper version. Current examples of such co-existence are the ACM Digital Libraries, Kluwer online, and INFORMS online. In hybrid journals, the material remains the traditional research paper. Articles are sequential in nature since they have to conform to both paper and electronic media. The means of distribution are mixed. Publishers use physical distribution for paper copies and Internet access for the electronic version. Paper and electronic articles are bundled into issues and delivered periodically. E-versions of the articles can include extensions with additional modes such as hyperlinks, images, video and audio (e.g., the International Journal of Robotics Research).[18] This approach not only justifies the additional fees charged but also adds value to the combined access.

4.2.3 Advanced Electronicity E-Journal

In advanced electronicity e-journals, the material is innovative[19] compared to p-journals. Using the additional space available, e-journals introduce additional material such as programs, algorithms, test data, experimental data, and videos of experiments or talking heads. Articles are intuitive in nature using hyperlinks. Portions of the articles can be stored in various locations and linked (e.g., [36]). Articles are posted when they are ready, reducing cycle time. The modes are multiple and include three-dimensional images, video, audio, color, or pictures (for example see [57]). Articles can also be published in several versions, at several levels of complexity (e.g., [21]) each targeting a different audience. For example, an article might contain two levels of theory and two levels of practical information. A researcher chooses to read the expanded theoretical section and the summary of the implications to practice, while a practitioner reads a summary of the theory and a detailed section on practical implications.

Advanced electronicity e-journals arise when scholars need to publish innovative material. In addition, publishing these types of articles in paper forms does not make

---

[17] Kluwer estimates the start-up cost to create the first issue of a p-journal to be of the order of $200,000. We estimate that adding a web version should involve an investment of less than $30,000 for 3 months of web developer time, a server, and miscellaneous startup and advertising costs.

[18] http://www.ijrr.org/electronic.html [last accessed June 16th, 2005].

[19] Here the term innovative refers to the inclusion of new formats, networked structure or living scholarship. Advanced electronicity e-journals like replacement e-journals can also include innovative (unconventional) content.

economic sense. The advanced electronicity e-journals develop despite some resistance to change by stakeholders (e.g., tenure committees, gatekeepers).

4.3   Challenges Solved by E-Journals

As of 2005, all three forms are in existence. The paper replacement and the hybrid forms are more common whereas advanced electronicity e-journals are rare. As indicated in Table I, each e-journal type solves some of the challenges facing academic publishing.

Space. Effectively infinite space is only available to advanced and paper replacement e-journals since the hybrid journal is limited by the space constraints of the paper version. Some paper replacement journals, in attempt to look like traditional paper journals do not use their additional space (e.g., the length of all articles in *Foundations of Information Systems* is 15–20 pages which is the acceptable page limit in traditional p-journals).

New formats. For the same reasons, the hybrid journals and the paper replacement e-journals do not use new formats or interactivity. An exception is a hybrid journal that offers multi media extensions (e.g., the *International Journal of Robotics Research*).

Cycle-time. Both paper replacement and advanced electronicity e-journals reduce cycle time. Advanced e-journals publish accepted manuscripts, as they are ready. Paper replacement e-journals collect articles into issues and volumes.[20] This practice can increase the cycle-time somewhat. However, because paper replacement e-journals have unlimited available space, they do not need to create a backlog of accepted articles. Hybrid journals have the option to publish the electronic version of manuscripts, as they are ready and the paper version when an issue is due. This practice can create some confusion in citation (Section 4.4).

Accessibility. Ease of access seems to be the main driver for the existence of hybrid journals. Articles can be read at any time and from anywhere. Scholars do not have to carry hard copies of an entire issue or borrow an entire volume from the library; they can print articles of interest. Therefore, e-journals (regardless of the form they take) provide easier access to scholarly work. Traditionally, scholars used to subscribe to a few journals in their discipline and that is mostly what they read and referenced. Today scholars search for articles based on a topic of interest. Because more and more articles are available electronically (not just the abstracts), the following occurs:

- scholars drop individual paper subscriptions because the paper accumulates and clutters their offices and their homes,

---

[20] In many cases, paper replacement e-journals post articles as they are ready. However, they send e-mail announcements periodically to reduce information overload. In addition, paper replacement e-journals arrange articles in volumes and issues to conform to traditional citation standards.

- scholars cite work from many different journals not only the few key ones,
- scholars read material from other disciplines.

In the late 1990s, scholars had to request numerous inter-library loans (ILL) to receive all the material they needed. Now almost everything is available online.

The cost benefits of each form are discussed in Section 5.

4.4   New Challenges

Each electronic form also introduces new challenges. For example, the prestige of academic journals is often associated with their acceptance rate. The lower the acceptance rate, the higher is the journal's prestige. The added space afforded by advanced electronicity and replacement e-journals allows an increase in their acceptance rate. Increasing acceptance rate increases publication opportunities for authors but at the cost of reduced reputation for the journal.

Hybrid journals can post the electronic versions of articles as soon as they are ready, thus reducing cycle time. However, such practice needs to consider timing. For example, a scholar with on-line access can cite an e-article not yet published in a p-version. If access to the e-version is restricted[21] (as it almost invariably is) non-subscribers to the e-version do not have access to the article for a period of time. Similarly, if electronic versions of articles contain value added information that is only available to e-version readers, subscribers to p-versions cannot access that information unless their library subscribes to the e-version.

For paper replacement and advanced electronicity e-journals, references can become invalid if a web site is moved and the URL is changed [45]. The current practice of stating the last access date helps readers determine when the site was last available. This practice will not help readers in the distant future to determine where the material then resides.

Each form of e-journal affects academic publishing stakeholders differently. This idea is discussed in Section 6.

5.   The Economics of E-Journals

The increasing cost of scholarly journals is a major concern for researchers and faculty members [50]. Thus, the economic benefits of e-journals were the first area of research to be addressed. Early studies analyzed the cost to produce journals in the hard sciences. Only recent studies expanded the cost analysis to all disciplines.

---

[21] The usual custom is to embargo access for non-subscribers for a period of time, such as a year.

The unique characteristics of academic journals (as discussed in Section 3.3) introduce added complexities to the cost and fee structures of the scholarly publishing industry. Early research on the topic concentrated on the cost/benefit to publishers. More recent research also considers the cost to the reader. From the perspective of the publisher, the economics of e-journals can be divided into the cost to publish and the revenue from fees and charges.

5.1   Cost Structure

The production cycle of an academic journal involves six steps (see Fig. 2):

Step 1. Manuscript creation.
Step 2. Submission.
Step 3. Refereeing.
Step 4. Editing.
Step 5. Production.
Step 6. Distribution.

Universities and other research institutions absorb the costs of step 1 and most of steps 2 and 3 regardless of the medium used to distribute the material. The costs of the first step are the same for both e-journals and p-journals. The costs of submission and refereeing are reduced for both p-journals and e-journals when (as is now common) electronic communication technology is used.

Once published in a p-journal, a paper cannot be altered. The best that can be done is to print an erratum or two in a subsequent issue. An electronic paper is not as final. If a typographical error is found, the text can be corrected and reposted. The finality of paper articles increase the need for very thorough proofreading function that is often done by professionals just as is done for books. Authors usually are asked for a final proof because the text may contain technical and specialized terms with which the proofreader is not acquainted. In e-journals, professional proofreaders are often not used, reducing the cost of step 4.

The publisher's main cost reduction for a replacement or advanced e-journal is in steps 5 and 6: the production and distribution functions. In production, typesetting is replaced by word processing. The cost reduction depends on the format used by the journal. For example, some e-journals post manuscript in HTML or in .pdf formats. These formats require some conversion efforts. The creation of a .pdf file from a word document can be automated. However, some features need to be edited manually. The conversion of a word processing file to HTML requires more manual work. This portion of the production function requires new skills and processes and is not completely eliminated. For example, Regier [46] estimated that the cost of the skills required to support electronic publishing is 20% per capita higher than the skills required to support print journals.

Producing copies is cheaper for e-journals. In p-journals, a press run incurs a fixed cost plus a variable cost per copy printed. In e-journals, copies are created on demand and at no incremental cost for the publisher.[22] For e-journals, the majority of the cost of distribution is shifted from the publisher to the consumer [15,4]. Internet-based e-journals do not require packaging, labeling, mailing, and storage of back issues. They do incur computer storage costs, server costs, and verification of passwords. The consumer requires broadband Internet access, disk storage and printing capabilities. The cost to the consumer is discussed in Section 5.1.2.

5.1.1   The Cost/Benefit of E-Journals

A hybrid journal is more costly than pure e-journals because it requires maintaining both paper and electronic infrastructures. Advanced electronicity e-journals are more costly than paper replacement e-journals if they use extensive multimedia capabilities. The extra cost is in human time, the skill required to implement the multimedia capabilities, the space allocated to this material, and the "horsepower" of the server used. For example, a one-minute video clip requires 60-100 Mb depending on the compression used while a page of text can be stored in 2 Kb.

Odlyzko [38] calculated the cost (in 1994) to the publisher to produce an article in a p-journal in Mathematics to range from $900 to $8,700 with a median of $4,000.[23] This figure is supported by Tenopir and King's [52] study which estimated the cost (to the publisher) of preparing the first copy to be $4,000. The cost to produce the same article in an e-journal is estimated to be much cheaper: $300 to $1,000.[24]

Clarke [7] describes four different business models for electronic journals and analyzes the cost to produce an e-journal in each case.[25]

1. The "Unincorporated Mutual Gratis e-journal." This journal is a pure e-journal that is published by an association or other not-for-profit organization as a service to its community and is funded by donations or sponsorship. The assumption is that senior academics, the editor, and the editorial committee do most of the work (including marketing, solicitation of manuscript, posting ar-

---

[22] In systemic terms, costs include such factors of production as communication, keeping records of subscribers, and more. However, many of these systemic costs occur for both p-journals and e-journals.

[23] This median is equal to median revenue calculated by Odlyzko [40].

[24] Odlyzko's work mostly refers to journals in mathematics where the cost to typeset complex formulas is high. A page containing such formulas can cost substantially more than a page containing text only.

[25] Clarke's analysis is based on the assumption that a traditional journal publishes four issues a year. Each issue contains 4–5 articles. Each article is 15–20 pages in length.

ticles, and similar functions). The cost of this type of a journal to the publisher is calculated to be zero [7].[26]

2. The "Association with a single e-journal." The assumption here is that the journal is a paper replacement journal that is published periodically with 7 to 8 articles per issue. The journal is published by an association as part of member services and is funded from member fees paid to the association. The estimated costs to publish such a journal are $5,500 per issue [7].

3. "Association with Multiple Journals." This model is similar to the previous model with the exception that the association offers a combination of paper and electronic journals. The total cost estimated for the paper journals is $28,000 per issue while the total estimated cost for the electronic journal is (same as above) $5,500 per issue [7]. The differences in cost are in the operation functions (e.g., editing,[27] producing, and distribution).

4. The "For-profit Publisher with a Subscription Based Access." The for-profit organization can be a commercial publisher or a subsidiary of a professional society that expects to profit from its journals.[28] The journal is assumed to be a "hybrid" journal that is published periodically with 7 to 8 articles per issue. Hard copies are available to subscribers while electronic versions are available on the WWW. The total estimated cost to publish this type of a journal is $34,250 per issue [7]. The main difference in cost is in the publisher's investments in marketing, brand name and content protection. Considering the importance of prestige for the scholarly community—these tasks should not be taken lightly and will be discussed later (Section 6).

Clarke's [7] results are consistent with prior studies (for example, [40,48,59,27]). Although the production and distribution costs of e-journals is lower than the production and distribution costs of paper journals, the skills required to maintain the infrastructure and post the articles online are greater than those of traditional production. E-journals may also reduce costs by transferring work to their editors and authors or, for non-commercial journals, eliminating some of the administrative and marketing functions that traditional, commercial publishers perform. The impact of this transfer of duties, on scholars, editors, and other stakeholders is discussed in Section 6.

---

[26] The actual costs are paid for by the hosting organization or via monetary or equipment donations.

[27] Clarkes [7] analysis assumes that the editing function is transferred to the senior scholars and therefore is free of cost.

[28] Studies show that most professional societies journal ventures are not profitable [59].

5.1.2   Cost of E-Journals to the Readers

Most early studies in this area concentrated on the economic benefits to the publisher and ignored the increased cost of e-publishing to the consumer. Regier [46], a director of John Hopkins University Press, studied the economics of electronic publishing at John Hopkins University and concluded that the cost to provide e-journals to students and faculty is not necessarily cheaper than p-journals. The cost of e-journals depends on the quality of the infrastructure, speed of access, dependability, ease of use and the administrative and technological support required to implement them. For example, Princeton invested an estimated $12 Million in 10 years in its effort to create and maintain the infrastructure required to provide Internet access [17] throughout the campus. Significant portions of that infrastructure are used to provide scholars and students with access to electronic information.

Three types of hidden costs are related to the implementation of any-time-any place access afforded by e-journals.

1. The initial cost to create the necessary infrastructure and enable access to e-journals by readers and by libraries. In addition, on-going expenses are incurred to support and maintain the library infrastructure and the long-term sustainability of the material by the publisher. Libraries may save on real estate costs by keeping journals electronically, but will incur technology, administration, and personnel costs.
2. The costs to scholars (and their departments) involved in producing e-journals. If the scholar and/or their institution edit and perform all the production functions to create a final copy prior to uploading to the server, they, rather than the publisher, bear these costs.[29]
3. The costs accrued by the reader. Readers downloading or reprinting articles will use their own (or departmental) material, hardware and software.
4. Internet Costs: In addition, a potential cost (mostly outside of the United States) is the fee charges for use of the Internet. All the economic analyses we have seen thus far assume that the use of the Internet will remain essentially free, once setup and connect fees are paid. The future fee structure of the Internet can change. Although previous proposals in the United States by telephone companies to charge users on a per unit time or on a bandwidth basis failed, there is no guarantee that subsequent attempts will also fail. In many countries around the world (e.g., Israel, France[30]) and in cybercafés users pay a per-

---

[29] It is unclear if the reduced cost on the library side is equal or greater than the increase cost on the department/school side. However, these costs are difficult to compare because library costs are separate from departmental budgets.

[30] In 2005, France Télécom, offers dial-up Internet access for €0.02 per minute without a monthly service fee or 120 connection hours for €25 a month.

minute charge to access the Internet. Therefore, what is assumed free in the United States may cost a considerable amount elsewhere.

5.2   Fee Structure

The initial conjecture was that the cost to produce an e-journal is minimal. Thus, some argued that these journals should be free of charge to readers.[31] By using existing infrastructure and other resources available in most universities, scholars were able to establish e-journals for no real cost to them.[32] Many of the early electronic journals were free of charge. This was especially true for entrepreneurial e-journals subsidized by research centers, universities and other sponsors. A survey by Hitchcock, Carr et al. [22] studied 83 science, technology and medicine (STM) e-journals. Most commercially published e-journals in the sample were subscription-based while the majority of the other e-journals did not charge. The study also found that approximately half of the journals had no stable source of funding.

In 2005, the two opposing philosophies about the fee structure of e-journals were: subscription based access (Section 5.2.1) and free access (also known as open access) to all e-journals regardless of their type or sponsor (Section 5.2.2).

5.2.1   Subscription Based E-Journals

E-journals (although cheaper) cannot be published without expense (Section 5.1.1) Therefore, publishers must obtain revenues by some means. Most commercial publishers and professional associations use some form of subscription.

Hybrid journals usually charge a (relatively) small additional fee to provide both a paper and an electronic version of the same journal. For example, IEEE/INSPEC charges $810 for a paper subscription to *Electronic Letters Online* and $1,215 for a combination subscription [1]. The American Mathematical Society charges 90% of the p-journal price for an e-journal version and 115% for both [39]. In 2004, Kluwer Academic Publishing charged $69 for a print only version of *Information Systems Frontiers* and $87 for both print and online. INFORMS charges its members $66 for a personal p-subscription and $47 for an e-subscription to *Information Systems Research*.[33] The price of both a p-subscription and an e-subscription is $86. Individuals can obtain all of INFORMS' 11 e-journals for $189 a year. By 2005, some

---

[31] This belief is exacerbated by the general assertion that all Internet resources should be provided free of charge.

[32] As discussed in Section 5.1.2, hidden costs are involved in the production of e-journals (e.g., the use of the infrastructure, the time of the scholar, the time of a graduate assistants, and secretarial staff). Some of these resources are already in place rather than being incremental. These costs are often absorbed by the hosting university.

[33] http://www.informs.org/Pubs/PubsInstitutional.pdf [last accessed on June 20, 2005].

publishers started offering one rate (eliminating the print only option). For example, INFORMS charges libraries, which usually pay more because of the multiple uses of their copies, $286 for both an e- and p-version; the society does not offer a p-only subscription to libraries.

In another market model, individual subscribers may choose to subscribe for a full year or they may choose to pay per article. For example, ADONIS, a CD-ROM based collection of biomedical journals,[34] charges subscription plus royalty payment per article accessed on a CD-ROM [50,2].[35] A similar subscription model is Pay-per-view (e.g., SpringerLink).[36] A reader pays for each viewing or downloading of an article. Berge and Collins [3] findings that scholars read individual articles rather than complete issues support this fee structure concept. One limitation of this method is that it discourages readers (especially students) from reading additional manuscripts because of the cost. We are not aware of any advanced electronicity e-journal that adopted the pay-per-view fee structure.

E-journals associated with professional societies collect subscription fees with membership dues. For example, the *Communications of AIS*, an e-journal established by the Association for Information Systems (AIS), is bundled with the society's membership fee.

E-journals (much like p-journals) can use advertising to recover some of the publishing costs and thus reduce subscription fees [41]. However, we are not aware of any e-journal that is currently using advertising as a source of income. In addition, many e-journals are a part of a consortium that provides full text access to libraries for a fixed monthly rate. An example is JSTOR. Therefore, instead of paying individual or institutional subscription for a given journal, universities pay a fixed fee to the consortium, which in turns pays royalties to the individual journals.

5.2.2   The Free Access Movement

The open access movement is growing. It is estimated that as of 2003, 10–20 percent of online journals provide free access to their content [59]. Several articles by proponents describe ways to support free access [59,54,7]. An analysis of the elec-

---

[34] ADONIS is part of an electronic publishing initiative developed by a consortium of well-established scientific, technical, and medical publishers [50].

[35] CD-ROMs were available on the library network. Users can select articles and download them to their own computers. The library paid a flat (subscription fee) and a fee for every article downloaded [50].

[36] For information on how to purchase a per-per-view article from SpringerLink see http://www. springerlink.com/app/home/faq.asp?wasp=70a2fb54f260418c8b7c98dccce49091#21.

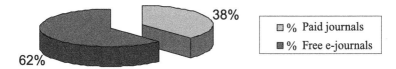

FIG. 3. Percentage of paid e-journals.

tronic journals listed in the "Miner" at the Colorado Alliance of Research libraries (http://www.coalliance.org/) shows that even in 2005, a large percentage of pure e-journals are free of charge (Fig. 3). The database lists over 6700 electronic journals. Sixty two percent of the journals listed are free.

The open access movement suggests that e-journals cover their expenses by charging authors [27]. In this model, authors pay per page published or per article published. Some scholars also recommend that e-journals should charge for reviewing articles since the review process is costly. Charging authors runs the risk of creating a vanity press and involves the following limitations.

- Established, high-reputation journals in fields such as physics do require page charges. However, these charges are often covered by federal and other research grants. In other disciplines (such as business), research is rarely funded by grants and therefore fewer sources of funds are available to pay for publications.
- Scholars in less endowed universities, students, and researchers in countries where the currency (compare to the US Dollar or the Euro) is weak are at a great disadvantage. Such a "pay to play" system would create a disparity in publishing and reduce scholarly communication.
- It can hinder the knowledge base and sense of community of a discipline. Scholars in disadvantaged countries can be expected to stop publishing or reading journals that charge authors. These trends are counterproductive and curtail the benefits gained by the introduction of e-journals (Table I).
- Established authors do not have incentives to pay page charges unless publishing in the journal adds to their reputation. Emerging e-journals would have difficulty attracting reputable authors.

Free access also involves negative implications for the reputation and prestige of the journal. These issues are discussed in Section 6.

5.3   Copyrights Payments

Copyright payments are a source of income for publishers. To reuse an article or distribute an article one must obtain permission from the publisher and pay a fee.[37] Although, copying complete articles violates copyright laws, professors and students copied material for years, often by photocopying sections from the original text or by creating notes and handouts summarizing written work. Electronic material is much easier to duplicate and distribute. Manuscripts can be posted on a class list-serv, e-mailed, downloaded, and printed. Therefore, it was assumed that e-journals would relax copyright policies, thus erode sales, and damage commercial publishers. Gold [18] suggested that electronic publishing could benefit publishers. Work can remain active longer, marginally profitable work can turn beneficial[38] and the cost of production and distribution can be reduced. In addition, it is to the university's benefit to support electronic publishing. The relationships between universities and publishing houses should develop to allow implementation of electronic distribution of academic work. Arrangement like Kluwer online and the ACM Digital Library provide scholars and students with an unlimited access to material while preserving copyright laws. Finally, some e-journals changed their copyright requirements. For example, *IPCT-J* [8] does not require exclusive rights from its contributors but only first publishing rights. Authors may republish their work in other outlets as long as there is a mention that the article first appeared in *IPCT-J*.

6.   The Effects of E-Journals on Stakeholders

E-journals introduce several technological advantages such as increased space and reduced cycle time (Section 4). E-journals are also cheaper to produce and distribute although not cost free as was initially assumed. However, one needs to consider their potential influence on the academic community and the various stakeholders involved. Two stakeholders that have been largely ignored by electronic publishing researchers are the editors of the journals (Section 6.1) and the authors who submit their work to electronic journals[39] (Section 6.2).

---

[37] Fees are charged even for educational use. Fees for most journals are handled through the Copyright Clearance Center (www.copyright.com). Some societies, such as ACM and AIS allow educational use without a fee.

[38] An example of such marginal work is the: "Women Writers Project" at Brown University [34, p. 218].

[39] Two exceptions are the work by the authors of this chapter on the management of electronic journals and some work on hazards of publishing in e-journals for authors' tenure and promotion prospects by [51].

6.1   Editors of E-Journals

An argument made by some people, particularly those who believe that e-journals should be free, is that many administrative, marketing, and editing functions performed by professionals in publishing houses should be transferred to the academics who serve as editors. While a romantic notion, the idea does not match reality. Here are some of the reasons:

1. Journal editors are senior academics who teach, do research, and even some service functions in addition to running the journal. Many editors do some of the work in the evenings, on the weekend, and on plane flights. They insist on an honorarium, even a small one, since they follow the dictum that what is worth doing is worth doing for money.
2. Senior academics are paid much more than administrative staff, yet are much further down the learning curve. They are therefore not cost-effective by any measure.
3. Many scholars are inexperienced with the processes required to accomplish administrative tasks. Interviews with several editors of e-journals, conducted by the first author over a period of five years indicate that most editors know little about the mechanics or the importance of promoting their journals through abstracting and indexing services. Similarly, many assume that e-journals can not be included in some of the citation impact data bases when in fact they can be.[40]
4. The assumption that administrative tasks can be transferred to the editor, editorial boards or other senior scholars is misleading. Senior scholars get some credit for scholarly activities related to academic journals (e.g., reviewing, associate editors). However, administrative activities almost never receive any credit.

Therefore, the conjecture that e-journals can be as successful as paper journals without the support staff (and the cost associated with it) is also misleading.

6.1.1   An Example

The following example illustrates some of the administrative steps taken by the editors of *Communications of AIS* (CAIS) to ensure its success, reputation, and brand name recognition:

---

[40] In an interview with a senior executive of Information Science Institute (ISI), a premier indexing service, it was made clear that electronic journals that publish high quality papers consistently are considered for indexing. ISI does not require paper versions of articles nor does it require a traditional volume/issue type publication cycle. ISI is a division of Thompson Publishing (http://www.isinet.com/).

1. *Reputation.* To ensure the journal's reputation, an international, elite editorial board was established, consisting of 40 leading academics in information systems from around the world. The associate editors are asked to obtain an article a year for consideration by the journal. An advisory board of eight "household names" in the field and a senior editorial board of people holding publications positions were also created. Articles are solicited from well-established and highly reputable authors. To date, most senior, prominent scholars in the Information Systems discipline authored or co-authored at least one article in the journal. This strategy is designed to signal to potential authors (particularly junior and middle level faculty) that CAIS is a place where people with top reputation publish.

2. *Acceptance by gatekeepers.* CAIS adopted measures to increase acceptance by tenure committees (who are often scholars outside the IS discipline). At its inception, the President of AIS undertook to inform tenure committees and deans in business schools, information systems, and computer science departments and Schools of Information, of the journal and its quality control measures. In its third year, the journal adopted a look and feel that increases its appeal to T&P committees. CAIS also uses a traditional citation format.

3. *Innovation and unorthodox work.* Information Systems is a volatile field. It is well served by publications that provide quality. Yet unorthodox works that include innovative content and are in line with the rapid changes of the field are difficult to publish quickly or even at all. The CAIS vision is to create a place for non-traditional papers. To overcome the cautiousness of referees about non-traditional work, authors are offered a choice of what is called "Editorial Board Review" and "Peer Review" In Editorial Board Review, only an Associate Editor and the Editor review the paper; in Peer review two outside referees are added. If a paper undergoes Peer Review, that is noted in the article. This process increases the workload of the editors because more rides on their judgment. The editors were chosen because they are each expert in a broad range of topics.

However, even the editors of CAIS, who are experienced and established a methodical process to increase the prestige of the journal, faced obstacles. It took almost five years to get the journal indexed anywhere. This long time was partially due to the time constraints of the editorial board. For example, Information Systems Frontiers (ISF), a hybrid journal that was established at the same time that CAIS, was indexed within three years. Since that journal is published by a commercial publisher, a staff member is dedicated to indexing and abstracting. In contrast, a member of the senior editorial board who is also a professor and a scholar was a volunteer responsible for obtaining indexing for CAIS. In addition, Communication of AIS is not registered with Journal Citation Reports while ISF is registered.

6.2   Authors of E-Articles

Authors of e-articles benefit from:

1. Added space for long articles (Section 6.2.1) and
2. Reduced cycle time (Section 6.2.2).

However, they must be concerned by two detriments of e-journals:

1. E-journal prestige and acceptance (Section 6.2.3).
2. Added work required to publish (Section 6.2.4).

6.2.1   Added Space

The added space afforded by advanced electronicity e-journals allows additional material to be included. This benefit is especially important for qualitative research where long case studied and in-depth descriptions can increase the value of the work. The added space also supports the inclusion of unorthodox material and unorthodox media. Researchers that study innovative areas or new streams of research are given a potential outlet for their work.[41] For example, *Communications of AIS* includes tutorials in the journal. Tutorials are often considered merit worthy for scholars in teaching universities and are useful teaching tools for professors in research and teaching universities.

6.2.2   Reduced Cycle Time

In the sciences (e.g., computer science, biology, physics, chemistry) and in medicine it is common to send preprints of work, to establish priority claims because the competition for recognition is high. In behavioral science, preprints are rare. However, databases like the Social Science Research Network and Web sites like the IS World working paper series[42] allow readers access to working papers in various disciplines. However, working papers are rarely cited in subsequent work. When a topic is "hot," having the first published article can increase recognition and citation (assuming the journal is read and referenced). Therefore, the speed of publication afforded by e-journals is an incentive for authors.

---

[41] For example, Koenig and Harrel [29] predicted that the added space afforded by e-journals would increase the odds of scholars to publish. However, as of 2005, it is unclear if the distribution of published authors as depicted by Lotka [33] has changed.

[42] http://www.is.cityu.edu.hk/research/resources/isworld/workingpapers/index.htm [last accessed June 25, 2005].

6.2.3 Prestige and Acceptance

In general, electronic journals are perceived to be inferior to p-journals even if they maintain the same rigorous quality control of their paper counterparts [51]. These perceptions vary depending on the type of e-journal (hybrid versus advanced electronicity) and the publisher (commercial, association, or entrepreneurial). Palmer et al. [42] found that T&P committee members often do not grant articles in e-journals the same credit they would for an equal quality article in a print journal. They also found that scholars who were educated regarding the review process of e-journals were more accepting of these journals. These perceptions of lower quality are due to several trends and vary by the form of the e-journal and its sponsors:

- The lack of extensive marketing and brand name efforts (Section 5.1.1). Brand name is rarely an issue for the hybrid e-journals since the publisher promotes the paper version of the journal. Advanced electronicity and paper replacement e-journals that are run by associations and entrepreneurial ventures are more likely to have branding issues.

- The ease of which an e-journal can be established is primarily a concern for the advanced electronicity and paper replacement e-journals. Because an e-journal can be established with ease, it creates a perception of a flighty existence. The general notion is that any one can establish an e-journal and start publishing articles regardless of their quality.

- The survival rate of e-journals. The authors have been following the progress of six journals between 1998 and 2005. Of these six, only three survived. To our dismay, the published work of one of the journals is no longer accessible.[43] Thus, a large body of knowledge can be lost to the academic community.

- Many e-journals are not abstracted or indexed (Section 6.1). Some journals assume that they can be accessed and searched via Internet search agents and thus do not need to be abstracted. However, scholars rarely use Internet search agents to locate scholarly material. Rather they use the traditional abstracting services (e.g., ABI/Inform, or Business Source Premier). E-journals that rely only on web searches are perceived as low quality [51]. Whether the attitude toward web searching would change as Google's Scholar (http://scholar.google.com/) takes hold was still unknown in 2005.

---

[43] During the first part of 2005, the Website of the journal was unavailable. In the later part of 2005, the access to the site was unpredictable.

Peer reviewed e-journals

FIG. 4. Percentage of e-journals that are peer reviewed.

Most free journals are not peer reviewed

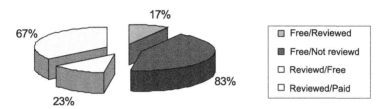

FIG. 5. Paid versus reviewed e-journals.

- The open access movement is a noble idea. However, establishing reputation and prestige incurs costs. Prestige is often associated with price.[44] Therefore, the concept of free e-journals adds to the perceptions of lower quality.
- Fifty five percent of e-journals are not peer reviewed (Fig. 4) supporting the prevailing assumption that e-journals are of lower quality. Data gathered by the first author shows that[45] (Fig. 5):

1. Only eleven percent of all e-journals are free and peer-reviewed.
2. Only seventeen percent of the free e-journals are peer reviewed.
3. Only twenty three percent of peer-reviewed e-journals are free.

The existence of a large number of free non-reviewed e-journals supports Sweeney's [51] findings that e-journals are believed to be of lesser quality than other journals.

---

[44] For example, one would rarely find a multi-millionaire shopping at a discount store. The price tag on an item adds to its perceived quality although it might have been manufactured at the same plant as its less expensive counterpart.

[45] This analysis is based on the electronic journals listed in the *Miner* at the Colorado Alliance of Research libraries (http://www.coalliance.org/ consulted May 2005).

Many universities do not have clear policies regarding publishing in electronic outlets. Authors often engage in a "guessing game" when they elect to publish in an e-journal [51].

One of the main differences between for profit publishers and other type of publishers is the investment in marketing, brand naming, competitive stance and protection of content [7]. These marketing mechanisms aim to promote the publisher and the journal but they are essential for the future of the contributing scholar. Productivity is partially measured by the prestige of the journals. Scholarly reputation is also measured by the number of times work is cited (impact factor). If an e-journal is indexed, recognized and is cited, authors can feel more confident that it will be recognized as a valid scholarly outlet.

6.2.4 Additional Work

Depending on the e-journal, articles may require additional work by the author. Universities rarely reward authors for these extra efforts. Added space (Section 6.2.1) allows authors to include additional material, even in hybrid journals. However, that material has to be prepared, written, and edited. The quality of the article is improved but at a cost to the author. In departments that simply count the number of articles, the incentive is to write a lot of short articles. Similarly, departments that value high impact articles do not necessarily encourage length or added material.

Sometimes electronic journals assume that authors should be responsible for some of the formatting (similar to what is expected of a conference paper) and some of the copyediting (proofreading). This is due to the fact that manuscripts are written in digital form, and due to the availability of spelling and grammar checks in word processors (e.g., Microsoft Word). Other journals (e.g., FIS) provide authors with a formatting template. The extensive reliance on proofing using a word processor is a dangerous business. If a word is recognized by the word processor, it is accepted whether it is correct or not. For example, an author wanting to say read who types red would see no error. The limited administrative staff employed by some e-journals and the lack of a finality of the digital product (compare with a paper product) can result in a poorly edited manuscript.

In the case of advanced electronicity e-journals, authors are often expected to implement new formats or use new media. This expectation causes added work for the authors who may not have the technical skills necessary. For example, a highly reputable, interactive e-journal in the area of Management Information Systems (MISQ Discovery) found it difficult to attract submissions. In an interview with the editor, lack of incentives and lack of rewards were cited as the main reasons. Authors were not receiving added benefit from submitting to that journal but had to invest more time in constructing the articles. Similarly, the idea of living scholarship (for additional discussion see Section 6.5.3) requires added work by the author with little added reward. Universities do not recognize each version as a new publication regardless of the extent of variation.[46] The time required to maintain the living article comes in place of writing additional new manuscripts.

E-journals allow increasing interactivity and communications among scholars. However, the activities surrounding that idea are time consuming and also not rewarded by the academic system. For example, one e-journal attempted to increase interactivity by attaching a discussion stream to each article and by soliciting comments to be posted. The e-journals received very few comments. Authors considered such comments as being equivalent to a Letter to the Editor.

In summary, the current academic system does not reward scholars for the extra activities required to make use of the e-journal's advances in publishing. From the authors' perspective, paper replacement e-journals where the publisher invests time and money in marketing, branding, indexing and abstracting the journal are superior to other types of e-journals. These journals provide added space and reduced cycle time and can gain the prestige necessary for the scholar's future and advancement. The current reward system does not give authors enough incentives to include new formats, living scholarship and interactivity in their work.

6.3   Academia as a Community

A discipline, its scholars, and members, operate as a community. Members of a discipline share professional associations, publication outlets, professional meetings and social events. Journals are one way that a discipline builds itself as a community and builds its credibility as a discipline to the outside world. It is important for the growth of a discipline, that articles are read, referenced, and cited by external scholars [6]. E-journals can support the development of small or relatively new disciplines in the following ways.

1. Small, un-endowed professional societies can not afford the production of paper journals [7]. Yet journals are the prime engine of communications for the development and growth of relatively new disciplines. E-journals enable such professional societies to produce their own publications without relying on commercial publishers (e.g., *Communications of AIS and Journal of AIS*).

2. E-journals enable a discipline to expand its scope by affording new outlets for unorthodox material. For example, *Foundations of Information Systems* (an e-journal dedicated to the philosophical foundations of information systems) started in the late 1999 as an entrepreneurial venture. The goal of the editorial board was to introduce a venue for work that was not part of the core paradigm

---

[46] Much the same as universities do not recognize a new edition of a book as equal to the original although the book may be changed completely between editions.

of IS research. Since then, the topic of Philosophy of IS became a mainstream topic with several publication outlets and conference tracks, thus expanding the scope of IS research.

3. E-journals enable a discipline to increase its external reach. Through the 1980s, scholars typically read three to four leading p-journals in their own discipline. Most scholars in well-established disciplines would rarely encounter an article in a new referent discipline. The existence of electronic journals and search mechanisms changed the way scholars read. Today, scholars searching for articles on a given topic are more likely to find manuscripts relevant to their work that appear in journals from other disciplines (Section 4.3). Thus, the existence of e-journals aids the development of new disciplines and encourages multidisciplinary research.

At the same time, academic communities need to be aware of some pitfalls. Since it is easy to start an e-journal, it is possible that a large number of new e-journals will be initiated within a given discipline. This capability can create dispersed knowledge instead of cumulative knowledge. Dispersion is especially a concern when the e-journal is not indexed and the work is rarely referenced. In addition, if the e-journal's material is not sustainable, knowledge may be lost.

6.4   Libraries

Libraries are moving from carrying individual serials to offering access to electronic collections. Electronic collections usually carry a group of titles in one or more disciplines. Libraries pay a fixed annual fee for access to the electronic collection. Scholars and students can access any journal in the collection at no cost to them. These collections are either a digitization of paper articles or access to electronic journals [10]. Examples are ABI/Inform, Business Source Premier, ScienceDirect, and JSTOR. This transition to digital collections is evident by the increase in access as depicted on JSTOR's web site.[47] In 1997, JSTOR reported a peak usage of 0.5 Million hits. In 2005, the number of hits reached 30 Million (see Fig. 6).

6.4.1   The Advantages of Electronic Collections

The advantages of electronic collections are:

1. Fixed, known cost and increased number of serials.
2. Ability to introduce serials on new disciplines.
3. Fewer Interlibrary Loans.

---

[47] JSTOR usage statistics can be found at: http://stats.jstor.org [last accessed June 20, 2005].

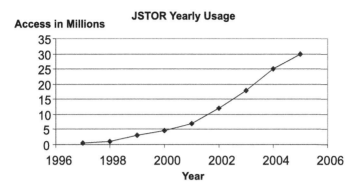

FIG. 6. Increase in the usage of JSTOR from 1997 to 2005.

4. Reduced Real Estate.
5. Increased access by students and teaching faculty.

Fixed subscription cost. The cost of the collection is the same no matter how often the electronic collection is accessed. However, some collections limit the number of simultaneous users; in that case, large libraries buy more 'seats' than small libraries. The providers of collections (who act as intermediaries) are able to negotiate low access fees with publishers of individual journals by leveraging economies of scale. The result is that scholars can gain any-time-any-place access to a large number of journals from their personal computers while libraries are able to contain their costs. For example, a university that subscribes to the ACM Digital Library provides access to a total of six journals, 23 transactions, ten magazines, publications by 42 Special Interest Groups (SIGs) and 16 affiliated organizations newsletters and conference proceedings (http://portal.acm.org/dl.cfm).

New and expanding disciplines. Libraries with budget shortfalls drop subscriptions when publishers raise their prices (Section 3.4.5). Shrinking budgets makes it difficult to add publications that serve emerging areas of research. Electronic collection providers can create a portfolio of new titles together with more established titles for marginally higher fees. In such cases, electronic collections increase accessibility to new areas of research.

Interlibrary loans. Collections reduce the need for interlibrary loans. When libraries carry only a certain number of paper journals, scholars often request copies of articles via interlibrary loan (ILL) services. Because it usually takes a week or two to obtain a paper copy of an article through interlibrary loan, this process delays the scholars' ability to access the material. With collections and full text access to a large of number of journals, scholars rarely need to rely on ILL services.[48]

Reduced real estate cost. The availability of e-journals reduces the library's real estate costs. Currently, libraries preserve thousands of volumes of serials placed on hundreds of shelves. Given the physical limitations on sharing paper articles among libraries, each library must maintain their own copies of a given serial. Often libraries hold several copies of books and other printed material so that multiple persons can check them out. That is, universities allocate a large amount of physical space for their libraries' archives. Electronic material obviously requires much less physical space.[49] Electronic material is also less sensitive to humidity and heat but requires attention to damage caused by fire, flood and other natural disasters, much like paper material.

Increased access by students and teaching faculty. A study of the usage pattern of JSTOR indicates a major increase during semester months and a major drop in usage during the months of December, January, June, July and August. In some cases, the drop is substantial (over 50%). Assuming that research faculty does most of their research in the summer,[50] one can conclude that during the semester months, majority of the access is for teaching purposes by research and teaching faculty and by students.

6.4.2   The Challenges of Electronic Collections

Covi and Cragin [10] point out that while providers often add titles, they also drop titles, leading to a lack of continuity in the material a library carries. In the past, when a library dropped a subscription, it traditionally kept prior issues (archives). With electronic collection services, when a provider drops a title, access to all previous material to that journal is discontinued. Past issues are not archived.

To accommodate e-journals and collections, libraries require a different set of skills. For example, scholars need less help with searches. However, some scholars may require more help in accessing web sites and configuring their Internet browsers. Libraries need information technologists that can help with the installation and maintenance of the library's Web site, configure network infrastructure and servers, and set up backup and recovery systems. Whether electronic skills are more expensive than traditional librarian skills and whether any added technology expenses are being offset by reduced real estate costs depends on individual situations.

---

[48] In addition, current inter-library loan services send articles in digital form, reducing the time and cost of delivery.

[49] Space reduction is true even if we include the need for a server room, networking and switching closets and other Internet related technology.

[50] Therefore, we assume that the access to JSTOR during the summer months is predominately by research faculty and postgraduate students conducting research.

6.4.3   Backwards Compatibility

Paper was the medium of choice for publishing in the last several hundred years because it is highly stable. It is unchanged in form since Gutenberg's first printing press. Journals published in the 18th century are still readable today. Backwards compatibility (the idea that when a new medium appears previous media can still be read) was never an issue. Information technology, however, changes every five to seven years. For example, material that was saved on $5'25''$ diskettes is not readable by a 2005 computer unless someone saved an old $5.25''$ disk drive and the software to read it (i.e., the diskette drivers). Material that was posted using versions 1 and 2 of Microsoft Word is no longer readable on current machines. Material stored in older formats will have to be converted or it will become inaccessible to new technology. The challenge is determining who will be responsible for the conversion: the library or the publisher? Although large commercial publishers could afford to fund such conversions, they have no incentives unless back issues are still being ordered. Professional societies (especially small ones) and entrepreneurial ventures most likely would not have the resources to perform complex conversions. Similarly, while large libraries are able to convert the material they hold for specific requests, small libraries face financial difficulties. The net effect would be a loss of knowledge unless copies were kept or could be obtained from the Library of Congress.[51]

We found no studies that quantify the cost of conversions. We do know, however, that backwards compatibility is not included in assessing the total cost of ownership of e-journals.

6.5   Reviewers, Gatekeepers and Other Stakeholders

Each type of e-journal affects stakeholders differently. Hybrid journals are likely to cause the least impact while advanced electronicity e-journals are likely to cause the most change. For example, for a hybrid journal the effect on article peer reviewing[52] is limited since these journals follow the same review process they used in the past. Similarly, hybrid journals are less likely to affect the gate keeping system or the Tenure and Promotion (T&P) process. Because hybrid e-journals publish in both p- and e-versions, T&P committees treat articles in these journals as p-journals. The following discussion concentrates on paper replacement and advanced electronicity e-journals.

---

[51] This applies to paper replacement e-journals. Often, advanced electronicity e-journals can not be replicated in print.

[52] Reviewing is sometimes referred to as refereeing.

6.5.1   Paper Replacement E-Journals

Paper replacement e-journals can be divided into two groups:

1. E-journals run by commercial publishers or professional societies. These e-journals are often peer-reviewed and indexed.
2. E-journals run by entrepreneurs, research centers, or privately. These e-journals are usually not peer-reviewed and not indexed.

Peer review process. Paper replacement e-journals are unlikely to involve major changes to the review process since the articles are similar in their look and structure to traditional paper manuscripts. A possible exception for some is that in their attempt to reduce cycle time, they may ask for speedier reviews, thus increasing reviewers' pressure and workload.

T&P committees are more likely to treat articles in paper replacement (unlike advanced electronicity) e-journals as traditional paper articles since the articles look and feel like traditional articles. Articles can be printed and included as part of the portfolio presented to the committee. Therefore, T&P committees are not expected to change their guidelines for these journals. However, e-articles that appear in non-indexed and non-reviewed journals will not be accepted by T&P committees as a scholarly publication.

Gatekeepers who control what is published will want to exert the same control as they currently exert over traditional p-journals. Because space in highly ranked journals is a rare and costly commodity, pages in these journals are highly valued.[53] Scholars that control this commodity are powerful. The unlimited space available to e-journals (regardless of their acceptance rate) de-values the worth of the scarce commodity, thereby de-valuating the importance of the gatekeepers. In addition, gatekeepers are more likely to object to e-journals run by entrepreneurial ventures because these journals usually target markets and topics outside of the discipline's main paradigm. Therefore, if these journals are successful, they are more likely to diminish the gatekeepers' power and control.

6.5.2   Advanced Electronicity E-Journals

Advanced electronicity e-journals present the same challenges as paper replacement e-journals (Section 6.5.1) for reviewers, T&P committees and gatekeepers. In addition, the use of multimedia, network structure, and living scholarship require changes to reviewers' approaches and potentially to T&P guidelines.

---

[53] The availability of pages in highly ranked journals can be compared to beach front properties. Since the buildable coastline is limited, these properties are much more expensive than comparable properties two streets over.

Refereeing journal articles is a service to the community with limited rewards. Finding high quality reviewers is often difficult. Yet articles in advanced electronicity e-journals require additional efforts from reviewers. They contain more material (e.g., videos of lab experiments, raw data). Reviewers must be technically knowledgeable to evaluate some of this material and the media used. In addition, some articles may not be printable on a conventional printer[54] or are not written sequentially (i.e., they use hypertext).[55] The reviewers would have to follow a variety of links and read the article on-line rather than in print, making it more difficult to review. Increasing the workload of reviewers without some apparent return would create resistance and reduce the number of available reviewers. The review process may become the new bottleneck of scholarly publishing.

Current T&P guidelines are not equipped to handle advanced electronicity e-journals. For example, MISQ Discovery expects submissions to be theoretically rigorous and to use the features afforded by the technology. These types of journals will require changes in the typical T&P committee's view of electronic scholarship. If T&P committees do not recognize and reward the added effort required, most authors would be reluctant to contribute to these journals (see Section 6.2.4) and reviewers would be reluctant to referee these articles.

Gatekeepers are likely to face similar challenges (loss of control and de-valued status) as they would with paper replacement e-journals. Therefore, the added media should have little effect on gatekeepers.

6.5.3   Skywriting and Community Reviews

Harnad [19] suggested the concepts of "*scholarly skywriting*" and an open, interactive refereeing process as ways to restore the communication function of academic journals. In scholarly skywriting, a paper is, in effect, never formally finished but continually reviewed by all its readers. Authors are able to change a manuscript at any time based on readers' comments. Thus, the work becomes a living entity rather than a static product. In Harnad's scenario, this ongoing refereeing process becomes an integral part of the formation of the article.[56]

The basic idea behind the concept is to shift the control (of accepting or rejecting articles) from the gatekeepers back to the community. Articles are posted as they are

---

[54] For example see Hars [21].

[55] For example see Myers [36] at: http://www.misq.org/discovery/MISQD_isworld/index.html.

[56] The difficulty of implementing such a system is great. It requires people to be willing to make and send comments, authors willing to make changes, electronic repositories keeping both comments and revisions, and people using the work to review the repository periodically. Living scholarship in general did not gather much support in the years since it was first discussed. An example is the few contributions that came to MISQ Discovery which sought to encourage periodic revision. The Wikipedia (www.wikipedia.com) is an example of successful skywriting, although it is not an element of scholarly publication.

submitted. Readers may comment and critique the work. The authors, at their discretion or by request from the editor will modify the article. The comments become an integral part of the manuscript. Skywriting can transfer much of the work from the reviewers to the community. This transfer can reduce the need to find qualified reviewers but it also puts a great deal of responsibility on the editors and the community. The response from the community is usually weak (Section 6.3) since engaging in "unofficial" reviews is not rewarded.

6.5.4   Conclusions on Stakeholders

The higher the electronicity of an e-journal, the more work, time and skills are required for submitters and reviewers. As a result, e-journals (particularly advanced electronicity journals) require a major social change for their acceptance. The existence of e-journals is expected to diminish the control of gatekeepers because these journals can be created rapidly, increase the number of pages published, and ultimately reengineer the review process. Skywriting and community reviews, described in Section 6.5.3 are examples of reengineering the process.

7.   Conclusions

In this chapter, we described the development of academic publishing as a means of knowledge building and dissemination, communication among scholars and as an instrument to measure scholarly productivity and to grant rewards. We detailed the forces that affect that development and the challenges facing the paper-based publishing industry. We classified e-journals into three categories, which we term paper replacement, hybrid, and advanced electronicity and list their prospective benefits and challenges. We concluded by examining the effect of e-journals on their stakeholders, the authors, editors, libraries, reviewers, and gatekeepers. From our analysis, we conclude that:

A rose is (not) a rose. Most studies assume either that all electronic journals are the same or they neglect to define the type of e-journal they are investigating. The three types of e-journals we defined each resolves a different set of challenges and introduces a different set of issues. We found that at present, the two dominant designs are the commercial publisher's hybrid journal and the paper replacement journal published by professional societies and entrepreneurial ventures. These designs require the least social and cultural changes and are likely to remain the dominant design for some time. Advanced electronicity e-journals offer additional advantages but require major changes in the academic reward system. Although they may dominate in the future, they are still rare.

There is no free lunch—you get what you pay for. The assumption that e-journals can be offered free of charge is naïve. Most financial analyses of e-journals ignore the administrative costs involved in producing academic journals or presume that senior editors are available to undertake them at no cost. Neither presumption passed the test of time. To survive economically while maintaining the reputation and prestige that will draw authors, e-journal publishers need to invest funds in editorial work, marketing, indexing, and infrastructure.

Science is cumulative. Because science builds upon its history, it depends on maintaining archives of prior work. Paper is a remarkably stable medium. Although it is sensitive to natural mishaps (e.g., fire, water, sun damage), it is easily accessible and portable. Over the years society established safety measures to protect paper (e.g., smoke detectors). E-journals are at the mercy of the continually changing digital world. New technologies replace old ones with a life cycle of 5 to 7 years. Old storage media (think of 5.25″ disks or even 3.5″ disks) and old formats are no longer readable by new equipment. Backward compatibility is a serious, technical and economic issue that requires cooperation among all the stakeholders to resolve.

To peer or not to peer. To increase the speed of communication, make it easier to publish non-standard, innovative work, and increase interactivity, proposals abound for reengineering the current peer review system. We found:

1. Academia is a self-regulating industry. Its reputation depends on a self-imposed system of checks and balances of which the review process is an important and integral part. Despite its many faults, it is necessary. That is not to say that it cannot or has not been improved. For example, electronic messaging reduces cycle time, although only marginally.
2. The integrity of the review process depends on the voluntary time of scholars and on their domain knowledge. It is scholar time and willingness to review that is the scarcest resource.
3. The review process also introduces a time delay that even e-journals cannot resolve.

Thus, peer review may be the worst way to ensure quality, yet to paraphrase Winston Churchill, it is still the best of systems.

Who is No. 1?[57] Journals' ranking and prestige largely depends on their low acceptance rate (5–10% in some journals) and on their impact. Two major evolutions, driven by electronic media are likely to transform the current journal ranking system:

1. The added space afforded by e-journals reduces the need for high rejection rates. For p-journals, these rates result from the fixed amount of space available and the increasing flood of research as scientific work expands.

[57] "The Prisoner," circa 1967 ITC TV in the UK and 1968 CBS in United States.

2. Changes in authors' search processes enable them to find any work relevant to the topic of interest published in reputable journals. Authors no longer limit their search and subsequent citations to a few leading journals in their own discipline. This change is likely to create a more even impact index than currently exists.

We believe that these two factors will drive a major change in the scholarly merit system where innovation (in content and communication) is rewarded. Journals will be ranked based on the quality of the material published rather than on extraneous factors such as acceptance rates. However, being in academia, this evolutionary process is bound to take considerable time.

8. Summary

Commercial and society publishers invest large sums to initiate and maintain a scholarly journal. Much like any other business that wants to succeed and make a profit, a publisher does not invest in a new journal without a solid business plan. Once the investment is made, the publisher markets and brands it to achieve success (high ratings, prestige and high circulation).

Although the initial investment and operating cost can be less, e-journals require the same care and planning as p-journals. They also need to solve institutional issues resulting from the divide between culture and social norms, and technological advancements. We believe that, over time, these problems will be resolved.

REFERENCES

[1] "New pricing and product enhancements for IEEE/INSPEC's electronics letters online", *Information Today* **12** (4) (1995) 19.
[2] "ADONIS electronic journal subscription service goes live", *Information Today* **14** (5) (1997) 28.
[3] Berge Z., Collins M., "IPCT journal readership survey", *Journal of the American Society for Information Science* **47** (9) (1996) 701–710.
[4] Bot M., Burgemester J., Roes H., "The cost of publishing an electronic journal", *D-Lib Magazine* (November 1998), http://www.dlib.org/dlib/november98/11roes.html.
[5] Campanario J.M., "Have referees rejected some of the most-cited articles of all times", *Journal of the American Society for Information Science* **47** (4) (1996) 302–310.
[6] Cheon M.J., Lee C.C., Grover V., "Research in MIS—points of work and reference: A replication and extension of the Culan and Swanson study", *Data Base* **23** (2) (1992) 21–29.

[7] Clarke R., "The cost-profiles of alternative approaches to journal-publishing", in: *Fiesole Collection Retreat*, Melbourne, 2005.

[8] Collins M., Berge Z., "IPCT journal: A case study of an electronic journal on the Internet", *Journal of the American Society for Information Science* **45** (10) (1994) 771–776.

[9] Covi L.M., "Social worlds of knowledge work: Why researchers fail to effectively use digital libraries", in: *Proceedings of ASIS Mid-Year Conference, San Diego, CA*, 1996.

[10] Covi L.M., Cragin M.H., "Reconfiguring control in library collection development: A conceptual framework for assessing the shift toward electronic collections", *Journal of the American Society for Information Science and Technology* **55** (4) (2004) 312–325.

[11] Cronin B., Overfelt K., "E-journals and tenure", *Journal of the American Society for Information Science* **46** (9) (1995) 700–703.

[12] Cummings L.L., Frost P. (Eds.), *Publishing in the Organizational Science, Foundations for Organizational Science*, Sage Publishing, Thousands Oaks, 1995.

[13] Drott C., "Reexamining the role of conference papers in scholarly communication", *Journal of the American Society for Information Science* **46** (4) (1995) 299–305.

[14] Fisher J., "Traditional publishers and electronic journals", in: Peek R., Newby G. (Eds.), *Scholarly Publishing: The Electronic Frontier*, The MIT Press, Cambridge, 1996, pp. 231–241.

[15] Freeman L., "The university press in the electronic future", in: Peek R., Newby G. (Eds.), *Scholarly Publishing: The Electronic Frontier*, The MIT Press, Cambridge, 1996, pp. 147–163.

[16] Frost P., Taylor R., "Partisan perspective: A multiple level interpretation of the manuscript review process in social science journals", in: Cummings L.L., Frost P. (Eds.), *Publishing in the Organizational Sciences*, vol. 1, Sage Publishing, Thousands Oaks, 1995, pp. 13–43.

[17] Fuchs I., "Networked information is not free", in: Peek R., Newby G. (Eds.), *Scholarly Publishing: The Electronic Frontier*, The MIT Press, Cambridge, 1996, pp. 165–180.

[18] Gold J., "An electronic publishing model for academic publishers", *Journal of the American Society for Information Science* **45** (10) (1994) 760–764.

[19] Harnad S., "Implementing peer review on the net: Scientific quality control in scholarly electronic journals", in: Peek R., Newby G. (Eds.), *Scholarly Publishing: The Electronic Frontier*, The MIT Press, Cambridge, 1996, pp. 103–118.

[20] Harrison T., "Faxon's 1997 preliminary subscription price projection", *Newsletter on Serial Pricing Issues* **153** (2) (1996), http://sunsite.unc.edu/reference/prices/prices.html.

[21] Hars A., "Web-based knowledge infrastructures for the sciences: An adaptive document", *Communications of the AIS* **4** (1) (2000).

[22] Hitchcock S., Carr L., Hall W., "A survey of STM online journals 1990–1995: The calm before the storm", in: *Directory of Electronic Journals, Newsletters and Academic Discussion Lists*, vol. 1, Association of Research Libraries. Office of Scientific and Academic Publishing, Washington, DC, 1996, pp. 7–32.

[23] Houghton B., *Scientific Periodical: Their Historical Development, Characteristics and Control*, Linnet Books, Hamden, CT, 1975.

[24] Hovav A., Gray P., "Future penetration of academic electronic journals: Four scenarios", *Information Systems Frontier* **4** (2) (2002) 229–244.

[25] Introna L., Whittaker L., "Journals, truth and politics: the case of MIS quarterly", in: Wood-Harper T., DeGross J.I., Kaplan B., Truex D.P., Wastell D. (Eds.), *Information Systems Research: Relevant Theory and Informed Practice*, Dordrecht, Kluwer Academic Publishers, 2004, pp. 103–120.

[26] King D.W., Roderer N.K., "The electronic alternative to communication through paper-based journals", *The Information Age in Perspective: Proceedings of the ASIS Annual Meeting, 1978, White Plains, NY*, 1978.

[27] King D.W., "Should commercial publishers be included in the model for open access through author payment?", *D-Lib Magazine* **10** (6) (2004), http://www.dlib.org/dlib/june04/king/06king.html.

[28] Kling R., Covi L., "Electronic journals and legitimate media in the system of scholarly communications", *The Information Society* **11** (4) (1995) 261–271.

[29] Koenig M., Harrel T., "Lotka's law, price urn, and electronic publishing", *Journal of the American Society for Information Science* **46** (5) (1995) 386–388.

[30] Lesk M., "How can we get high-quality electronic journals?", *IEEE Intelligent Systems* **13** (1) (1998) 12–13.

[31] Libraries, *Directory of Electronic Journals, Newsletters and Academic Discussion Lists*, Association of Research Libraries, Washington, DC, 1991.

[32] Libraries, *Directory of Electronic Journals, Newsletters and Academic Discussion Lists*, Association of Research Libraries, Washington, DC, 1996.

[33] Lotka J.A., "The frequency distribution of scientific productivity", *Journal of the Washington Academy of Sciences* **16** (12) (1926) 317–323.

[34] Manoff M., "The politics of electronic collection development", in: Peek R., Newby G. (Eds.), *Scholarly Publishing: The Electronic Frontier*, The MIT Press, Cambridge, 1996, pp. 215–229.

[35] McEldowney P., "Scholarly electronic journals, trends and academic attitude: A research proposal", Department of Library and Information Studies, Greensboro, University of North Carolina, 1995, p. 18.

[36] Myers D.M., "Qualitative research in information systems", *MIS Quarterly Discovery* (1997), http://www.misq.org/discovery/contents.html.

[37] Nord W., "Looking at ourselves as we look at others: An exploration of the publication system for organizational research", in: Cummings L., Frost P. (Eds.), *Publishing in Organizational Science*, vol. 1, Sage Publishing Inc., Thousands Oaks, 1995, pp. 64–78.

[38] Odlyzko A.M., "Tragic loss or good riddance? The impending demise of traditional scholarly journals", *International Journal of Human–Computer Studies* **42** (1) (1995) 71–122.

[39] Odlyzko A., "On the road to electronic publishing", *Euromath Bull.* **2** (1) (1996) 49–60.

[40] Odlyzko A., "The economics of electronic journals", *First Monday* **2** (8) (1997).

[41] Okerson A., "University libraries and scholarly communications", in: Peek R., Newby G. (Eds.), *Scholarly Publishing: The Electronic Frontier*, The MIT Press, Cambridge, 1996, pp. 181–199.

[42] Palmer J., Speier C., Wren D., Hahn S., "Electronic journals in business schools: Legitimacy, acceptance, and use", *Journal of the Association for Information Systems* **1** (2) (2000).

[43] Peek R., "Scholarly publishing, facing the new frontier", in: Peek R., Newby G. (Eds.), *Scholarly Publishing: The Electronic Frontier*, vol. 1, The MIT Press, Cambridge, 1996, pp. 3–15.

[44] Peek R., "Where are electronic journals going?", *Information Today* **14** (1997) 44–46.

[45] Peffers K., Avison D., Ein-Dor P., Zmud R.W., "Scholarly products in IS: Will advances in electronic media promote evolutionary or radical change?", *Communication of AIS* **11** (2003) 498–512.

[46] Regier W., "Economics of electronic publishing: Cost issues", Scholarly Communications and Technology, Emroy University, 1997.

[47] Roberts P., "Scholarly publishing, peer review and the Internet", *First Monday* **4** (4) (1999), http://firstmonday.org/issues/issue4_4/proberts/index.html.

[48] Rowland F., McKnight C., Meadows J., Such P., "ELVYN: The delivery of an electronic version of a journal from the publisher to libraries", *Journal of the American Society for Information Science* **47** (9) (1996) 690–700.

[49] Schaffner A.C., "The future of scientific journals: Lesson from the past", *Information Technologies & Libraries* **13** (4) (1994) 239–247.

[50] Schauder D., "Electronic publishing of professional articles: Attitudes of academic and implications for the scholarly communication industry", *Journal of the American Society for Information Science* **45** (2) (1994) 73–100.

[51] Sweeney A.E., "Should you publish in electronic journals?", *Journal of Electronic Publishing* **6** (2) (2000), http://www.press.umich.edu/jep/06-02/sweeney.html.

[52] Tenopir C., King D.W., "Trends in scientific scholarly journal publishing in the United States", *Journal of Scholarly Publishing* **28** (3) (1997) 135–170.

[53] Tenopir C., King D.W., "Lessons for the futures of journals", *Nature* **413** (6857) (2001) 672–674.

[54] Tenopir C., "Open access alternatives", *Library Journal* **129** (12) (2004) 33.

[55] Turoff M., "The EIES experience: Electronic information exchange system", *Bulletin of the American Society for Information Science* **4** (5) (1978) 9–10.

[56] Turoff M., Hiltz R., "The electronic journal: A progress report", *Journal of the American Society for Information Science* **33** (1982) 195–202.

[57] Watson H., Wixom B., Buonamici J., Revak J., "Sherwin–Williams' data mart strategy: Creating intelligence across the supply chain", *Communications of the AIS* **5** (9) (2001).

[58] Willcocks L., Dube L., Pare G., Robey D., "Pointers in doing writing up case research", in: *Proceedings of the International Conference on Information Systems*, December 15–17, 1997, p. 531.

[59] Willinsky J., "Scholarly associations and the economic viability of open access publishing", *Journal of Digital Information* **4** (2) (2003), Article No. 177.

[60] Zmud B., "Editor's comments—reducing the cycle time of MIS quarterly review process", *MIS Quarterly* **21** (3) (1997).

Web Testing for Reliability Improvement

JEFF TIAN* AND LI MA

Southern Methodist University
Dallas, TX
USA
tian@engr.smu.edu

Abstract

In this chapter, we characterize problems for web applications, examine existing testing techniques that are potentially applicable to the web environment, and introduce a strategy for web testing aimed at improving web software reliability by reducing web problems closely identified with web source contents and navigations. Using information about web accesses and related failures extracted from existing web server logs, we build testing models that focus on the high-usage, high-leverage subsets of web pages for effective problem detection and reliability improvement. Related data are also used to evaluate web site operational reliability in providing the requested pages as well as the potential for reliability growth under effective testing. Case studies applying this approach to the web sites www.seas.smu.edu and www.kde.org are included to demonstrate its viability and effectiveness. We also outline extensions to our approach to address testing, defect analysis, and reliability improvement issues for the constantly evolving web as a whole by analyzing the dynamic web contents and other information sources not covered in our current case studies.

*For correspondence, contact Dr. Jeff Tian, Computer Science & Engineering Dept., Southern Methodist University, Dallas, TX 75275, USA. Phone: +1-214-768-2861; fax: +1-214-768-3085.

ADVANCES IN COMPUTERS, VOL. 67
ISSN: 0065-2458/DOI 10.1016/S0065-2458(05)67004-0

177

1. Introduction

Web-based applications provide cross-platform universal access to web resources for the massive user population. With the prevalence of the world wide web (WWW) and people's reliance on it, testing and quality assurance for the web is becoming increasingly important. To help us test web-based applications and improve their reliability, we would like to adapt existing techniques that have been used effectively to assure and improve quality and reliability for traditional software systems [16,38, 48]. As a prerequisite to successful adaptation, we must have a good understanding of the differences between the web environment and the traditional software systems, as well as a good understanding of the existing techniques, their applicability to different domains, and their effectiveness in dealing with different problems.

Quality in software is generally associated with good user experiences commonly characterized by the absence of observable problems and satisfaction of user expectations, which can also be intimately related to some internal characteristics of the software product and its development process [23,38,48]. A quantitative measure of quality meaningful to both the users and the developers is product *reliability*, which is defined as the probability of failure-free operations for a specific time period or input set under a specific environment [27,34]. Some testing and quality assurance techniques work directly to assure product reliability by detecting and correcting problems that are likely to be experienced by target customers and users [30,33], while others work indirectly to ensure some internal integrity for the product under development or in operation [5,35].

In subsequent sections, we review basic concepts and testing techniques, examine the characteristics of the web, discuss the use of existing models and techniques for web testing, and introduce an integrated web-testing strategy that ensures web reliability. In particular, Section 2 defines some basic terms related to defect and reliability to ensure a consistent interpretation of quality, and surveys major testing techniques and reliability models; Section 3 analyzes the web environment and its impact on web testing and quality assurance, particularly its challenges and opportunities, and focuses our attention on web problems closely identified with web source contents and navigations; Section 4 examines strategies for testing individual web elements and basic web navigation; Section 5 presents an integrated strategy for large-scale web testing that uses statistical testing models to selectively test important and frequently used web pages and to guide in-depth testing using traditional testing techniques; Section 6 uses defect and usage data from web logs to assess web site operational reliability and the potential for reliability growth under effective statistical testing, which also provide an external validation for our integrated testing strategy; and finally, we present our summary, conclusions, and future work in Section 7.

2. Basic Concepts and Techniques

As noticed above, various terms related to problems or defects are commonly used in discussing software quality and reliability. Several standard definitions [19] related to these terms include:

- *Failure*: The inability of a system or component to perform its required functions within specified performance requirements. It is an observable behavioral deviation from the user requirement or product specification.

- *Fault*: An incorrect step, process, or data definition in a computer program, which can cause certain failures.

- *Error*: A human action that produces an incorrect result, such as the injection of a fault into the software system.

Failures, faults, and errors are collectively referred to as *defects*. Testing plays a central role in assuring product quality by running the software, observing its behavior, detecting certain behavior deviations as failures, and helping us locate and fix the underlying faults that caused the observed failures.

Depending on whether external functions or internal implementation details are tested, we have two generic types of testing: *Functional* or *black-box* testing focuses on the external behavior of a software system, while viewing the object to be tested as a black-box that prevents us from seeing the contents inside [18]. *Structural* or *white-box* testing focuses on the internal implementation, while viewing the object to be tested as a white-box that allows us to see the contents inside [5].

Most of the traditional testing techniques and testing sub-phases use some coverage information as the stopping criteria [6,35], with the implicit assumption that higher coverage means higher quality or lower levels of defects. On the other hand, product reliability goals can be used as a more objective criterion to stop testing. The use of this criterion requires the testing to be performed under an environment that resembles actual usage by target customers so that realistic reliability assessment can be obtained, resulting in the so-called usage-based statistical testing [30,34].

The steps in most systematic testing include [7,48]:

(1) information gathering, with the internal implementations or external functions as the main information sources giving us white-box testing and black-box testing, respectively;
(2) test model construction, with models based on checklists, partitions, equivalence classes, and various forms of finite-state machines (FSMs) such as control flow graphs and data dependency graphs;
(3) test case definition and sensitization, which determines the input to realize a specific test;
(4) test execution and related problem identification; and
(5) analysis and followup, including making decisions such as what to test next or when to stop.

For usage-based statistical testing that play a critical role to ensure product reliability, the following particular steps are involved:

- The information related to usage scenarios, patterns, and related usage frequencies by target customers and users is collected.
- The above information is analyzed and organized into some models—what we call operational profiles (OPs)—for use in testing.
- Testing is performed in accordance with the OPs.
- Testing results is analyzed to assess product reliability, to provide feedback, and to support follow-up actions.

Both the failure information and the related workload measurements provide us with data input to various software reliability models that help us evaluate the current reliability and reliability change over time [27,34,44]. Two basic types of software reliability models are: input domain reliability models (IDRMs) and time domain software reliability growth models (SRGMs). IDRMs can provide a snapshot of the current product reliability. For example, if a total number of f failures are observed for n workload units, the estimated reliability R according to the Nelson model [36], one of the most widely used IDRMs, can be obtained as:

$$R = \frac{n - f}{n} = 1 - \frac{f}{n} = 1 - r.$$

Where r is the failure rate, which is also often used to characterize reliability. When usage time t_i is available for each workload unit i, the summary reliability measure, mean-time-between-failures (MTBF), can be calculated as:

$$\text{MTBF} = \frac{1}{f} \sum_i t_i.$$

If discovered defects are fixed over the observation period, the defect fixing effect on reliability (or reliability *growth* due to defect removal) can be analyzed by using various SRGMs [27,34]. For example, in the widely used Goel–Okumoto model [17], the failure arrival process is assumed to be a non-homogeneous Poisson process [22]. The expected cumulative failures, $m(t)$, over time t is given by the formula:

$$m(t) = N\left(1 - e^{-bt}\right)$$

where the model constants N (total number of defects in the system) and b (model curvature) need to be estimated from the observation data.

3. Web Characteristics, Challenges, and Opportunities

Web applications possess various unique characteristics that affect the choices of appropriate techniques for web testing and reliability improvement. We next examine these characteristics in relation to existing software testing techniques and address general questions about web quality and reliability.

3.1 Characterizing Web Problems and Web Testing Needs

One of the fundamental differences between web-based applications and traditional software is the *document and information focus* for the former as compared to the computational focus for the latter. Although some computational capability has evolved in newer web applications, document and information search and retrieval still remain the dominant usage for most web users. Most of the documents and information sources are directly visible to the web users, as compared to the complicated background computation associated with traditional software systems. Consequently, the line that distinguishes black-box testing from white-box testing is blurred for the web environment.

A related difference between the development of web sites or web-based applications and that for traditional software systems is the increasingly faster pace and evolving nature of the former. Traditionally, large software systems take years to develop by a large group of professional developers, with the testing part typically consuming from a quarter to over half of the total development time and/or resources. In contrast, web sites and web-based applications can be set up and start running within a few weeks or even a few days by a small group of web developers. The dynamic web environment allows web site owners and contents providers to add, update, or change web contents, functions, and structures incrementally. All the testing sub-phases before product release for traditional software systems are condensed for the web environment, but post-release web site maintenance and related testing play an increasingly important role. This environment also provides opportunities for us to capture actual usage scenarios and patterns for effective web testing and reliability improvement for operational web site, as we describe in Section 5.

In addition, navigational facility is a central part of web-based applications, with the most commonly used HTML (hyper-text markup language) documents playing a central role in providing both information and navigational links. In this respect, web-based applications resemble many traditional menu-driven software products. The most commonly used testing technique for menu-driven software is the one based on finite-state machines (FSMs), where each menu is represented as a state in an FSM [6,48]. We next compare web-based applications to traditional menu-drive software products:

- Traditional menu-driven software still focuses on some computation; while web-based applications focus on information and documents.

- Traditional menu-driven software usually separates its navigation from its computation; while the two are tightly mingled for web-based applications.

- In traditional menu-driven software, there is usually a single top menu that serves as the entry point; while for web-based applications, potentially any web page can be the starting point. Similar differences exist for the end points or final states, with traditional menu-driven software having limited exits while web-based applications typically can end at any point when the user chooses to exit the web browser or stop browsing.

- There is a qualitative difference in the huge number of navigational pages even for moderately sized web sites and the limited number of menus for traditional menu-driven applications. We will revisit this key difference in Section 5 in connection with selective web testing.

- Web-based applications typically involve much more diverse support facilities than traditional menu-driven software. Web functionalities are typically distributed across multiple layers and subsystems, ranging from web browsers at the

Client–web browsers
Web server
Middleware
Database–backend

FIG. 1. Multi-layered web applications.

client side to web servers, middleware, and backend at the server side, as illustrated in Fig. 1. We need to make sure all different versions of web browsers, servers, and their underlying support infrastructure work well together to deliver the requested web contents.

Similar to general testing, testing for web applications focuses on reducing the chances for web failures by removing the underlying faults or defects. Therefore, we need to examine the common problems and associated concepts such as web failures, faults, and errors, before we can select, adapt, or develop appropriate testing techniques for this environment.

Based on the above characterization of the web environment, we can adapt some standard definitions of quality, reliability, defect, and related concepts to this new application environment. We define a web failure as the inability to correctly deliver information or documents required by web users [20]. This definition also conforms to the standard definition of failures as the behavioral deviations from user expectations [19] (correct delivery expected by web users). Based on this definition, we can consider the following failure sources:

- *Source or content failures*: Web failures can be caused by the information source itself at the server side.

- *Host or network failures*: Hardware or systems failures at the destination host or home host, as well as network failures, may lead to web failures. These failures are mostly linked to the web server layer and below in Fig. 1. However, such failures are not different from the regular system or network failures, and can be analyzed by existing techniques [43,54].

- *Browser failures*: Browser failures are linked to problems at the highest layer in Fig. 1 on the client side. These failures can be treated the same way as software product failures, thus existing techniques for software testing and quality assurance can be used [5,34,48].

- *User errors* can also cause problems, which can be addressed through user education, better usability design, etc. [3,11,42].

The last three groups of problems above can be addressed by the "global" web community using existing techniques, while web source or content failures are typically directly related to the services or functions that web-based applications are trying to provide. In addition, although usability is one of the primary concerns for novice web users, reliability is increasingly becoming a primary concern for sophisticated web users [55]. Therefore, we focus on web source failures and trying to ensure *reliability* of such web-based applications in this chapter.

With the above differentiation of different sources for web problems and the focus of source contents problems, we need to test the web (1) to ensure that individual components behave as expected, and (2) to ensure that the overall navigational facility works as expected. We will first describe testing models that attempt to "cover" those basic elements and navigation patterns in Section 4. However, such coverage-based testing would soon run into difficulties for web sites with numerous functions or diverse usage patterns, leading us to usage-based web testing in Section 5.

3.2   Information Sources for Testing and Analyses: New Opportunities

Information sources for testing models can generally be divided into two broad categories: (1) internal components and structures and (2) external functions and related usages. For the web environment, the easy access to source files (primarily HTML documents) is a significant difference from traditional software systems where the users typically do not have access to program source code. This difference would blur the distinction between black-box testing and white-box testing, and allow independent testers and users to perform white-box testing for different web components in addition to black-box testing.

Although external functions for web-based applications and web sites are rarely formally specified, we do have abundant information about web usages available, typically recorded in various server log files. In fact, monitoring web usage and keeping various logs are necessary to keep a web site operational. Therefore, we would only incur minimal additional cost to use the information recorded in these logs for testing and reliability analyses.

Two types of log files are commonly used by web servers: Individual web accesses, or hits, are recorded in *access logs*, and related problems are recorded in *error logs*. A "hit" is registered in the access log if a file corresponding to an HTML page, a document, or other web content is explicitly requested, or if some embedded content, such as a graphic file or a Java class within an HTML page, is implicitly requested or activated. Some sample entries from the access log for the www.seas.smu.edu web site using Apache Web Server [4] is given in Fig. 2. Specific information in this access log includes:

```
129.119.4.17 - - [16/Aug/1999:00:00:11 -0500] "GET
/img/XredSeal.gif HTTP/1.1" 301 328 "http://www.seas.smu.edu/"
"Mozilla/4.0 (compatible; MSIE 4.01; Windows NT)"

129.119.4.17 - - [16/Aug/1999:00:00:11 -0500] "GET
/img/ecom.gif HTTP/1.1" 304 - "http://www.seas.smu.edu/"
"Mozilla/4.0 (compatible; MSIE 4.01; Windows NT)".
```

FIG. 2. Sample entries in an access log.

- The reverse-DNS hostname of the machine making the request. If the machine has no reverse-DNS hostname mapped to the IP number, or if the reverse-DNS lookup is disabled, this will just be the IP number.
- The user name used in any authentication information supplied with the request.
- If "identd" checking is turned on, the user name as returned by the remote host.
- Date and time that the transfer took place, including offset from Greenwich Mean Time.
- The complete first line of the HTTP request, in quotes.
- The HTTP response code.
- Total number of bytes transferred.
- The referrer, or the source page that lead to the current access.
- The agent, or the information that the client browser reports about itself.

If the value for any of these data fields is not available, a "−" will be put in its place. Most of the above information is available from most web logs despite minor variations in web log configurations and information contents across different web servers.

Error logs typically include details about the problems encountered. The format is simple: a time-stamp followed by the error or warning message, such as in Fig. 3.

```
[Mon Aug 16 13:17:24 1999] [error] [client 207.136.6.6]
File does not exist: /users/seasadm/webmastr/htdocs/
library/images/gifs/homepage/yellowgradlayers.gif

[Mon Aug 16 13:17:37 1999] [info] [client 199.100.49.104]
Fixed spelling: /img/XredSeal.gif to /img/xredSeal.gif
from http://www.seas.smu.edu/
```

FIG. 3. Sample entries in an error log.

Analyzing information stored in such logs can help us capture the overall web usages for testing, as described in Section 5. Various measurements can be derived to characterize web site workload at different levels of granularity and from different perspectives. These workload measurements are used together with failure information in Section 6 to evaluate web site operational reliability and the potential for reliability improvement. Web logs also give us a starting point to characterize common problems for web-based applications, as we discuss below.

3.3   Preliminary Analysis of Common Problems for Two Web Sites

We next analyze common problems for www.seas.smu.edu, the official web site of the School of Engineering and Applied Science at Southern Methodist University (SMU/SEAS). This web site utilizes Apache Web Server [4], a popular choice among many web hosts, and shares many common characteristics of web sites for educational institutions. These features make our results and observations here and in the rest of this chapter meaningful to many application environments. Server log data covering 26 consecutive days in 1999 were used.

The use of this web site continues the trend of most previous studies that overwhelmingly focus on academic sites [39], which may not be a good representative for many other web sites. For example, most of the SMU/SEAS web pages are static ones, consisting primarily of the HTML documents and embedded graphics [25], and the web site operates under fairly light traffic. In e-commerce and other applications, workload types may be more diverse, with dynamic pages and context-sensitive contents play a much more important role, and traffic volume can be significantly larger [39]. Therefore, we obtained recent (2003) web logs from the open source KDE project web site www.kde.org to cross-validate our results [52]. The overall user population and traffic volume are significantly larger, and changes are continuously committed to the web site in order to provide the developers and users with the most up-to-date information. These characteristics make it a good choice for our validation study. On the other hand, this web site also uses Apache Web Server [4], which makes our data extraction and analysis easy due to the same data format used.

Common web problems or error types are listed in Table I. Notice that most of these errors conform closely to the source content failures we defined above, making them suitable for our web problem characterization and reliability evaluation. Table I also gives the summary of different types of errors for SMU/SEAS. The most dominant error types are type A ("permission denied") and type E ("file does not exist"), which together account for 99.9% of the recorded errors.

TABLE I
GENERIC ERROR TYPES AND THE RECORDED ERRORS
BY TYPE FOR SMU/SEAS

Type	Description	# of errors
A	permission denied	2079
B	no such file or directory	14
C	stale NFS file handle	4
D	client denied by server configuration	2
E	file does not exist	28,631
F	invalid method in request	0
G	invalid URL in request connection	1
H	mod_mime_magic	1
I	request failed	1
J	script not found or unable to start	27
K	connection reset by peer	0
All types		30,760

Type A errors, accounting for 6.8% of the total recorded errors, involve improper access authorization or problems with the authentication process. These errors are more closely related to security problems instead of reliability problems we focus on in this chapter. Further analyses of them may involve the complicated authentication process. In addition, type A errors also account for much less of a share of the total recorded errors than type E errors. Therefore, we decided not to focus on these errors in our study.

Type E errors usually represent bad links. They are by far the most common type of problems in web usage, accounting for 93.1% of the total recorded errors. This is in agreement with survey results from 1994–1998 by the Graphics, Visualization, and Usability Center of Georgia Institute of Technology (see http://www.gvu.gatech.edu/user_surveys). The surveys found that broken link is the problem most frequently cited by web users, next only to network speed problem. Therefore, type E error is the most observed web content problem for the general population of web users. Further analysis can be performed to examine the trend of these failures, to guide web testing, and to provide an objective assessment of the web software reliability.

For the KDE web site, only access logs are used but not the error logs. However, from the HTTP response code, we can extract the general error information. For example, type E (missing file) errors in the error logs are equivalent to access log entries with a response code 404. The access logs for the KDE web site for the 31 days recorded more than 14 million hits, of which 793,665 resulted in errors. 785,211 hits resulted in response code 404 (file-not-found), which accounted for 98.9% of all the errors. The next most reported error type was of response code 408, or "request timed out," which accounted for 6225 or 0.78% of all the errors. This dominant share of 404 errors, which is equivalent to type E errors, justifies our focus on this type of errors in our study.

We performed a preliminary analysis of the originators of these bad links [28] and discovered that the majority of them are from internal links, including mostly URLs embedded in some web pages and sometimes from pages used as start-ups at the same web site. Only a small percentage of these errors are from other web sites (4.3%), web robots (4.4%), or other external sources, which are beyond the control of the local site content providers, administrators, or maintainers. Therefore, the identification and correction of these internal problems represent realistic opportunities for improved web software reliability based on local actions such as testing and other quality assurance activities. In addition, we also need to test for problems beyond what is reported in web logs, as we describe next.

4. Testing Individual Web Elements and Navigations

For the web functionalities distributed across multiple layers and subsystems, we need to make sure that all the components work well individually as well as together. We next examine the techniques to test these individual web components and the basic web navigations.

4.1 Web Components, Aspects, and Testing

Web components [29] that need to be tested for conformance to some standards or user expectations include the following:

- *HTML document*, still the most common form for documents on the web.
- *Java, JavaScript, and ActiveX* commonly used to support platform independent executions.
- *Cgi-Bin Scripts* used to pass data or perform some other activities.
- *Database*, a major part of the backend.
- *Multi-media components* used to present and process multi-media information.

All these components need to be tested. Fortunately, many existing testing techniques and tools can be used to perform such testing. In fact, most existing work on web testing focuses on *functionality testing* to test web components to ensure that the web site performs its intended functions as expected [9,15]. This type of testing usually involves analyzing given web components and checking their conformance to relevant standards and external specifications. Specific types of functionality testing include:

- *HTML syntax and/or style checking*: HTML validators, such as Weblint (www. weblint.org), W3C Validator (validator.w3.org), and CSSCheck (www.htmlhelp. com/tools/csscheck/), can parse HTML files and check their conformance to relevant language specifications and document standards.

- *Link checking* can be performed to check the entire site for broken links, with the help of tools like Net Mechanic (www.netmechanic.com). This is similar to link coverage testing in FSM-based testing described later in this section for testing web navigations, but without formally constructing an FSM.

- *Form testing* checks input types and variable names in various forms, with the help of tools such as Doctor HTML (www2.imagiware.com/RxHTML). This can be considered as rudimentary input domain testing based on a simple check-list [48].

- *Verification of end-to-end transactions*, which is similar to testing complete execution paths in control flow testing or transaction processing in transaction flow testing [6].

- *Java and other component testing*: Java applets, which work on the clients side, or other Java applications, which work on the server side, need to be tested, similar to traditional software testing. Similarly, other programming languages used for various web-based facilities, such as C/C++, Visual Basic, etc., can also be checked for syntax, decisions, etc.

Various tools or tool suites are also available to support a combination of various functionality and regression testing, including SilkTest (www.segue.com), Astra QuickTest (www.mercury.com), eTester (www.rswsoftware.com), etc. Besides the basic web elements that need to be tested above, some specific web aspects that cut through several web elements also need to be tested, including:

- *Load testing* is a subset of stress (or performance) testing. It verifies that a web site can handle a large number of concurrent users while maintaining acceptable response time.

- The focus of *usability testing* is the ease-of-use issues of different web designs, overall layout, and navigations [3,11,29], which is different from our reliability focus in this chapter. Such testing relies heavily on subjective preferences of selected users.

- *Browser rendering* problems may affects the delivery as well as presentation of web contents. For example, HTML files that look good on one browser may look bad on another. We need to make sure that the web site functions appropriately with different browser versions. However, the browser checking is done manually to assess the "look & feel" of the GUI, etc., similar to usability testing discussed above.

- Other specialized testing include accessibility for blind and disabled people, runtime error detection, web security testing, etc. [29,37].

4.2   Modeling and Testing Web Navigations as Finite-State Machines (FSMs)

As mentioned in Section 3, web navigations have many similarities with menu selections in traditional menu-driven software systems, and the most commonly used testing technique for such systems is based on finite-state machines (FSMs) [5,48]. From the web users' point of view, each web-based application or function consists of various components, stages, or steps, visible to the web users, and typically initiated by them, making FSM-based testing an appropriate choice. We next consider the basic elements of FSMs and map them to web-based applications:

- Each web page corresponds to a state in an FSM. When we start a web browser, the default starting page or our customized starting page will be loaded, which corresponds to the initial state. Therefore, potentially any page can be the initial state. Similarly, we can stop anytime by exiting the web browser, or implicitly by no longer requesting pages. This last page visited, which can be potentially any page, is then the final state.

- State transitions correspond to web navigations following hypertext links embedded in HTML documents and other web contents.

- The input and output associated with such navigations are fairly simple and straightforward: The input is the clicking of the embedded link shown as highlighted content. The corresponding output is the loading of the requested page or content with accompanying messages indicating the HTML status, error or other messages, etc.

One special case in the state transition modeling above is that a user may choose to follow a previous saved link (bookmarked favorites) or to directly type a URL (universal resource locator, the address of a specific page). The use of these external navigation tools makes state transitions more unpredictable. However, there are also two factors worth noting in modeling web navigations as state transitions in FSMs:

- From the point of view of Internet- and web-based service providers, it is more important to ensure that the "official" embedded links on the providers' web site are correct than to ensure that the users' bookmarks or typed URLs are up-to-date or correct.

- There is empirical evidence that the vast majority of web navigations are following embedded hypertext links instead of using bookmarked or typed URLs. For example, for the www.seas.smu.edu web site, 75.84% of the navigations are originated from embedded links within the same web site, only 12.42% are user originated, and the rest from other sources [28].

Consequently, we choose to focus on the embedded navigation links and capture them in FSMs for web testing.

Once these FSMs are constructed, they can be used in testing. FSM-based testing typically attempts to achieve the following coverage goals [5,48]:

- *State or node coverage*: We need to make sure that each state can be reached and visited by some test cases. This is essentially a state or node traversal problem in graph theory [13,24], and test cases can be derived accordingly. In fact, web robots used by various Internet search engines or index services commonly "crawl" the web by systematically following the embedded hypertext links to create indexes or databases of the overall web contents, much like the state traversal for FSMs.

- *Transition or link coverage*: We need to make sure that each link or state transition is covered by some test cases. Although this problem can also be treated as link traversal in graph theory, the above state coverage testing already helped us reach each reachable state. It would be more economical to combine the visit to these states with the possible input values to cover all the links or transitions originated from this current state, which would also help us detect missing links (some input not associated with any transitions) [48]. Existing link-checkers can also be used to help us perform link coverage testing by checking bad links ("file-not-found"), which represent extra links in FSMs or missing states (pages).

In trying to reach a specific state, each test case is essentially a series of input values that enables us to make the transitions from an initial state to some target state, possibly through multiple hops by way of some intermediate states. The key in this sensitization is to remember that in FSM-modeled systems, input and output are associated with individual transitions instead of as an indistinguishable lump of initial input for many other systems. Consequently, the input sequencing is as important as the correct input values.

One useful capability for test execution is the ability to save some "current state" that can be restored. This would significantly shorten the series of state transitions needed to reach a target state, which may be important because in some systems these transitions may take a long time. This capability is especially useful for link coverage testing starting from a specific state: If we can start from this saved state, we can go directly into link coverage testing without waiting for the state transitions to reach this state from an initial state. Fortunately for web testing, most web pages can be saved or "bookmarked" to enable us to perform such testing easily. For a subset of dynamic and embedded pages, a more complicated navigation sequence will probably be needed.

The result checking is easy and straightforward, since the output for each transition is also specified in FSMs in addition to the next state. The key to this result checking is to make sure that both the next state and the output are checked.

4.3   Limitations and Motivation for Usage-Based Web Testing

We characterized web-based applications in Section 3 by their information/document focus, integration between information and navigation, and multi-layered support infrastructure to derive checklist- and FSM-based testing above for web-based applications. Additional characteristics of web-based applications include:

- *Massive user population*: Virtually anyone from anywhere with an Internet access can be a user of a given web-site. Although some traditional software systems, such as operating systems, also serve a massive user population, the systems are usually accessed locally, thus scattering the user population into sub-groups of limited size.

- *Diverse usage environments*: Web users employ different hardware equipments, network connections, operating systems, middleware and web server support, and web browsers, as compared to pre-specified platforms for most traditional software.

Any reliability problem of the web-based applications will be magnified by the massive user population, requiring us to address reliability problems effectively and directly. The diverse usage environment requires thorough testing to be performed for a huge number of situations. However, traditional coverage-based testing adapted for web testing in this section cannot be used directly to ensure reliability for web-based applications, and the combinatorial explosion resulted from the above diverse environments would make "coverage" an unattainable goal, as discussed below.

There is one obvious drawback to web testing using techniques covered in this section: The number of web pages for even a moderate-sized web site can be thousands or much more. Consequently, there would be significant numbers of unorganized individual testing activities when we attempt to test the individual items or aspects, which would overwhelm testing resources. If FSMs are used, the large number of states makes any detailed testing impractical, even with some automated support, because FSM-based testing can generally handle up to a few dozen states at most [5,48].

Hierarchical FSMs can be used to alleviate the problem associated with the large numbers of states and transitions by limiting transactions across boundaries of different FSMs in the hierarchy: In lower-level models, we generally assume a common source and common sink as its interface with higher-level models. However, the interactions may well be cutting through hierarchy boundaries in real systems. For large web sites, the complete coverage of all these hierarchical FSMs would still be impractical.

Another alternative to deal with state explosion problem of FSMs is to use selective testing based on Markov operational profiles (Markov OPs) [30,56] by focusing on highly used states and transitions while omitting infrequently used ones or grouping them together. The combination of these hierarchical FSMs and Markov OPs led us to unified Markov models (UMMs) [20,49] described in Section 5. On the other hand, loosely related collections of web pages can be more appropriately represented and tested by using some simpler usage models based on a flat list of operations and associated probabilities, such as Musa's operational profiles (OPs) [33]. The introduction of statistical testing strategies based on such OPs or UMMs is not to replace traditional testing techniques, but to use them selectively on important or frequently used functions or components.

On the other hand, as a general rule, usage and problem distribution among different software components is highly uneven [8], which is also demonstrated to be true among different web contents [25]. Consequently, some kind of selective testing is needed to focus on highly-used and problematic areas to ensure maximal web site reliability improvement, such as through usage-based statistical testing we discuss in the next section. These techniques can help us prioritize testing effort based on usage scenarios and frequencies for individual web resources and navigation patterns to ensure the reliability of web-based applications.

5. A Hierarchical Approach for Large-Scale Web Testing

We next describe an integrated strategy that combines several existing testing techniques in a hierarchical framework for web testing [48,50]. We first outline the overall framework and then describe its individual tiers in detail.

5.1 Overall Framework: A Three-Tiered Web Testing Strategy

Once we have decided to use usage-based statistical web testing, the immediate question is then the choice between two commonly used usage models or operational profiles (OPs): Musa's flat OP [33] and Markov OP [30,56] or its variation, unified Markov models (UMMs) [20,49]. Musa OP's key advantage is its simplicity, allowing us to focus on frequently used individual pages or web components. On the other hand, Markov models such as UMMs are generally more appropriate for selective testing of web navigations. Therefore, we have selected UMMs as the central testing models to work under the guidance of high-level Musa OPs in our overall web testing framework, to form a three-tiered strategy [50]:

1. The high-level operational profile (OP) enumerates major functions to be supported by web-based applications and their usage frequencies by target customers. This list-like flat OP will be augmented with additional information and supported by lower-level models based on unified Markov models (UMMs). The additional information includes grouping of related functions and mapping of major external functions to primary web sources or components.

2. For each of the high-level function groups, a UMM can be constructed to thoroughly test related operation sequences and related components. UMMs capture desired behavior, usage, and criticality information for web-based applications, and can be used to generate test cases to exhaustively cover high-level operation sequences and selectively cover important low-level implementations. The testing results can be analyzed to identify system bottlenecks for focused remedial actions, and to assess and improve system performance and reliability.

3. Critical parts identified by UMMs can be thoroughly tested using lower-level models based on traditional testing techniques. Other quality assurance alternatives, such as inspection, static and dynamic analyses, formal verification, preventive actions, etc. [38,48], can also be used to satisfy user needs and expectations for these particular areas.

Therefore, existing techniques that attempt to "cover" certain web aspects or elements, particularly those we described in Section 4, can still be used, but under the guidance of our mid-level UMMs as well as our top-level Musa OPs. Our hierarchical strategy can also accommodate other quality assurance activities, mostly at the bottom-level, much like for coverage-based testing:

• Support for software inspection can be provided in two ways: (1) selective inspection of critical web components by relating frequently used services to specific web components; (2) scenario based inspection [40] guided by our UMMs where usage scenarios and frequencies can be used to select and construct inspection scenarios.

• Selective formal verification can be carried out similar to the way inspection is supported above. Specific formal verification models can also be associated with highly critical parts of UMMs, and much of the UMM information can help us work with formal verification models, particularly those based on symbolic executions [31,57].

- The ability to identify reliability bottlenecks can also help the selective application of corrective and preventive actions, system analyses, damage containment, etc. [48].

To implement the above strategy, quantitative web usage information needs to be collected. Fortunately, the availability of existing web logs offers us the opportunity to collect usage information for usage model construction and for statistical web testing. The following reports can be easily produced from analyzing the web access logs kept at the web servers:

- *Top access report* (TAR) lists frequently accessed (individual) services or web pages together with their access counts.
- *Call pair report* (CPR) lists selected important call pairs (transition from one individual service to another) and the associated frequency.

TAR is important because many of the individual services can be viewed as stand-alone ones in web-based applications, and a complete session can often be broken down into these individual pieces. This report, when normalized by the total access count or session count, resembles the flat OP [33]. Each service unit in a TAR may correspond to multiple pages grouped together instead of a single page, such as in Fig. 2. Such results provide useful information to give us an overall picture of the usage frequencies for individual web service units, but not navigation patterns and associated occurrence frequencies.

CPR connects individual services and provides the basic information for us to extract state transition probabilities for our UMMs. For a web site with N pages or units, the potential number of entries in its global CPR is N^2, making it a huge table. Therefore, we generally group individual pages into larger units, similar to what we did above for TAR. Alternatively, we can restrict CPR to strong connections only, which is feasible because the $N \times N$ table is typically sparsely populated with only a few entries with high cross-reference frequency, as we will see empirically in Fig. 9 at the end of this section.

We can traverse through CPR for strong connections among TAR entries, which may also include additional connected individual services not represented in TAR because of their lower access frequencies or because they represent lower-level web units. A UMM can be constructed for each of these connected groups. In this way, we can construct our UMMs from TAR and CPR.

Notice that multiple OPs, particularly multiple UMMs in addition to TAR, our top-level OP, usually result for a single set of web-based applications using the above

Top Level:	Top Access Report (TAR)
	a flat list of frequently accessed services in ranking order
	(may be grouped by interconnection in customer usage scenarios)
Middle Level:	Unified Markov Models (UMMs)
	for groups of TAR entries linked by CPR (call-pair report)
	(may be expanded into lower-level UMMs or other models)
Bottom Level:	Detailed UMMs or other Models
	associated with frequently visited or critical nodes of UMMs
	(may correspond to testing models other than UMMs)

FIG. 4. Hierarchical implementation of an integrated web testing strategy.

approach. This implementation of our integrated strategy in a hierarchical form is discussed below:

- At the top level, TAR can be used directly as our flat OP for statistical usage-based testing.

- Entries in TAR can be grouped according to their connections via CPR, and a UMM can be constructed for each of these groups, forming our middle-level usage models, or our individual UMMs.

- The hierarchical nature of our UMMs will allow us to have lower-level UMMs as well as other lower-level testing models to thoroughly test selected functions or web components.

This hierarchical implementation of our integrated strategy is graphically depicted in Fig. 4. We focus on testing frequently used individual functions or services at the top level, testing common navigation patterns and usage sequences at the middle level, and covering selected areas at the bottom level. Specific low-level UMMs or other coverage-based testing models can be built to thoroughly test the related features or critical components in the higher-level flat OPs or UMMs. Coverage, criticality, and other information can also be easily used to generate test cases using lower-level models under our OPs.

5.2 Testing High-Level Component Usage with Musa Operational Profiles

According to Musa [33], an operational profile (OP) is a list of disjoint set of operations and their associated probabilities of occurrence. It is a quantitative characterization of the way a software system is or will be used. Table II gives an example OP for the web site, www.seas.smu.edu, listing the number of requests for differ-

TABLE II
USAGE FREQUENCIES AND PROBABILITIES BY
FILE TYPES FOR SMU/SEAS

File type	Hits	% of total
.gif	438,536	57.47
.html	128,869	16.89
directory	87,067	11.41
.jpg	65,876	8.63
.pdf	10,784	1.41
.class	10,055	1.32
.ps	2737	0.36
.ppt	2510	0.33
.css	2008	0.26
.txt	1597	0.21
.doc	1567	0.21
.c	1254	0.16
.ico	849	0.11
Cumulative	753,709	98.78
Total	763,021	100

ent types of files by web users over 26 days and the related probabilities. This OP can also be viewed as a specialized TAR above, where individual web pages are grouped by file types to form individual service units. The adaptation and application of OP-based testing would ensure that frequently used web pages and components are adequately tested, which in turn, would have a great impact on web site reliability improvement.

The "operations" represented in the operational profiles are usually associated with multiple test cases or multiple runs. Therefore, we typically assume that each "operation" in an OP can be tested through multiple runs without repeating the exact execution under exactly the same environment. In a sense, each operation corresponds to an individual sub-domain in domain partitions, thus representing a whole equivalence class [48]. In this example, each item in the table, or each operation, represents a type of file requested by a web user, instead of individual web pages. Of course, we could represent each web page as an operation, but it would be at a much finer granularity. When the granularity is too fine, the statistical testing ideas may not be as applicable, because repeated testing may end up repeating a lot of the same test runs, which adds little to test effectiveness. In addition, such fine-granularity OPs would be too large to be practical. For example, the SMU/SEAS web site has more than 11,000 individual web pages, while the number of file types is limited to a hundred or so, including many variations of the same type, such as HTML files with extensions of ".HTML," ".html," ".htm," etc.

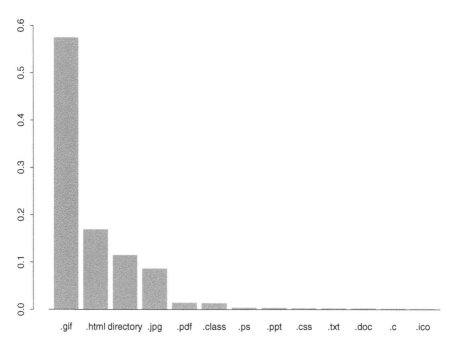

Fɪɢ. 5. An operational profile (OP) of requested file types for the SMU/SEAS web site.

There are also several other key points worth noting about Musa OPs, including:

- It is customary to sort the operations by descending probabilities of usage and present the results in that order. This sorted OP is often represented visually as a histogram, such as in Fig. 5, to make the results easy to interpret.

- It is common to have quite uneven distribution of usage probabilities, with a few frequently used ones account for most of the usage frequencies. In Table II, the top 13 out of a hundred or so file types account for more than 98% of the web hits for SMU/SEAS.

- Related to the uneven distribution of usage probabilities is the probability threshold for individual operations. The basis of statistical testing is to perform more testing for those operations that are used more by the customers. Therefore, if some operations have very low probability of usage, we could omit them in the OP. This probability threshold plays an important role in limiting the numbers of operations to represent in the OP, especially when there are a large number of possible operations.

There are three generic methods for information gathering and OP construction, in decreasing accuracy: actual *measurement* of usage at customer installations, *survey* of target customers, and usage estimation based on *expert opinions*. Fortunately, the availability of existing web logs offers us the opportunity to collect usage information for OP construction without incurring much additional cost. For new web sites or new web-based applications, similar information about the "intended" customer usage can be obtained by surveying potential customers or from experts.

Once an OP is constructed, it can be used to support statistical testing by some random sampling procedure to select test cases according to the probability distribution and execute them. Essentially, each operation in the OP corresponds to certain test cases specifically constructed or selected from existing ones to test a specific system operation.

The actual test runs are sampled from these test cases according to the probability of associated operations. The number of test runs for each operation in the OP is proportional to its probability. Under most circumstances, these test cases and associated runs can be prepared ahead of time, so that some test procedure can be employed to sequence the multiple test runs according to various criteria. In some cases, truly random sampling can be used, to dynamically select test cases to run next. However, such dynamic random sampling will slow down test execution and the system performance because of the overhead involved in managing the test case selection in addition to monitoring the test runs. Therefore, unless absolutely necessary, we should prepare the test cases and test procedures ahead of time to reduce the impact of testing overhead on normal system operations.

In addition to or in place of proportional sampling, progressive testing is often used with the help of OPs. For example, at the beginning of testing, higher probability threshold can be used to select a few very important or highly used operations for testing. As testing progresses, the threshold can be lowered to allow testing of less frequently used operations so that a wide variety of different operations can be covered. In a sense, the use of OPs can help us prioritize and organize our testing effort so that important or highly used areas are tested first, and other areas are progressively tested to ensure good coverage.

5.3   Unified Markov Models (UMMs) for Usage-Based Testing

As mentioned in Section 4, the primary limitation of FSM-based testing for the web is its inability to handle large number of states or individual web pages. We can augment FSMs with probabilistic usage information to focus our testing effort on usage scenarios and navigation sequences commonly used by target customers, while reduce or eliminate testing of less frequently used ones. The use of this approach would help us ensure and maximize product reliability from a customer's perspective, and at the same time make it scalable. Such augmented FSMs are our OPs, which typically form Markov chains, as we describe below.

A Markov chain can be viewed as an FSM where the probabilities associated with different state transitions satisfy the so-called *Markovian* or *memoryless* property: From the current state $X_n = i$ at time n or stage n, the probability of state transition to state $X_{n+1} = j$ for the next time period or stage $n + 1$ is denoted as p_{ij}, which is independent of the history, i.e.,

$$P\{X_{n+1} = j \mid X_n = i, \ X_{n-1} = s_{n-1}, \ \ldots, \ X_0 = s_0\}$$
$$= P\{X_{n+1} = j \mid X_n = i\}$$
$$= p_{ij} \quad \text{where } 0 \leqslant p_{ij} \leqslant 1 \text{ and } \sum_j p_{ij} = 1.$$

In other words, the probability that the system will be in state j only depends on the current state i and the history-independent transition probability p_{ij}. Equivalently, the complete history is summarized in the current state, thus removing the need to look back into the past to determine the next transition to take. This property is call the memoryless or Markovian property in stochastic processes [22]. A simplified test of memoryless property has been proposed and successfully used to verify that web usages can be accurately modeled by Markov chains [26].

Figure 6 is a sample Markov chain, with probabilistic state transitions. For example, after state B the next state to follow is always C, as represented by the transition probability of $p(B, C) = 1$. While the states to follow C could be D, with probability $p(C, D) = 0.99$ for the normal case, or B, with probability $p(C, B) = 0.01$ for the rare occasion that MS is unable to receive paging channel. Notice that we omitted the input/output information in such Markov OPs to keep the illustration simple, with the understanding that the input/output information is available for us to sensitize testing.

Much of the previous work with statistical testing used individual Markov chains [30,56]. For large systems, a collection of Markov chains might be used for testing, organized into a hierarchical framework called unified Markov models (UMMs) [20, 49,50]. For example, the top-level Markov chain for call processing in a cellular communication network is represented in Fig. 6. However, various sub-operations may be associated with each individual state in the top-level Markov chain, and could be modeled by more detailed Markov chains, such as the one in Fig. 7 for expanded state E. Notice that in some of these Markov chains, the sum of probabilities for transitions out from a given state may be less than 1, because the external destinations (and sources) are omitted to keep the models simple. The implicit understanding in UMMs is that the missing probabilities go to external destinations.

The higher-level operations in a UMM can be expanded into lower-level UMMs for more thorough testing. Therefore, UMMs are more suitable for large systems

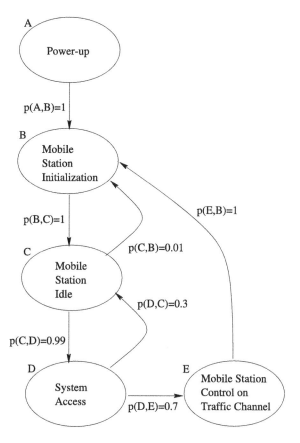

FIG. 6. An example Markov chain.

with complex operational scenarios and sequences than Musa's OPs above or deterministic FSMs described in Section 4. This hierarchical structure and the associated flexibility set this approach apart from earlier approaches to statistical testing using Markov chains.

Test cases can be generated by following the states and state transitions in UMMs to select individual operational units (states) and link them together (transitions) to form overall end-to-end operations. Possible test cases with probabilities above specific thresholds can be generated to cover frequently used operations. In practical applications, thresholds can be adjusted to perform progressive testing, similar to that used with Musa OPs we described earlier. Several thresholds have been initially proposed [2] and used in developing UMMs [20,49]:

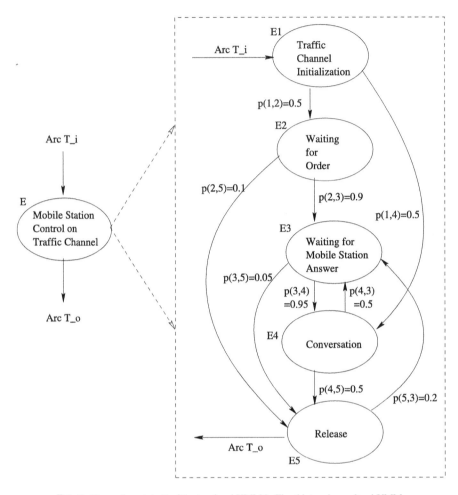

FIG. 7. Expanding state E of the top-level UMM in Fig. 6 into a lower-level UMM.

- *Overall probability threshold* for complete end-to-end operations to ensure that commonly used complete operation sequences by web users are adequately tested.
- *Stationary probability threshold* to ensure that frequently visited states are adequately tested.
- *Transition probability threshold* to ensure commonly used operation pairs, their interconnections and interfaces are adequately tested.

In our hierarchical strategy for web testing, information captured in our TAR and CPR is similar to the stationary probability and transition probability above. Consequently, we rely less on the last two thresholds above, and instead primarily use the overall probability threshold for our testing with UMMs. To use this threshold, the probability for possible test cases need be calculated and compared to this threshold. For example, the probability of the sequence ABCDEBCDC in Fig. 6 can be calculated as the products of its transitions, that is,

$$1 \times 1 \times 0.99 \times 0.7 \times 1 \times 1 \times 0.99 \times 0.3 = 0.205821.$$

If this is above the overall end-to-end probability threshold, this test case will be selected and executed.

Coverage, importance and other information or criteria may also be used to generate test cases. In a sense, we need to generate test cases to reduce the risks involved in different usage scenarios and product components, and sometimes to identify such risks as well [14]. The direct risks for selective testing include missing important areas or not covering them adequately. These "important" areas can be characterized by various external or internal information. The coverage requirement can be handled similarly by adjusting the probabilities to ensure that all things we would like to cover stays above a certain threshold, or by adjusting our test case selection procedures. Similar adjustments as above can be used to ensure that some critical functions of low usage frequencies are also thoroughly tested.

The hierarchical structure of UMMs also gives us the flexibility to improve test efficiency by avoiding redundant executions once a subpart has been visited already. This is particularly true when there are numerous common sub-operations within or among different end-to-end operations. When revisiting certain states, exact repetition of the execution states that have been visited before is less likely to reveal new problems. The revisited part can be dynamically expanded to allow for different lower-level paths or states to be covered. For example, when state E is revisited in the high-level Markov chain in Fig. 6, it can be expanded by using the more detailed Markov chain in Fig. 7, and possibly execute different subpaths there. In general, to avoid exact repetition, we could expand revisited states with operations of finer granularity, and more thoroughly test those frequently used parts.

5.4   Constructing and Using UMMs for Web Testing

Since UMMs are enhanced FSMs, FSM construction described in Section 4 can be reused as the first step to construct UMMs. The additional step involves assigning transition probabilities. Similar to the construction for Musa OPs described above, transition probabilities could be obtained by several methods, including: subjective evaluation based on *expert opinions*, *survey* of target customers, and *measurement* of actual usage. UMMs can be constructed based on existing access logs, using a combination of existing tools and internally implemented utility programs. However, as with most model construction activities, fully automated support is neither practical nor necessary. Human involvement is essential in making various modeling decisions, such as to extract UMM hierarchies and to group pages or links:

- Not every higher-level state needs to be expanded into lower-level models, because testing using lower-level model are to be performed selectively. Therefore, a threshold should be set up so that only the ones above it need to be expanded with their corresponding lower-level UMMs constructed.

- For traditional organizations, there is usually a natural hierarchy, such as university-school-department-individual, which is also reflected in their official web sites. There are generally closer interconnections as represented by more frequent referrals within a unit than across units. This natural hierarchy is used as the starting point for the hierarchies in these UMMs for web testing, which are later adjusted based on other referral frequencies.

- For links associated with very small link probability values, grouping them together to form a single link would significantly simplify the resulting model, and highlight the frequently used navigation patterns. A simple lower-level model for this group can be obtained by linking this single grouped node to all those it represents to form a one-level tree.

- Web pages related by contents or location in the overall site structure can also be grouped together to simplify UMMs.

Although any web page can be a potential entry point or initial state in an FSM or its corresponding Markov chain, one basic idea in statistical testing is to narrow this down to a few entry points based on their usage frequencies. The destinations of incoming links to a web site from external sources or start-ups are the entry points for UMMs. These links include URL accesses from dialog boxes, user bookmarks, search engine results, explicit links from external pages, or other external sources. All these accesses were recorded in the access log, and the analysis result for SMU/SEAS is summarized in the entry page report in Table III. For this web site, the root page "/index.html" outnumber other pages as the entry page by a large margin. In addition, these top entry pages are not tightly connected. These facts lead us to build a single set of UMMs [20] with this root page as the main entry node to the top-level Markov chain.

The issue with exit points is more complicated. Potentially any page can be the exit point, if the user decides to end accessing the web site. That is probably why

TABLE III
TOP ENTRY PAGES TO SMU/SEAS

Entry page	Occurrences
/index.html	18,646
/ce/index.html	2778
/co/cams/index.html	2568
/ce/smu/index.html	2327
/netech/index.html	2139
/disted/phd/index.html	1036
/co/cams/clemscam.html	963
/disted/index.html	878
/cse/index.html	813

no such exit page report is produced by any existing analyzer. This problem can be handled implicitly by specific usage sequences associated with specific test cases: The end of a usage sequence is the exit point from the UMM. This decision implies that frequently visited pages are also more likely to be the exit node than infrequently visited pages, which makes logical sense.

Figure 8 shows the top-level Markov chain of the UMM for the SMU/SEAS web site. The following information is captured and presented:

- Each node is labeled by its associated web file or directory name, and the total outgoing direct hits calculated. For example, out = 2099 for the root node "/index.html," indicates that the total direct hits from this node to its children pages is 2099.

- Each link is labeled with its direct hit count, instead of branching probability, to make it easier to add missing branching information should such information become available later. However, relative frequencies and conditional branching probabilities for links originating from a given node can be deduced easily. For example, the direct hit count from the page "/index.html" to the page "gradinfo.html" is 314; and the conditional branching probability for this link is $314/2099 = 20.5\%$.

- Infrequent direct hits to other pages are omitted from the model to simplify the model and highlight frequently followed sequences. However, the omitted direct hits can be calculated by subtracting out direct hits represented in the diagram from the total "out" hits of the originating node. For example, there are direct hits to nine other pages from the root page "/index.html." The combined direct hits are: $2099 - 431 - 314 - 240 - 221 = 893$.

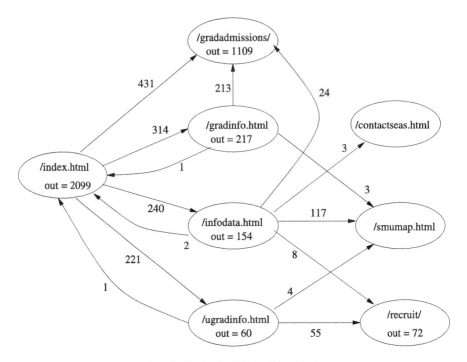

FIG. 8. Top-level UMM for SMU/SEAS.

Lower-level models are also produced for the nodes "/gradadmission/" and "/recruit/" in the top-level model. These models can be used to support our hierarchical strategy for statistical usage-based testing.

The test sensitization and outcome prediction are relatively simple and straightforward, similar to that for testing based on FSMs in Section 4. We can prepare all the input and specify the anticipated output and transitions ahead of time for most test situations. However, sometimes it would be hard to anticipate the input and the next state. Under such situations, dynamic test cases may be generated in the following way: From a current state, the transition or branching probabilities can be used to dynamically select the next state to visit, and sensitize it on the spot. Such dynamic test cases also have their own drawbacks, primarily in the reduced system performance due to the overhead to dynamically prepare and sensitize them.

The usage-based testing based on UMMs also yield data that can be used directly to evaluated the reliability of the implemented system, to provide an objective assessment of product reliability based on observation of testing failures and other related information. Unique to the usage of UMMs is that the failures can be associated with specific states or transitions. We can use such information to evaluate individual state reliability as well as overall system reliability, to extrapolate system reliability to different environments, and to identify high risk (low reliability) areas for focused reliability improvement.

5.5 Internal Validation via Cross-Reference Characterization

To validate the soundness of our integrated testing strategy above and its various decisions, we examined the cross-references recorded in the access log for the official pages of SMU/SEAS. The results are plotted in Fig. 9, which can be considered as a specific CPR introduced earlier in this section. As discussed in Section 4, embedded links in official pages are the primary responsibilities of the web site hosts, and consequently the focus of our study and the object of our analysis here. The sorted names of individual official pages are used as indexes in Fig. 9. Each point represents a cross-reference from a specific page indexed by its x-axis value to another

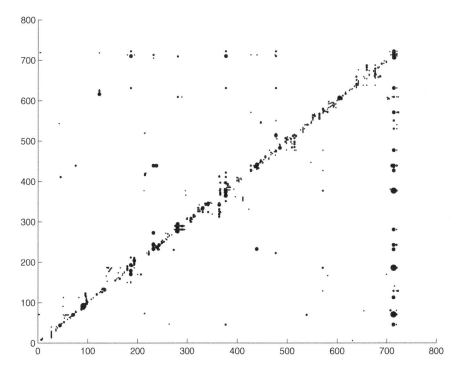

FIG. 9. Cross-references for sorted individual web pages.

specific page indexed by its y-axis value. A propositionally larger dot represents the number of duplicate cross-references. The references within a unit is then typified by the short distance between their indexes due to the same leading string in their names. The associated cross references would be represented by points close to the diagonal.

We examined the characteristics of high-level operations, and found that many items are loosely connected. This can be seen by the sparse points plotted in Fig. 9, particularly after we group some of the related pages together. Therefore, independent and individual probabilities used in Musa OPs are appropriate for high-level statistical web testing. For example, most of the pages with the highest access frequencies are index pages for individual academic units within SMU/SEAS, not tightly linked with each other and with little cross-references. Further analysis of expanded list of frequently visited pages follow similar patterns. In addition, the usage frequencies as well as the cross-reference frequencies are very unevenly distributed, as shown by the uneven distribution of points and masses in Fig. 9, thus justifying our use of statistical testing to focus on high-risk/high-leverage areas.

The exception to the loose connection above among the top access index pages is the hierarchical structure reflected, where there are numerous "up" and "down" references between the index page for SMU/SEAS and those for its individual departments and other academic units. In fact, there is a cluster of cross-references representing the common links followed from the site index page and other related pages to individual sub-sites or units, as represented by the cluster of points that form a vertical band to the right of Fig. 9. This can be tested using a high-level UMM to test the interaction between SMU/SEAS and its academic units.

While investigating the transition from top-level Musa OPs to middle-level UMMs, we noticed some natural clusters, which would be handled by individual UMMs. There is a close link and high cross-reference frequencies within a cluster but low visit frequencies across pages from different clusters. For example, within each academic department or unit, there are numerous cross-references but few across boundaries, as illustrated by the dominance of diagonal clusters in Fig. 9. Consequently, a UMM can be associated with each academic unit in statistical testing of this web site.

On the other hand, completely (or nearly completely) isolated operations can be tested by the top-level Musa OP alone, or if necessary, can bypass the middle level and go directly to the bottom-level model for further testing. This latter finding would require minor adjustments to our initially proposed approach and make our three-tiered testing strategy more flexible. In effect, we have modified our model to provide a bypass from top-level Musa OP to bottom-level structural testing.

6. Web Workload Characterization and Reliability Analyses

For software systems under normal operation or in testing, the execution results can be analyzed to assess test effectiveness and product reliability. In general, the failure information alone is not adequate to characterize and measure the reliability of a software system, unless there is a constant workload [27,34]. Due to the vastly uneven web traffic observed in previous studies [1,39], we need to measure both the web failures and related workload for reliability analyses. We next adapt existing techniques that characterize workload for traditional software systems and analyze their reliability to the web environment [52]. These measurement and analysis results also provide external validation or effectiveness assessment for our integrated testing strategy described in the previous section.

6.1 Defining Workload Measures for Reliability Assessment

The characteristics of the web environment discussed in Section 3 require us to measure actual web workload to ensure its satisfactory reliability instead of indiscriminately using generic measures suitable for traditional computation-intensive workload. The user focus and substantial amount of idle time during browsing sessions make any variation of execution time [34] unsuitable for web workload measurement. Similarly, the dominance of non-computational tasks also makes computational task oriented transactions [51] unsuitable for web workload measurement. Instead, other workload measures may be more suitable for characterizing workload at web sites.

From the perspective of web service providers, the usage time for web applications is the actual time spent by every user at the local web site. However, the exact time is difficult to obtain and may involve prohibitive cost or overhead associated with monitoring and recording dynamic behavior by individual web users [39]. One additional complication is the situation where a user opens a web page and continues with other tasks unrelated to the page just accessed. In this situation, the large gap between successive hits is not a reflection of the actual web usage time by this user. To approximate the usage time, we can consider the following workload measures [52]:

- *Number of hits, or hit count.* The most obvious workload measure is to count the number of hits, because (1) each hit represents a specific activity associated with web usage, and (2) each entry in an access log corresponds to a single hit, thus it can be extracted easily.

- *Number of bytes transferred, or byte count.* Overall hit count defined above can be misleading if the workload represented by individual hits shows high variability. Consequently, we can choose the number of bytes transferred, or byte count, as the workload measure of finer granularity, which can be easily obtained by counting the number of bytes transferred for each hit recorded in access logs.

- *Number of users, or user count.* User count is another alternative workload measure meaningful to the organizations that maintain the web sites and support various services at the user level. When calculating the number of users for each day, we treat each unique IP address as one user. So, no matter how many hits were made from the same computer, they are considered to be made by the same user. This measure gives us a rough picture of the overall workload handled by the web site.

- *Number of user sessions, or session count.* One of the drawbacks of user count is its coarse granularity, which can be refined by counting the number of user sessions. In this case, along with the IP address, access time can be used to calculate user sessions: If there is a significant gap between successive hits from the same IP address, we count the later one as a new session. In practice, the gap size can be adjusted to better reflect appropriate session identification for the specific types of web applications.

The number of user sessions per day may be a better measure of overall workload than the number of users, because big access gaps are typically associated with changes of users or non-web related activities by the same user. Each user who accesses the same web site from the same computer over successive intervals will be counted by user sessions, as long as such a gap exists in between. Even for a single user, a significant access gap is more likely to be associated with different usage patterns than within a single time burst. Therefore, by using user sessions, we can count the users' active contribution to the overall web site workload more accurately.

To summarize, the above measures give us workload characterization at different levels of granularity and from different perspectives. Hit count is more meaningful to web users as they see individual pages; byte count measures web traffic better; while number of users or sessions provide high-level workload information to web site hosts and content providers.

6.2   Measurement Results and Workload Characterization

On the average, each day for the SMU/SEAS web site is associated with 301.6 Mbytes, 29,345 hits, 2338 sessions, and 2120 users; each user is associated with 13.8 hits; each user session is associated with 11.6 hits; and each hit is associated with 10,279 bytes. We used the standard two-hour gap [32] to identify user sessions here.

The overall traffic at the KDE web site is significantly heavier than that for SMU/SEAS, with a daily average of 3563 Mbytes, 455,005 hits, 24,656 users, 29,029 s1 sessions, and 104,490 s2 sessions. Two different variations of session count were used in dealing with the KDE data: the same two-hour gap cut-off we used for the SMU/SEAS web site (labeled s1), and the 15 minutes cut-off more appropriate for dynamic pages (labeled s2) [39].

No matter which workload measure is used, the daily workload shows several apparent characteristics for both web sites, as follows:

- *Uneven distribution and variability*: The distribution is highly uneven and varies from day to day, as represented by the peaks and valleys in workload plots, which conforms to previously observed traffic patterns [1,21,39]. Among the four workload measures, daily bytes and daily hits show larger variability in relative magnitudes than daily users or daily sessions. This result indicates that although the number of users or user sessions may remain relatively stable, some users may use the web much more intensively than others, resulting in larger variations in detailed web site workload measurements over time. The relative differences for KDE tends to be smaller than that for SMU/SEAS, likely due to the heavier traffic by a larger and more diverse user population world-wide.

- *A periodic pattern that synchronize with error profile*, which is characterized by weekdays normally associated with heavier workload than during the weekends. This pattern seems to conform to the self-similar web traffic [12]. In addition, this periodic pattern are correlated or synchronized with daily error profile. This fact indicates that these workload measures are viable alternatives for web software reliability evaluation, because of the direct relation between usage and possible failures for the web site's source contents demonstrated in such synchronized patterns.

- *A long term stability for the overall trend*, which can be cross-validated by examining the trend over a longer period. All the workload measures traced over a year for SMU/SEAS showed long-term stability. This is probably due to the stable enrollment for SMU/SEAS and web site stability where no major changes were made to our web-based services over the observation period.

Of the four workload measures, hits, users, and sessions can be extracted from access logs easily and consistently. However, byte counting was somewhat problematic, because "byte transferred" field was missing not only for the error entries but also for many other entries. Further investigation revealed that most of these missing entries were associated with files or graphics already in the users cache ("file not modified," therefore no need to resend or reload). Since the total number of entries with missing bytes information represented about 15% of the total number of entries (hits), we simply used the rest to calculate the number of bytes transferred.

Workload measurements associated with periods shorter than calendar days, such as by the hour or by some short bursts, can also be used in reliability analysis. With time-stamped individual hits and related information available in the access log, such measurements can be easily obtained. As for reliability analysis, data with less variability, usually through data grouping or clustering, are generally preferable, because they typically produce more stable models that fit the observations better and provide better reliability assessments and predictions [41,47]. In our case, daily data have much less variability than hourly ones, yet give us enough data points for statistical analyses and model fitting. Consequently, we only use daily data in subsequent reliability analyses.

6.3   Analyzing Operational Reliability

As mentioned in Section 2, a workload profile with considerable variability, such as the web traffic for our two web sites studied here, is a clear indication that measuring failures alone over calendar time is not suitable for reliability analysis. The number of problems encountered per day is expected to be closely related to the usage intensity. When we combine the measurement results for the web failures, in this case type E errors extracted from the error log, and workload measured by the number of users, sessions, hits, and bytes transferred, we can perform analyses to evaluate web software reliability.

As observed earlier, the peaks and valleys in errors generally coincide with the peaks and valleys in workload. This close relationship between usage time and failure count can be graphically examined as in Fig. 10, plotting cumulative errors vs. cumulative bytes transferred over the observation period. An essentially linear relation can be detected between the two. Similar observations can be obtained if we plot cumulative errors vs. cumulative hits, users, or sessions.

This relationship can also be characterized by the daily failure rate, as defined by the number of errors divided by the workload measured by bytes transferred, hits, users, or sessions for each day. These daily failure rates also characterize web software reliability, and can be interpreted as applying the Nelson model [36] mentioned in Section 2 to daily snapshots. Table IV gives the range (min to max), the mean, and the standard deviation (std.dev.), for each daily error rates defined above. Because these rates are defined for different workload measurement units and have different magnitude, we used the relative standard error, or *rse*, defined as: $rse = std.dev./mean$, to compare their relative spread in Table IV. We also included the daily error count for comparison. All these daily error rates fall into tighter spread

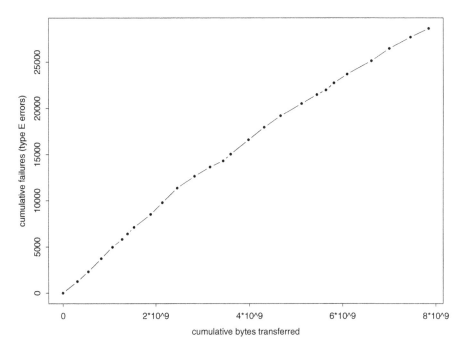

FIG. 10. Cumulative errors vs. cum. bytes transferred for SMU/SEAS.

TABLE IV
DAILY ERROR RATE (OR FAILURE RATE) FOR SMU/SEAS

Error rate	min	max	mean	std.dev.	rse
errors/bytes	2.35×10^{-6}	5.30×10^{-6}	3.83×10^{-6}	9.33×10^{-7}	0.244
errors/hits	0.0287	0.0466	0.0379	0.00480	0.126
errors/sessions	0.269	0.595	0.463	0.0834	0.180
errors/users	0.304	0.656	0.5103	0.0859	0.168
errors/day	501	1582	1101	312	0.283

than daily error count, which indicates that they provide more consistent and stable reliability estimates than daily error count alone.

Since individual web failures are directly associated with individual hits, we can use the Nelson model [36] to evaluate the overall web software reliability using failures and hits for the complete 26 days. This gives us the site software reliability of $R = 0.962$, or 96.2% of the individual web accesses will be successful. This model also give us an MTBF = 26.6 hits, or averaging one error for every 26.6 hits.

TABLE V
DAILY ERROR RATE (OR FAILURE RATE) FOR KDE

Error rate	min	max	mean	std.dev.	rse
errors/bytes	3.608×10^{-6}	1.246×10^{-5}	7.210×10^{-6}	1.81×10^{-6}	0.251
errors/hits	0.04178	0.09091	0.05519	0.0117	0.211
errors/s1s	0.6335	1.4450	0.8648	0.189	0.219
errors/s2s	0.1665	0.4041	0.2403	0.0554	0.231
errors/users	0.7428	1.7060	1.0180	0.228	0.223
errors/day	15,510	44,160	25,330	6833	0.270

Modeling with other workload measures is also possible. For example, the above MTBF can be re-calculated for other workload units, giving us an MTBF = 273,927 bytes, an MTBF = 1.92 users, or an MTBF = 2.12 sessions. That is, this site can expect, on the average, to have a problem for every 273,927 bytes transferred, for every 1.92 users, or for 2.12 sessions. The web software reliability R in terms of these workload measures can also be calculated by the Nelson model. However, result interpretation can be problematic, because web failures may only be roughly associated with these workload measures. For example, because of the missing byte transferred information in the access logs for failed requests, the failures can only be roughly placed in the sequence of bytes transferred, resulting in imprecise reliability assessments and predictions. On the other hand, individual web failures may be roughly associated with certain users or user sessions through the particular hits by the users or within the sessions. In this case, each user or session may be associated with multiple failures, and appropriate adjustments to modeling results might be called for. For example, it might be more appropriate to separate failure-free sessions from sessions with failures, instead of comparing the number of failures in a session.

Table V gives the evaluation results of operational reliability for the KDE web site. Expectedly, the same patterns hold, i.e., all the daily failure rates fall into tighter bands than that for the daily errors, to give consistent and stable assessments of the operational reliability of this web site's contents. The overall reliability values are also roughly the same as that for SMU/SEAS. For example, on average, 5.76% of the hits would result in 404 errors, or the web site was 94.2% reliable as compared to 96.2% for SMU/SEAS.

6.4 Evaluating Potential Reliability Improvement

Under the idealized environment, the fault(s) that caused each observed failure can be immediately identified and removed, resulting in no duplicate observations of identical failures. This scenario represents the upper limit for the potential reliability improvement if we attempt to fix operational problems on-line or if we attempt to test the system and fix problems under simulated customer operational environment using our integrated testing strategy described in Section 5. This upper bound on reliability growth may not be attainable under many circumstances because of the large number of transient faults that usually take place whose origins are usually very difficult to be identified and removed because of their dependency on the context. Nevertheless, this upper limit gives us an idea about the potential reliability growth. Should quantitative information become available about the faults that are hard to fix, it can be used to fine tune the above limit to provide more accurate estimate of reliability growth potential.

This limit on potential reliability improvement can be measured by the reliability change (or *growth*) through the operational duration or testing process where such defect fixing could take place. Under the web application environment, each observed failure corresponds to a recorded type E error in the error log, and the idealized defect fixing would imply no more observation of any duplicate type E errors. In other words, failure arrivals under this hypothetical environment would resemble the sequence of unique type E errors extracted from the error log, which can be calculated by counting each type E error only once at its first appearance but not subsequently.

In general, reliability growth can be visualized by the gradual leveling-off of the cumulative failure arrival curve, because the flatter the part of the curve, the more time it takes to observe the next failure. To visualize this, we plotted in Fig. 11 cumulative unique failures versus different workload measurements we calculated above. Relative scale is used to better compare the overall reliability growth trends. The individual data points in the middle depict the failure arrivals indexed by cumulative hits. The (top) solid line depicts failure arrivals indexed by the cumulative bytes transferred. The (bottom) dashed line depicts failure arrivals indexed by the cumulative number of users. The user session measurement resulted in almost identical curve shape as that for the number of users, thus was omitted to keep the graph clean. As we can see from Fig. 11, there is an observable effect of reliability growth for this data, with the tail-end flatter than the beginning for all three curves.

Quantitative evaluation of reliability growth can be provided by software reliability growth models (SRGMs) we described in Section 2, which commonly assume instantaneous defect fixing [27,34]. In this chapter, we use a single measure, the purification level ρ [45] to capture this reliability change:

$$\rho = \frac{\lambda_0 - \lambda_T}{\lambda_0} = 1 - \frac{\lambda_T}{\lambda_0}$$

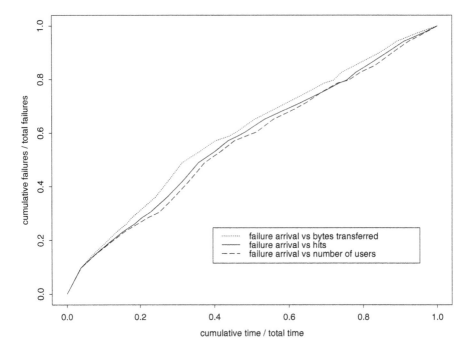

FIG. 11. Reliability growth comparison for different workload measures for SMU/SEAS.

where λ_0 and λ_T are the initial and final failure rates, respectively, estimated by a fitted SRGM. Complete elimination of all potential defects would result in $\rho = 1$, and no defect fixing would result in $\rho = 0$. Normal reliability growth is associated with ρ values ranging between these two extremes, with larger ρ values associated with more reliability growth. $(1 - \rho)$ gives us the ratio between λ_T and λ_0, or the final failure rate as a percentage of the initial failure rate.

We fitted the widely used Goel–Okumoto (GO) model [17] introduced in Section 2 to relate cumulative unique failures ($m(t)$) to cumulative workload measurements (t) in the formula:

$$m(t) = N\left(1 - e^{-bt}\right).$$

Table VI summarizes these modeling results, giving estimated model parameters N and b, λ_0, λ_T, and ρ. The ρ values based on models using different workload measurements indicate that potential reliability improvement ranges from 57.9 to 74.8% in purification levels. In other words, effective web testing and defect fixing equiv-

TABLE VI
RELIABILITY MODELING RESULTS FOR SMU/SEAS

Time/workload measurement	Model parameters & estimates				Reliability growth ρ
	N	b	λ_0	λ_T	
bytes	3674	1.76×10^{-10}	6.45×10^{-7}	1.63×10^{-7}	0.748
hits	4213	1.38×10^{-6}	0.00583	0.00203	0.632
sessions	4750	1.42×10^{-5}	0.0675	0.0284	0.579
users	4691	1.60×10^{-5}	0.0752	0.0311	0.587

alent to 26 days of operation could have reduced the failure rate to between slightly less than half ($1 - 57.9\%$) and about one quarter ($1 - 74.8\%$) of the initial failure rate. Other SRGMs we tried also yield similar results: A significant reliability improvement potential exists if we can capture the workload and usage patterns in log files and use them to guide software testing and defect fixing.

We also repeated the assessment of reliability growth potential for the KDE web site. However, when we extracted the unique failures (unique 404 errors), we noticed an anomaly at the 24th day, which was associated with more than 10 times the maximal daily unique errors for all the previous days. Further investigation revealed that this is related to a planned beta release of the KDE product, when the web contents were drastically changed and many new faults were injected. Since our reliability growth evaluation is for stable situations where few or none new faults are injected, as is the assumption for all the software reliability growth models [27,34], we restricted our data to the first 22 days in this analysis.

Figure 12 plots the reliability growth evaluation we carried out for the KDE data. Among the five workload measures we used, bytes, hits, users, s1 and s2 sessions, all produced almost identical results in the reliability growth visualization, when we plotted relative cumulative unique errors against relative cumulative workload, similar to what we did in Fig. 11. The comparative visualization is omitted here because all the relative reliability growth curves would closely resemble the actual curve represented by the actual data points in Fig. 12. A visual inspection of Fig. 12 also revealed more degrees of reliability growth, or more bending of the data trend and fitted curve, than that in Fig. 11. Reliability growth potential as captured by ρ for the KDE web site ranged from 86.7 to 88.9% (with the model in Fig. 12 gave us $\rho = 87.1\%$). In other words, effective web testing and defect fixing equivalent to 22 days of operation could have reduced the failure rate to about 11 to 13% (calculated by $1 - \rho$) of the initial failure rate; or, equivalently, almost all the original problems could have been fixed.

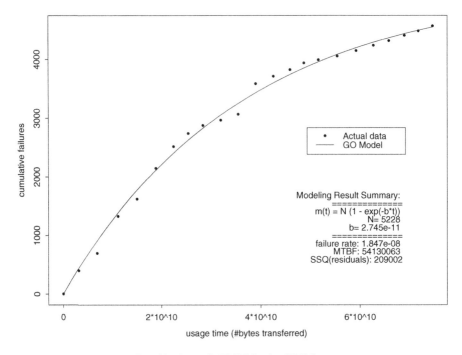

FIG. 12. A sample SRGM fitted to KDE data.

6.5   General Observations about Web Reliability and Test Effectiveness

As demonstrated in this section through case studies, web software reliability and test effectiveness can be evaluated based on information extracted from existing web server logs. Our key findings and related observations are summarized below:

- *Measure derivation and data extraction*: Four workload measures, bytes transferred, hit count, number of users, and number of sessions, were derived in this section for web workload characterization and reliability evaluation. Hit count, byte count, and user count can be easily extracted from access logs, due to their direct correspondence to access log entries and the data fields "bytes transferred" and "IP address." Session count computation may involve history information for individual users or unique IP addresses, but properly identified user sessions with appropriate time-out values can reflect web usage better than simply counting the users. Detailed failure data can be extracted from error logs. When such logs are not available, rough failure data can be extracted from access logs.

- *Assessing the operational reliability for web software*: When used with failure data to estimate failure rate or reliability, all four workload measures used in this section produced more consistent and stable reliability estimates than using daily errors alone. They offer reliability assessments from different perspectives, and each may be suitable for specific situations. For example, byte count might be more suitable for traffic measurement and related reliability interpretations; hit count might be more meaningful to web users as they browse individual pages; while number of users or sessions might be more suitable for high-level web site reliability characterization.

- *Assessing the potential for reliability improvement under effective testing*: Also demonstrated in both case studies is the significant potential for reliability improvement if defect can be fixed using our testing strategy described in Section 5. For www.seas.smu.edu, the failure rate could be reduced to 42.1–25.2% of the initial failure rate through such testing equivalent to 26 days of operation. Similarly for www.kde.org, the failure rate could be reduced to about 11–13% of the initial failure rate through testing equivalent to 22 days of operation; or, equivalently, almost all the original problems could have been fixed. These results provide external validation for our integrated testing strategy described in Section 5.

- *Some generalization beyond our two case studies*: Many of the results we obtained and patterns we observed concerning workload measurements for the SMU/SEA and the KDE web sites are remarkably similar to that for other Internet traffic [1,12,21,39], which indicates that web traffic characteristics have remained fairly stable for almost a decade. Although re-confirming these existing results and patterns is not our intention or our focus, this confirmation lends further validity to our primary purpose of using these measurements as part of the data input to evaluate web software reliability.

7. Conclusions and Perspectives

To summarize, a collection of appropriate testing techniques can be selected, adapted, and integrated to help us perform effective web testing and to ensure web reliability. As we demonstrated in this chapter through our case studies using the web sites for the School of Engineering and Applied Science, Southern Methodist University (SMU/SEAS) and for the large-scale open source KDE project, hierarchical testing of web-based applications is both viable and effective:

- The user focus of web-based applications is supported in this integrated strategy by testing functions, usage scenarios, and navigation patterns frequently used by web users under our top-tier usage models based on the list-like Musa operational profiles [33] as well as our middle-tier usage models based on Unified Markov Models (UMMs) [20,49].

- Individual web functions and internal components can be thoroughly exercised by using our bottom-tier models based on traditional coverage-based testing [6, 35], under the guidance of our upper-level usage models.

- Appropriate workload measures [52] can be extracted from access logs to capture the overall workload at different levels of granularity and from different perspectives. When used in conjunction with failure measurements, they can provide an objective and stable evaluation of web site operational reliability. A potentially significant reliability gain could be achieved under effective usage-based testing, leading to reliability growth ranging from 58 to 89% in purification levels [45] within a month of such improvement actions.

- The techniques and tools used by us for data collection, model construction and application, and result analysis and presentation can provide automated support that is essential for practical implementation and deployment of our strategy in industry.

There are some limitations to our approach, primarily in data availability and granularity, assumption of web stability in reliability evaluations, and lack of analyses based on detailed defect information. Related issues we plan to address in future studies include:

- *Overcoming data availability limitations*: Some information useful to support our integrated strategy is missing from existing web logs, such as the bytes transferred for failed or cached accesses, web navigation based on cached web contents at the users' side, ambiguity with "empty" referral information, other types of problems not isolated to the web server alone, etc. A logical next step is to search for alternative information sources to provide such information for more effective web testing and reliability improvement. The availability of such additional data will better support our integrated strategy.

- *Overcoming limitations of static web contents*: Our analyses are based on the default access logs of web servers, where dynamic errors concerning execution of dynamic web logic are not recorded. With more and more web sites providing dynamic information, dynamic logs will become widely available. We plan to expand and validate our approach on diverse web sites and make use of dynamic web logs in our future studies.

- *The impact of web site changes and related fault injections*: Our testing and reliability analyses in this chapter assumed the stability of the web sites under study, and our evaluation of reliability growth potential additionally assumed that none or few new faults were injected. Therefore, a direct generalization of this study is to study the impact of web changes and injection of new faults on test effectiveness and web reliability.

- *Detailed defect analysis and risk identification for reliability improvement*: Web error distribution is highly uneven, as shown in this chapter and in related studies [25,28,52]. To analyze them further, we plan to adapt detailed defect classification and analysis schemes such as ODC (orthogonal defect classification) [10] for traditional systems to the web environment. We also plan to apply appropriate risk identification techniques [46] and related models [45,53] to identify high-defect or low-reliability areas for focused web software reliability improvement.

In addition, we also plan to identify better existing tools, develop new tools and utility programs, and integrate them to provide better implementation support for our strategy. All these efforts should lead us to a more practical and effective approach to achieve and maintain high reliability for web applications.

ACKNOWLEDGEMENTS

The work reported in this chapter was supported in part by NSF grant 0204345 and THECB/ATP grant 003613-0030-2001. We thank our system administrator, Merlin Wilkerson, for his help in gathering and interpreting the web logs for the SMU/SEAS web site, and Dirk Mueller from the KDE project who helped us obtain and interpret the access logs for the KDE web site and deal with various data problems. We also thank Chaitanya Kallepalli and Omar Shahdad for their previous work in developing many of the Perl programs used in this study, and A. Güneş Koru and Zhao Li for their help and suggestions.

REFERENCES

[1] Arlitt M.F., Williamson C.L., "Internet web servers: Workload characterization and performance implications", *IEEE/ACM Trans. Networking* **5** (5) (Oct. 1997) 631–645.
[2] Avritzer A., Weyuker E.J., "The automatic generation of load test suites and the assessment of the resulting software", *IEEE Trans. Software Engrg.* **21** (9) (Sept. 1995) 705–716.

[3] Bachiochi D.J., Berstene M.C., Chouinard E.F., Conlan N.M., Danchak M.M., Furey T., Neligon C.A., Way D., "Usability studies and designing navigational aids for the World Wide Web", *Computer Networks and ISDN Systems* **29** (8–13) (Sept. 1997) 1489–1496.

[4] Behlandorf B., *Running a Perfect Web Site with Apache*, second ed., MacMillan Computer Publishing, New York, 1996.

[5] Beizer B., *Software Testing Techniques*, second ed., International Thomson Computer Press, Boston, MA, 1990.

[6] Beizer B., *Black-Box Testing: Techniques for Functional Testing of Software and Systems*, John Wiley & Sons, Inc., New York, 1995.

[7] Black R., *Critical Testing Processes*, Addison–Wesley, Reading, MA, 2004.

[8] Boehm B., Basili V.R., "Software defect reduction top 10 list", *IEEE Computer* **34** (1) (Jan. 2001) 135–137.

[9] Bowers N., "Weblint: Quality assurance for the World-Wide Web", *Computer Networks and ISDN Systems* **28** (7–11) (May 1996) 1283–1290.

[10] Chillarege R., Bhandari I., Chaar J., Halliday M., Moebus D., Ray B., Wong M.-Y., "Orthogonal defect classification—a concept for in-process measurements", *IEEE Trans. Software Engrg.* **18** (11) (Nov. 1992) 943–956.

[11] Constantine L.L., Lockwood L.A.D., "Usage-centered engineering for web applications", *IEEE Software* **19** (2) (Mar. 2002) 42–50.

[12] Crovella M.E., Bestavros A., "Self-similarity in world wide web traffic: Evidence and possible causes", *IEEE/ACM Trans. Networking* **5** (6) (Dec. 1997) 835–846.

[13] Deo N., *Graph Theory with Applications to Engineering and Computer Science*, Prentice Hall, Englewood Cliffs, NJ, 1974.

[14] Frankl P.G., Weyuker E.J., "Testing software to detect and reduce risk", *J. Systems Software* **53** (3) (Sept. 2000) 275–286.

[15] Fromme B., "Web software testing: Challenges and solutions", in: *InterWorks'98*, Apr. 1998.

[16] Ghezzi C., Jazayeri M., Mandrioli D., *Fundamentals of Software Engineering*, second ed., Prentice Hall, Englewood Cliffs, NJ, 2003.

[17] Goel A.L., Okumoto K., "A time dependent error detection rate model for software reliability and other performance measures", *IEEE Trans. Reliability* **28** (3) (1979) 206–211.

[18] Howden W.E., "Functional testing", *IEEE Trans. Software Engrg.* **SE-6** (2) (1980) 162–169.

[19] IEEE, *IEEE Standard Glossary of Software Engineering Terminology*, Number STD 610.12-1990, IEEE, 1990.

[20] Kallepalli C., Tian J., "Measuring and modeling usage and reliability for statistical web testing", *IEEE Trans. Software Engrg.* **27** (11) (Nov. 2001) 1023–1036.

[21] Karagiannis T., Molle M., Faloutsos M., "Long-range dependence: Ten years of Internet traffic modeling", *IEEE Internet Computing* **8** (5) (Sept. 2004) 57–64.

[22] Karlin S., Taylor H.M., *A First Course in Stochastic Processes*, second ed., Academic Press, New York, 1975.

[23] Kitchenham B., Pfleeger S.L., "Software quality: The elusive target", *IEEE Software* **13** (1) (Jan. 1996) 12–21.

[24] Knuth D.E., *The Art of Computer Programming*, Addison–Wesley, Reading, MA, 1973.

[25] Li Z., Tian J., "Analyzing web logs to identify common errors and improve web reliability", in: *Proc. IADIS International Conference on E-Society, Lisbon, Portugal*, June 2003, pp. 235–242.

[26] Li Z., Tian J., "Testing the suitability of Markov chains as web usage models", in: *Proc. 27th Int. Computer Software and Applications Conf., Dallas, TX*, Nov. 2003, pp. 356–361.

[27] Lyu M.R., *Handbook of Software Reliability Engineering*, McGraw-Hill, New York, 1995.

[28] Ma L., Tian J., "Analyzing errors and referral pairs to characterize common problems and improve web reliability", in: *Proc. 3rd International Conference on Web Engineering, Oviedo, Spain*, July 2003, pp. 314–323.

[29] Miller E., *The Website Quality Challenge*, Software Research, Inc., San Francisco, CA, 2000.

[30] Mills H.D., "On the statistical validation of computer programs", Technical Report 72-6015, IBM Federal Syst. Div., 1972.

[31] Mills H.D., Basili V.R., Gannon J.D., Hamlet R.G., *Principles of Computer Programming: A Mathematical Approach*, Alan and Bacon, Inc., Boston, MA, 1987.

[32] Montgomery A.L., Faloutsos C., "Identifying web browsing trends and patterns", *IEEE Computer* **34** (7) (July 2001) 94–95.

[33] Musa J.D., *Software Reliability Engineering*, McGraw-Hill, New York, 1998.

[34] Musa J.D., Iannino A., Okumoto K., *Software Reliability: Measurement, Prediction, Application*, McGraw-Hill, New York, 1987.

[35] Myers G.J., *The Art of Software Testing*, John Wiley & Sons, Inc., New York, 1979.

[36] Nelson E., "Estimating software reliability from test data", *Microelectronics and Reliability* **17** (1) (1978) 67–73.

[37] Peper M., Hermsdorf D., "BSCW for disabled teleworkers: Usability evaluation and interface adaptation of an Internet-based cooperation environment", *Computer Networks and ISDN Systems* **29** (8–13) (Sept. 1997) 1479–1487.

[38] Pfleeger S.L., Hatton L., Howell C.C., *Solid Software*, Prentice Hall, Upper Saddle River, NJ, 2002.

[39] Pitkow J.E., "Summary of WWW characterizations", *World Wide Web* **2** (1–2) (1999) 3–13.

[40] Porter A.A., Siy H., Votta L.G., "A review of software inspections", in: Zelkowitz M.V. (Ed.), *Advances in Computers*, vol. 42, Academic Press, San Diego, CA, 1996, pp. 39–76.

[41] Schneidewind N.F., "Software reliability model with optimal selection of failure data", *IEEE Trans. Software Engrg.* **19** (11) (Nov. 1993) 1095–1104.

[42] Shneiderman B., *Designing the User Interface: Strategies for Effective Human–Computer Interaction*, Addison–Wesley, Reading, MA, 1987.

[43] Stallings W., *High Speed Networks and Internets: Performance and Quality of Service*, second ed., Prentice Hall, Upper Saddle River, NJ, 2001.

[44] Thayer R., Lipow M., Nelson E., *Software Reliability*, North-Holland, New York, 1978.

[45] Tian J., "Integrating time domain and input domain analyses of software reliability using tree-based models", *IEEE Trans. Software Engrg.* **21** (12) (Dec. 1995) 945–958.

[46] Tian J., "Risk identification techniques for defect reduction and quality improvement", *Software Quality Professional* **2** (2) (Mar. 2000) 32–41.

[47] Tian J., "Better reliability assessment and prediction through data clustering", *IEEE Trans. Software Engrg.* **28** (10) (Oct. 2002) 997–1007.

[48] Tian J., *Software Quality Engineering: Testing, Quality Assurance, and Quantifiable Improvement*, John Wiley & Sons, Inc. and IEEE CS Press, Hoboken, NJ, 2005.

[49] Tian J., Lin E., "Unified Markov models for software testing, performance evaluation, and reliability analysis", in: *4th ISSAT International Conference on Reliability and Quality in Design, Seattle, WA*, Aug. 1998.

[50] Tian J., Ma L., Li Z., Koru A.G., "A hierarchical strategy for testing web-based applications and ensuring their reliability", in: *Proc. 27th Int. Computer Software and Applications Conf. (1st IEEE Workshop on Web-based Systems and Applications), Dallas, TX*, Nov. 2003, pp. 702–707.

[51] Tian J., Palma J., "Test workload measurement and reliability analysis for large commercial software systems", *Ann. Software Engrg.* **4** (Aug. 1997) 201–222.

[52] Tian J., Rudraraju S., Li Z., "Evaluating web software reliability based on workload and failure data extracted from server logs", *IEEE Trans. Software Engrg.* **30** (11) (Nov. 2004) 754–769.

[53] Tian J., Troster J., "A comparison of measurement and defect characteristics of new and legacy software systems", *J. Systems Software* **44** (2) (Dec. 1998) 135–146.

[54] Trivedi K.S., *Probability and Statistics with Reliability, Queuing, and Computer Science Applications*, second ed., John Wiley & Sons, Inc., New York, 2001.

[55] Vatanasombut B., Stylianou A.C., Igbaria M., "How to retain online customers", *Commun. ACM* **47** (6) (June 2004) 65–69.

[56] Whittaker J.A., Thomason M.G., "A Markov chain model for statistical software testing", *IEEE Trans. Software Engrg.* **20** (10) (Oct. 1994) 812–824.

[57] Zelkowitz M.V., "Role of verification in the software specification process", in: Yovits M.C. (Ed.), *Advances in Computers*, vol. 36, Academic Press, San Diego, CA, 1993, pp. 43–109.

Wireless Insecurities

MICHAEL STHULTZ AND JACOB UECKER

Internet Forensics Laboratory
Center for Cybermedia Research
University of Nevada, Las Vegas
USA

HAL BERGHEL

University of Canterbury
New Zealand

and

Internet Forensics Laboratory
Center for Cybermedia Research
University of Nevada, Las Vegas
USA

Abstract

The popularity of wireless networking is a function of convenience. It addresses one of the most important goals in advanced computing technology: mobility. When viewed conceptually, wireless technology can be seen as having a contemporaneous, parallel evolutionary path with remote login, distributed, and nomadic computing in the area of computing and car portable, car and cellular phones in the area of telecommunications.

This chapter provides an overview of the wireless landscape and the security mechanisms that have been introduced in an effort to protect Wireless Local Area Networks (WLANs). It then gives a detailed description of these mechanisms including a discussion of their inherent weaknesses. The conclusion is there is no effective WLAN security available in today's environment.

ADVANCES IN COMPUTERS, VOL. 67
ISSN: 0065-2458/DOI 10.1016/S0065-2458(05)67005-2

1. The Wireless Landscape

Wireless networking is one of the most recent technologies whose usage has exploded in the last decade. The operational metaphor behind wireless technology is mobility. The concept of wireless networking dates back at least as far as ALOHANET in 1970. While this project is now of primarily historical interest, the online overview is still worth reading (http://en.wikipedia.org/wiki/ALOHA_network). The concept of ALOHANET spanned many of the core network protocols in use today, including Ethernet and Wireless Fidelity (aka WiFi®). ALOHANET was the precursor of first generation wireless networks.

Wireless technologies may be categorized in a variety of ways depending on their function, frequencies, bandwidth, communication protocols involved, and level of sophistication (i.e., 1st through 3rd generation wireless systems). For present purposes, we'll lump them into four basic categories:

(1) Wireless Data Networks (WDNs),
(2) Personal Area Networks (PANs),
(3) Wireless Local Area Networks (WLANs), of which the newer Wireless Metropolitan Area Networks (WMANs) and Wireless Wide Area Networks (WWANs) are offshoots, and
(4) satellite networks.

WDN is a cluster of technologies primarily related to, developed for, and marketed by vendors in the telephony and handheld market. This market covers a lot of ground from basic digital cellular phones to relatively sophisticated PDAs and tablet PCs that may rival notebook computers in capabilities. WDN includes protocols such as the Cellular Digital Packet Data (CDPD), an older 19.2 Kbps wireless technology that is still in use in some police departments for network communication with patrol cars; General Packet Radio Service (GPRS) and Code Division Multiple Access 2000 (CDMA2000) which are multi-user, combined voice and data 2.5 generation technologies that exceed 100 Kbps; and Wireless Application Protocol (WAP) which provides wireless support of the TCP/IP protocol suite and now provides native support of HTTP and HTML. If you're using a cellular phone with text messaging and Web support, you're likely using some form of WAP.

PANs began as "workspace networks." Bluetooth, for example, is a desktop mobility PAN that was designed to support cable-free communication between computers and peripherals. Blackberry (http://www.blackberry.com) is like Bluetooth on steroids. It integrates telephony, web browsing, email, and messaging services with PDA productivity applications. As such it blurs the distinction between PAN and WLAN.

WLAN is what most of us think of as Wireless technology. It includes the now-ubiquitous 802.11 family of protocols, as well as a few others. Table I provides a quick overview of some of the 802.11 protocol space. Note that all but the first are derivative from the original 802.11 protocol introduced in 1997.

We note in passing that both the 802 and 802.11 landscape is somewhat more cluttered than our table suggests. For example, 802 also allows for infrared support at the physical layer. In addition, proprietary standards for 802.11 have been proposed. In

TABLE I
THE 802.11 PROTOCOL FAMILY

Standard	802.11	802.11a	802.11b	802.11g	802.11n
Year	1997	1999	1999	2003	2006
Frequency	2.4 GHz	5 GHz	2.4 GHz	2.4 GHz	?
Band	ISM	UNII	ISM	ISM	?
Bandwidth	2 Mbps	54 Mbps	11 Mbps	54 Mbps	300+ Mbps
Encoding techniques	DSSS/ FHSS	OFDM	DSSS	OFDM	?

"Year" denotes approximate year of introduction as a standard (e.g., 802.11a and 802.11b were introduced at the same time, though 802.11a came to market later). The two bands used for "WiFi" are Industrial, Scientific and Medical (ISM) and Unlicensed National Information Infrastructure (UNII). Bandwidth is advertised maximum. Encoding, aka "spectrum spreading" techniques appear at the physical or link layer and include frequency-hopping spread-spectrum (HPSS), direct-sequence spread-spectrum (DSSS), and orthogonal frequency division multiplexing (OFDM). (Source: [2].)

2001 Texas Instruments proposed a 22 Mbps variation of 802.11b called "b+," and Atheros proposed a 108 Mbps variant of 802.11g called "Super G." Further, there are standards for enhanced QoS (802.11e) and enhanced security (802.11i) that are actually orthogonal to the traditional 802.11 family in the sense that they deal with limitations rather than the characteristics of the protocol suite. To make comparisons even more confusing, there are 802.1x protocols like 802.16 (2001), 802.16a (2003) that are designed for wider area coverage, the so-called "Metropolitan Area Networks" or MANs. The 802.11n specifications are thin as of this writing, although the current attention is on increasing throughput at the MAC interface rather than the physical layer.

1.1   The WLAN Environment

WLAN offers many advantages: e.g., the ease and reduced expense of not having to run cabling through an existing building, communication between buildings, or just the convenience of not having to find a wall jack to establish a network connection. But this convenience comes at a price. While great care may have been taken through the use of firewalls and intrusion detection systems to secure a network's connection to the outside world, a WLAN creates another entrance into the network that is typically behind the firewall.

Wireless signals cannot be easily confined to their area of intended use. In fact, wireless communications can be monitored and captured from a mile or more away. And this covert monitoring activity is virtually undetectable.

A number of wireless security mechanisms have been introduced to address these problems. The first of these is an encryption and authentication standard called the Wired Equivalent Privacy, or WEP. More recent encryption and authentication protocols include EAP, WPA, and VPNs. Unfortunately, each of these has security vulnerabilities [1].

On a positive note, the 802.11i standard includes the Counter Mode/CBC-MAC Protocol (CCMP). CCMP is based on the Advanced Encryption Standard (AES) and should provide stronger encryption and message integrity than anything available now. Unfortunately, since CCMP will require new hardware that is incompatible with the older WEP-oriented hardware, it will probably be some time before this security mechanism is widely implemented.

It is important to note that nothing that is covered here isn't already understood and put into practice by the hacker and criminal communities. The people in the dark tend to be law-abiding citizens. It is hoped that the information presented here will raise awareness so that the defender stands a chance of protecting his digital assets against WiFi intrusion.

2. Basic Wireless Security

Some mention should be made of some basic wireless features that are often described as security mechanisms even though they are actually ineffective as deterrents.

(1) Disabling the Service Set Identifier (SSID) broadcast, and changing the name of the SSID to something other than the widely known default values. This will only serve to deter the inexperienced or lazy attacker since SSIDs can still be sniffed from association packets.

(2) MAC address filtering. Although MAC-based authentication is not a part of the 802.11 standard, it is a feature on many APs. MAC filtering can be easily bypassed though since the network traffic can be sniffed to determine which MAC addresses are being used. All an attacker has to do at that point is to force a host off of the wireless network (or just wait) and then assume that host's MAC address.

(3) Protocol filtering. Even if implemented on an access point, the range of attack vectors is so large at this point, that there are vulnerabilities that apply to whatever protocols are supported [15].

2.1 Wired Equivalent Privacy (WEP)

WEP is an algorithm that was a part of the original IEEE 802.11 specification with the design goals of preventing disclosure and modification of packets in transit and providing access control for the network. It uses the RC4 algorithm from RSA Security which was first designed in 1987 and kept as a trade secret until it was leaked on a mailing list in 1994. RC4 is a symmetric cipher, i.e., the key that encrypts the traffic is the same key that decrypts the traffic. It is also a stream cipher, meaning that it creates a stream of bits that are XORed with the plaintext (original data) to create the ciphertext (encrypted data). When the data reaches the other end, the same stream of bits is XORed with the ciphertext to retrieve the plaintext. RC4 uses a pseudo-random generation algorithm (PRGA) to create a stream of bits that are computationally difficult for an attacker to discover. This same stream of bits is reproduced at the other end to decrypt the data. Since RC4 is not supposed to be reused with the same key, the WEP designers added an Initialization Vector (IV) which is a value that changes for each packet. The IV is concatenated with the WEP key to form the WEP seed. Figure 1 outlines this process visually.

When a user inputs a key to configure the client wireless card, he or she must configure the same key on the opposite end of the communication (most likely an access point). Users provide either 40-bits or 104-bits of information for the secret

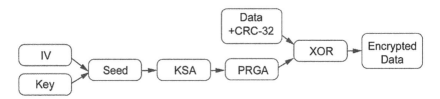

FIG. 1. The WEP encryption process.

key. While manufacturers may claim that the key is 64-bit or 128-bit, only 40 or 104 bits, respectively, are actually used for data. This remaining 24-bits are the IV which is pre-pended to the secret key before it is used in the key scheduling algorithm (KSA). This format is often symbolized by IV.SK, where IV symbolizes the 3 byte (24-bit) Initialization Vector, and SK symbolizes the 5 byte (40-bit) or 13 byte (104-bit) secret key from the user. This composite value is the input to the KSA which converts IV.SK into an initial permutation S of $\{0, \ldots, N-1\}$. The PRGA then uses this permutation to generate a pseudo-random output sequence. The algorithms can be seen in Fig. 2. Note that all additions are made modulo 256.

WEP contains a number of flaws in the implementation of RC4 that allows an attacker to completely compromise the intended security. This potential compromise is so well publicized and so complete, that WEP should never be considered a reliable form of security [3].

KSA(K)	PRGA(K)
Initialization:	Initialization:
$\quad$ for $i = 0 \ldots N-1$	$\quad i = 0$
$\qquad S[i] = i$	$\quad j = 0$
$\quad j = 0$	
	Generation loop:
Scrambling:	$\quad i = i + 1$
$\quad$ For $i = 0 \ldots N-1$	$\quad j = j + S[i]$
$\qquad j = j + S[i] + K[i \bmod l]$	$\quad$ Swap($S[i]$, $S[j]$)
$\qquad$ Swap($S[i]$, $S[j]$)	$\quad$ Output $z = S[S[i] + S[j]]$
Where—	Where—
$\quad N = 256$ (for WEP)	$\quad z$ is the byte used to XOR the
$\quad K[x] = $ value of key (IV.SK) at	plaintext
index x	
$\quad l$ is the length of IV.SK	

FIG. 2. The pseudocode of the Key Scheduling Algorithm and Pseudo-Random Generation Algorithm.

2.2   Brute Force/Dictionary WEP Cracking

The secret key can usually be entered in hex format or ASCII format. Since a number of hexadecimal characters are much harder to remember then half as many ASCII characters, most people will choose a word or phrase that they can easily remember. This might make the key management much easier, but it also facilitates a brute force attack. There are utilities that try to decrypt WEP encrypted packets. decrypt, a utility that comes with AirSnort, is one such tool. It tries a list of words from a wordlist (aka dictionary) against a saved encrypted packet capture. With each possible key, it decrypts a packet using that key and computes a checksum on the newly decrypted data. If the checksum matches the checksum that was transmitted with the packet, a potential secret key has been found. If that same potential key works with another packet, the correct secret key has been revealed.

Brute force cracking requires more time and resources to find the correct key than dictionary attacks. This is the process of trying all possible combinations of values until the correct key is found. With a 40-bit secret key, there are a total of $2^{40} = 1,099,511,627,776$ possible secret keys. If a computer could check 50,000 different secret keys per second, it would take over 250 days to find the correct key. The amount of time that would be required to brute force a 104-bit key is measured in centuries.

The time required to brute force a 40-bit secret key can be brought down to under a minute due to a flaw in the random WEP key generation programs that was discovered by Tim Newsham [11]. Unfortunately, this flaw has been implemented in firmware by many wireless vendors.

These programs are supposed to create a set of random keys based upon ASCII input. The algorithm that is often used by these programs is the Neesus Datacom key generation algorithm. This algorithm takes a string of ASCII characters as input, arranges them in a two dimensional array with four characters in a row, and then XORs all of the column values together in sequence to get a 32-bit output value. The 4 byte (32-bit) output value is then fed through a PRGA which generates the 40-bit secret keys. See Fig. 3 for a visual representation.

Note that the most significant bit of each ASCII character is always zero and therefore the resulting bytes from the XOR operation also have a most significant bit of zero. This, combined with the PRGA algorithm that is used, only produces unique keys for seeds 00:00:00:00 through 00:7F:7F:7F. This greatly reduces the amount of effort required for a brute force attack. To prove this concept, Newsham created the toolkit wep_tools which will brute force keys that have been generated by this type of "random" WEP key generation utility.

A utility called WEPAttack also makes claims to WEP cracking efficiency using both brute-forcing and dictionary attacks against the key. The claim is that only one WEP encrypted data packet is necessary to start the attack. This is possible because

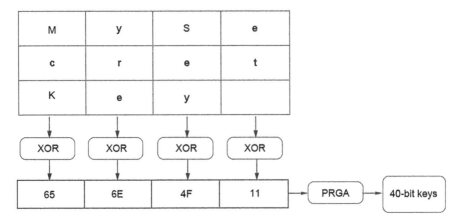

FIG. 3. XOR operation performed by the Neesus DataCom key generation algorithm.

each word in the dictionary is treated as the WEP key. WEPAttack uses the IV that is found in the encrypted data packet and prepends it to the words in the dictionary. This key is used to find the cipherstream which is XORed against the encrypted packet. If the decrypted packet starts with 0xAA (the standard SNAP header value), there is a good chance that the key has been found. More than one encrypted packet should be used for the processes since not all packets start with 0xAA. However, the chance that two packets, picked at random, are neither IP nor ARP (both start with 0xAA) is very unlikely.

2.3   The FMS Attack

The FMS attack is the most well known attack on WEP. It is derived from (and named after) Scott Fluhrer, Itsik Mantin, and Adi Shamir who published their research findings in a 2001 paper entitled "Weaknesses in the Key Scheduling Algorithm of RC4" [5]. The basis for this attack is a weakness in the way RC4 generates the keystream. Specifically:

1. The Initialization Vector (IV) that is always prepended to the key prior to the generation of the keystream by the RC4 algorithm is transmitted in cleartext.
2. The IV is relatively small (three bytes) which results in a lot of repetitions as the relatively small (16.78 million) number of unique IVs are re-used to encrypt of packets.
3. Some of the IVs are "weak" in the sense that they may be used to betray information about the key.

This weakness makes it possible, under certain conditions, to recover the input of RC4 (i.e., the key), knowing its first byte of output. This first byte of output is easy to determine since the first data to be encrypted in a WEP packet is usually the SNAP header (as with IP and ARP packets) and this header is almost always 0xAA.

A weak IV has a format of B+3:FF:X where B is the index of the shared key's byte currently being guessed, FF is 255, and X can be any number between 0 and 255.

Given a weak IV, the first several steps of the RC4 KSA that affect the leftmost positions of the table can be computed. There is then approximately a 5% chance that the remainder of the permutations of the KSA occur in the right part of the table. There is therefore a 5% chance that the portion of the table that was computed is the table that will be the input of the PRGA. Since the value determined for this shared key byte is only accurate 5% of the time, a number of weak IVs (usually about 60) with varying X's have to be used to compute guessed values for that byte. The value that is produced most often has a high probability of being the correct value. This process is then repeated to recover the remaining bytes of the shared key. As a rule of thumb, a few million packets generate enough weak IV traffic to recover 40-bit WEP keys. The attack is linear regardless of the key size so it does not take that much more traffic to recover a 104-bit key. A very good illustrated description of this process can be found in [6].

Since the IEEE standard of IV selection was so ambiguous, many wireless vendors use sequential IV generators that begin with 00:00:00 and wrap with FF:FF:FF. This is the worst of both worlds. Not only is this procedure guaranteed to generate weak IVs, but it does so predictably.

WEPCrack (http://wepcrack.sourceforge.net) was the first publicly released tool to use the FMS attack. Airsnort (http://airsnort.shmoo.com) is much better known and much easier to use. Since modern WiFi cards and appliances reduce the percentage of weak IVs that are generated (under the rubric of "WEP+" or "Advanced WEP Encryption," etc.), Airsnort is declining in importance as it takes an unreasonably long time to collect enough packets to break keys.

2.4   Enhancements to the FMS Attack

Subsequent to the original FMS research, a number of people have discovered that there are more ways that weak IV's can be used to speed up the WEP cracking process. "Using the Fluhrer, Mantin, and Shamir attack to break WEP," Stubblefield et al. [17] discusses an approach that deviates from the standard FMS algorithm methodology of finding all the previous values for B before finding the next value. The authors suggest that weak IVs associated with higher B values can be used to narrow down the beginning bytes of the secret key. This can be done by testing different values of the key and checking to see if the decrypted packet has a valid checksum. This can be facilitated by making assumptions about the range of possible values for a WEP key (users will often use ASCII characters).

Another whitepaper, written by David Hulton, "Practical Exploitation of RC4 Weaknesses in WEP environments" [7] describes a number of alternate approaches for expanding the FMS concepts including additional methods of finding weak IVs for secret key bytes beyond the first. Hulton claims it would be best to devise an algorithm which can determine whether or not a particular IV can be considered weak. His algorithm (implemented in a utility called dwepcrack) is shown in Fig. 4:

Using this algorithm, the search time for a weak IV is roughly 1/20 of the time it would take using the unmodified FMS algorithm. Notice that the line of code that is bolded tests to see whether the first byte of the IV is the byte of the secret key that is currently trying to be determined and whether the second byte of the IV is 255. Hulton includes a number of other tests to determine weak IVs resulting in a shorter cracking time and an overall smaller number of packets that need to be captured.

```
x = iv[0];
y = iv[1];
z = iv[2];

a = (x + y) % N;
b = AMOD((x + y) - z, N);

for(B = 0; B < WEP_KEY_SIZE; B++)
{
  /*
   * test to see if this key would apply to any of the bytes that
   * we're trying to crack.
   */
  if((((0 <= a && a < B) ||
    (a == B && b == (B + 1) * 2)) &&
    (B % 2 ? a != (B + 1) / 2 : 1)) ||
    (a == B + 1 && (B == 0 ? b == (B + 1) * 2 : 1)) ||
    (x == B + 3 && y == N - 1) ||
    (B != 0 && !(B % 2) ? (x == 1 && y == (B / 2) + 1) ||
    (x == (B / 2) + 2 && y == (N - 1) - x) : 0))
  {
    // It is a Weak IV
  }
}
```

FIG. 4. Dwepcrack's algorithm for determining weak IV's.

While these additions to WEP cracking algorithms can help to lower the time necessary to compromise a complete WEP key, they have not been widely implemented. This could be due to the overall low percentage of WEP enabled devices that are currently being implemented, or to the popularity of current WEP cracking utilities. These methods will most likely become more popular as newer devices avoid the usage of more commonly known weak IVs.

In August 2004, a hacker named KoreK published code in the NetStumbler forums that outlined expansions to the FMS attacks. These attacks have been implemented in both aircrack and WEPLab, both of which claim to crack WEP in record time. Essentially, these attacks work much like the FMS attack. The KSA is run as far as possible while looking at the values of the S array and the known keystream. Depending on the values that are found, the key bytes can be extracted. Appendix B contains KoreK's original code with comments added by the authors. Since the publication of this code on NetStumbler forums, KoreK has released a utility called chopper which expands upon this concept.

KoreK has since released another program called chopchop. This program exploits WEP in a different way to decrypt single packets. When an encrypted packet is captured, it can be decrypted one byte at a time by making a slight modification and attempting to retransmit it. The attacker will remove the last byte of the encrypted packet and replace it with a guess. To test to see if the guess was correct or not, the packet is sent to the access point. If the access point accepts the message and rebroadcasts it, the attacker can be sure that the guess was correct. The attacker can then use this byte and the corresponding cipherbyte to find the plaintext byte. Since there are only 256 choices for each byte, the packet can be decrypted in a relatively short period of time.

2.5   Injecting Packets for Faster WEP Cracking

The WEP cracking processes discussed so far require the capture of a large number of WEP encrypted data packets. For large wireless networks this requirement is easily met because of the large volume of traffic. However, there are other networks where the volume of traffic is not sufficient to allow the capture of enough packets in a reasonable period of time. It is possible to generate the necessary traffic on these networks by injecting packets to solicit responses. These packets do nothing to help the breaking of WEP, but the responses from a legitimate device on the network will increase the probability of generating weak initialization vectors. Some utilities like reinj and aireplay (part of the aircrack package) do this by capturing ARP requests. It then turns the packet around and injects it back into the network. Since the access point can't tell the difference between the injected packet and the original, the ARP request and response will give the attacker two more packets to work with. Other utilities (WEPWedgie; see Section 2.6) will use ICMP echo requests to a broadcast address. This could generate echo replies from hosts on the network using a possible weak initialization vector. It is also possible to use this approach with other types of packets (TCP RSTs, TCP SYN/ACKs, etc.) [4].

These utilities allow a remote attacker the ability to create traffic on parsimonious networks. Home wireless networks and small offices often are included in this category. No longer can security professionals claim wireless networks of this size "secure" due to the amount of traffic. If the traffic does not naturally exist, an attacker can create it.

2.6   Encrypted Packet Injection

WEP does not have an effective mechanism to ensure data integrity. It does use a cyclic redundancy check (CRC) which is calculated for the data that is sent over the network. This verifies that a packet has not become corrupt during transmission but it does not protect data integrity.

When a packet is sent, its CRC is calculated from the plaintext. The output of the CRC32 algorithm is a 4 byte value which is called the integrity check value (ICV). The ICV is appended to the plaintext and encrypted using the WEP algorithm. The ICV is run again against the data after it has been decrypted by the receiver. If the ICV value that was sent in the packet matches the value that was calculated by the receiver, then the packet is considered legitimate. However, due to the nature of WEP and stream ciphers, it's possible to create an encrypted packet with a correct ICV, without knowing the actual WEP key. The attacker must only determine the ciphertext and plaintext combination for data that is sent with a particular Initialization Vector (IV).

The attacker first takes a legitimate known plaintext and known ciphertext combination and XORs the two values together to recover the keystream that was used to encrypt the plaintext. This same keystream is used for all packets that are sent over the wireless network with the same Initialization Vector and secret WEP key. Since it is unlikely that the WEP key will be changed in a reasonable amount of time, the keystream will be the same for all packets using the same IV.

That keystream value is then XORed with the plaintext and ICV that the attacker wishes to inject into the datastream. The resulting value is an encrypted packet to be prepended with that same IV and injected on the network. This technique is called PRGA Injection. An attacker can use a number of mechanisms to recover an encrypted packet and its corresponding plaintext value.

Tools have been created that perform injection attacks on WEP encrypted networks. reinj was a tool created for BSD that finds what it considers to be a TCP ACK packet or an ARP request and sends it back onto the network. While this is technically the injection of encrypted packets onto a wireless network, it doesn't provide the attacker with the capability to customize the data. Another utility, WEP-Wedgie listens for WEP encrypted packets that are generated during a shared key authentication. This happens when a client wishes to connect to an access point. The access point will send the client a nonce which the client encrypts using the WEP key. This encrypted value is sent back to the access point for verification. If the value that the access point gets when it encrypts the nonce is the same as the value that the client returns, access is granted. This process provides a plaintext value and the corresponding ciphertext that is needed. WEPWedgie can now inject packets into a wireless network.

This attack can be expanded for even more malicious purposes. Once attackers gain the ability to inject packets into the wireless network, they can open connections to the internal servers, even if they are isolated by firewalls. The attacker will inject a packet into the wireless network asking for a connection to the server. This amounts to a TCP SYN packet with the source address of a computer that the attacker controls. The packet will be accepted into the network and sent to the unsuspecting server. The server will then do its part in opening the connection and send the attacker machine a TCP SYN/ACK packet. Assuming that the server can send a packet onto the Internet, it will send the packet through the firewall, onto the Internet and to the attacker's machine. The attacker's machine will then finish the 3-way handshake and a connection will be established. This approach can also be used to do port scans against the internal machines, do internal network mapping, etc. Being able to inject packets into a wireless network is an extremely powerful and dangerous tool.

2.7   802.1x Authentication

802.1x is a port authentication protocol that was originally created for wired networks. Switches, for example, can use 802.1x to authenticate a device before it allows the device access to a port. Once the authentication process has been successfully completed, access is granted to the device. There are three main components to the 802.1x authentication process: the supplicant, the authentication server, and the authenticator. The supplicant is the computer or device that wishes to have access on the network. The authentication server is the computer that performs the authentication. One of the most common types of servers that perform this task is a RADIUS server. The authenticator is the device that sits between the supplicant and the authentication server. In the example above, the authenticator is the switch. It is the point of access for the supplicant (Fig. 5).

Notice that there is two different sessions in Fig. 5. The supplicant starts the process by attempting to access the network resources. This triggers a request by

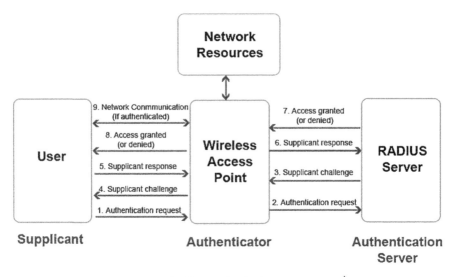

FIG. 5. 802.1x authentication process.

the authenticator for information about the identity of the supplicant. The supplicant provides this information and the authenticator forwards it to the authentication server. The authentication server then processes this information and usually sends a challenge to the supplicant through the authenticator. This challenge could be a nonce which needs to be encrypted or it could be some kind of token. The actual authentication mechanism is flexible and can vary between implementations. This is also the place where attacks can occur. When the supplicant responds to the challenge, the authenticator forwards this information on to the authentication server for processing. The authentication server then determines whether or not the supplicant should be granted access [16].

Although this process was originally developed for wired networks, it has been adopted by the 802.11i committee for use in wireless applications. In a wireless environment, the supplicant is a wireless client wishing to connect to the wireless network. The authentication server can still be a RADIUS server, but the authenticator is usually a wireless access point. Since one of the problems with WEP is key management, 802.1x can be very useful in a WEP environment. Any time a single key is used for an entire network, there will be security and scalability issues. The central server can provide clients with different keys, and even require a key change after a preset amount of time or data transmission. In a wireless environment, this is especially beneficial because it can change the secret key used by WEP and give different keys to clients [8].

2.8   EAP-LEAP Attack

802.1x uses a number of protocols to accomplish its goal of providing further security for wireless networks. The communication between the authentication server and the authenticator is logically separate from the communication between the authenticator and the supplicant. Extensible Authentication Protocol (EAP) is usually used for the authenticator/supplicant communication. EAP was created for point-to-point (PPP) authentication but has been adopted for use with wireless. EAP itself does not determine what method will be used to authenticate the supplicant, rather it allows the use of a server to facilitate the actual authentication. EAP-LEAP is one of the most popular types of EAP that is used today. It was developed by Cisco and has been implemented in a number of open-source RADIUS solutions [13].

EAP-LEAP is fundamentally flawed due to it's usage of MS-CHAPv2. This algorithm, and specifically the way that it was implemented in EAP-LEAP, allows an offline attack to be used to determine the password. When the usage of EAP-LEAP has been agreed upon, the authentication server sends the supplicant (by way of the authenticator) a nonce, or challenge text. Specifically it is an 8-byte random stream which the supplicant must encrypt. To encrypt the challenge text, the password is hashed using an NT hash and split up to generate three separate keys. The first key consists of the first seven bytes of the hashed password, the second key is the second seven bytes of the hashed password, and the third key is the final two bytes followed by five NULL values. These three keys are each used to encrypt the 8 byte challenge text. The three 8 byte results are then concatenated into one 24-byte value and this value is sent back to the authentication server for verification. Since EAP-LEAP supports mutual authentication, the process can be repeated in the opposite direction to authenticate the authentication server with the supplicant.

The problem with EAP-LEAP is that NT hashing does not use "salt." That means that the same plaintext value will hash to the same hashed value. So an attacker can hash a dictionary of plaintext passwords and store the corresponding hash values. If the password is one of the dictionary words, the hashes will match. Since the third hashed value that is used as a key to encrypt the 8 byte challenge consists of five null values, there is really only 2^{16} different possible values for the key. With so few possibilities, the two bytes can be found in less than a second. At this point, the last two NT hashed bytes of the password have been recovered. Using the precompiled dictionary, the attacker finds all hashed passwords where the last two bytes match what has been found. This usually narrows down the possible passwords to a number that can be brute forced against the authentication server. Now the attacker can achieve access to the wireless network.

There are a number of utilities that can perform this attack, the most famous of which is asleap, developed by Joshua Wright. Leapcrack and leap are two other utilities which help an attacker perform this attack against EAP-LEAP authentication [19].

2.9 EAP-MD5 Attack

EAP requires that EAP-MD5 be implemented to serve as a fallback authentication mechanism. It has a number of vulnerabilities including susceptibility to man-in-the-middle attacks, lack of dynamic key distribution, and the plaintext/ciphertext combination. The EAP-MD5 process is somewhat similar to EAP-LEAP. The authentication server sends a challenge to the supplicant that is then hashed using MD5 and the password. That hashed value is sent back to the authentication server. This hashed value is then compared to the server's hash of the challenge text and if they are equivalent, access is granted.

Since the authentication process happens in only one direction, a man-in-the-middle attack can be performed against the authenticator. All that is required is a fake access point with authentication server software installed. When a supplicant requires access, it contacts the rogue AP instead of the authentic AP.

3. WPA Background and Introduction

Since there have been so many vulnerabilities discovered in WEP, an 802.11i standard committee was formed to find a new method of securing wireless communication. As the development of the standard progressed, some parts were ready to be deployed and other parts were not. In 2002, the Wi-Fi Alliance decided to deploy the parts that were deemed ready to help alleviate some of the security problems that existed. The parts that were released were named Wireless Protected Access (WPA). WPA still uses the WEP algorithm, but it adds a stronger integrity checking algorithm and better key management as in 802.1x. It can be implemented with a centralized authentication server or using pre-shared keys (PSK), like WEP. WPA offers two things of value: Temporal Key Integrity Protocol (TKIP) and 802.1x. TKIP is the encryption algorithm that was created to provide more security than WEP. It is essentially a shell that was placed around the WEP RC4 algorithm to address the following weaknesses: replay attacks, forgery attacks, key collision attacks, and weak key attacks. It does this by improving the integrity checking function, adding initialization vector sequencing rules, and creating a per-packet key.

TKIP uses a master key (MK) which is either distributed using 802.1x or as the PSK to derive a pairwise master key (PMK). In turn, the PMK is used to derive four more keys. These four keys are used during various parts of the encryption. One of the keys is called the temporal key (TK), which is primarily used for the encryption of data that is sent over the wireless link. The TK is XORed with the sender's MAC

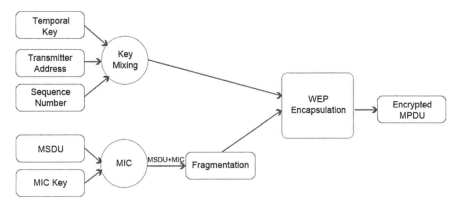

FIG. 6. Graphical diagram of TKIP Encapsulation. Note: MSDU is the MAC Service Data Unit and MPDU is the MAC Protocol Data Unit.

address, which is then mixed with a sequence number to produce a key that is used as input to the previous WEP algorithm. By adding all the extra steps the key is now much more secure against attack because it now depends on time and the sender's MAC address. TKIP also uses a sequence counter to prevent replay attacks and a Message Integrity Check (called MIC or Michael) to prevent message modification. Along with the sequence number, the source and destination addresses are added. Michael is also a one-way hash function rather than a simple linear CRC. This adds security to the algorithm because integrity verification is extremely difficult to forge. Figure 6 provides a graphical representation of TKIP [13,18].

More recently, the Wi-Fi alliance has announced the ratification of WPA2 which completely stops the use of WEP as an underlying protocol. Instead it uses the much stronger AES algorithm. As of this writing, WPA2 using AES does not share the same vulnerabilities as the original WPA.

3.1   The WPA-PSK Attack

There are two primary ways that TKIP can be used. The more secure way is to use 802.1x to distribute the keys and keep track of key management. The other way is to provide the client and access point with the same pre-shared key which is used as the pairwise master key (PMK) in the TKIP process. Although this shares many of the key management problems that WEP had, it does offer some "security through obscurity." One of the problems with TKIP is that if an attacker can determine what the PMK is for any one of the wireless clients, he or she can gain access to the network.

Researcher Robert Moskowitz discovered a problem with the WPA-PSK implementation when short passphrases are chosen [10]. When a pre-shared key is used, it is hashed with the SSID and the SSID length to create a 256-bit PMK. This key is then used to derive all the other keys that are used in the TKIP algorithm. The pre-shared key is appended with the SSID and the SSID length which are then fed into the hashing algorithm defined by the PKCS #5 v2.0: Password-based Cryptography Standard. The string is hashed a total of 4096 times to create a 256-bit Pairwise Transient Key (PTK) that is used to derive all the other keys used in the algorithm. Moskowitz states that the 802.11i standard declares that there are approximately 2.5 bits of security per PSK character. The formula becomes: $2.5n + 12$ bits = Security Strength in bits, where n is the number of characters in the pre-shared key. This means that a typical password of 10 characters will only provide 37 bits of security. Because of this, Moskowitz claims, a dictionary attack on the hash can be performed to recover the password.

Recently a utility called coWPAtty has been released which uses a hash comparison based attack to recover the pre-shared key. coWPAtty captures the four way handshake authentication packets that are sent between the access point and the client. In these packets, coWPAtty finds the SSID of the network, the addresses of the access point and the client, and the nonces sent between the two parties. The SSID information and the passphrase from the dictionary are used to find a PMK. Using the other information from the exchange, the PTK is found. Using the PTK, the attacker can try to decrypt a message and see if the integrity check value found in the packet matches the calculated value. If so, the passphrase has been found. If not, the next passphrase in the dictionary is tried.

4.   Other Attack Modes

4.1   VPNs: Point-to-Point Tunneling Protocol

A Virtual Private Network (VPN) allows an apparent "private" connection between two remote computers or networks. This is achieved by encrypting the traffic together with some sort of authentication. VPNs can be used by small office/home office users as well as large corporations.

Several standards have been developed to implement VPNs. One of these is the Point-to-Point Tunneling protocol (PPTP). This protocol allows a remote user to connect to another network using a VPN and it assures, or at least tries to assure, that the network that has been created is private. PPTP was created as an extension to point-to-point protocol (PPP) where dial-up users could connect to their Internet service provider (ISP) and then create a secure connection to the VPN server. Since it was pioneered by Microsoft, among others, PPTP is relatively simple to configure on Windows hosts and servers. As a result, a large number of VPN networks supporting PPTP are Windows networks. Like most other VPN protocols, PPTP employs authentication and encryption.

Wireless networking has adopted VPN protocols to add encryption and authentication security to its communications. Since WEP has been completely compromised and WPA has only recently been released as an upgrade to wireless devices, networks had to come up with another way to provide security. VPN's helped to fill this gap. Legitimate clients could be configured to connect to the wired network through a virtual private network which would encrypt the data that was being transferred. In this manner, wireless sniffers would only be able to capture encrypted data, which would then need to be decrypted before it became useful. Furthermore, the authentication process would help to shut out those people wishing to connect with the wireless network without legitimate access credentials [12].

Microsoft's original PPTP specified the use of Microsoft Challenge Handshake Authentication Protocol (MS-CHAP) for authentication. The design allowed someone to connect to a server, receive authentication based upon a password and gain access to the network resources. When a client connects to the network, it asks the authentication server for a login challenge. The server responds by sending the requesting client an 8 byte challenge nonce. The client then uses the LAN manager hash of the password that it has stored to derive three DES (Data Encryption Standard) keys. These keys are used to encrypt the challenge that the server sent. Each encryption results in an 8 byte encrypted string. All three encrypted strings are then concatenated to create a 24-bit reply. This same process is repeated with the Windows NT hash of the password. These two 24-bit blocks are sent to the server where they are compared. The server uses the stored client's password to decrypt the replies. If the decrypted blocks match the original challenge, access is granted. This process was used in the PPTP until vulnerabilities were found that compromise the authentication process. When these vulnerabilities became widely known, Microsoft re-worked the process and implemented a new version of MS-CHAP which was supposed to fix the problems that had been discovered.

MS-CHAP version 2, as it became known, added security to the process in the following ways: it stopped the use of the LM (LAN Manager) hash, introduced mutual authentication, replaced change password packets, and updated the encryption keys. To do this, it added a number of steps to the authentication process. When the client machine asks for a challenge, the server responds with a challenge of 16 bytes. The client then comes up with a 16-byte challenge itself which is called the "Peer Authenticator Challenge." The client then uses SHA-1 to hash the concatenation of the challenge from the server, the Peer Authenticator Challenge and the client's username. The first 8 bytes of the result then become the 8-byte challenge. Much like its predecessor, the 8 bytes are encrypted with the Windows NT hashed value of the password. This generates a 24-byte reply that is sent to the server where it is compared. To provide mutual authentication, the Peer Authenticator Challenge is sent to the server, where the server concatenates it with the 24-byte response from the client and the string "magic server to client constant." This value is hashed using SHA to generate a 20-byte result that is then concatenated with the original challenge that was sent to the client and the afore-mentioned string padded, if necessary, to force more than one iteration and then hashed once again with SHA. This value is sent back to the client where it can be verified. If all values match, the session has been authenticated. While MS-CHAPv2 is much more complicated than MS-CHAPv1, it does very little to add to the security [14].

4.2   Attacks on PPTP

The attacks on PPTP are predominately attacks on the MS-CHAP authentication. As mentioned above, this is easier to do with the older version of MS-CHAP. In this version, a number of attacks were possible. One of the attacks involved spoofing a message from the server telling the client to change his or her password. If the client did change the active password, the password hashes could be picked up and cracked using a program such as L0phtcrack (http://www.insecure.org/sploits/l0phtcrack.lanman.problems.html). It was also possible for password cracking utilities, like L0phtcrack, to take advantage of the fact that the LM hash was being sent along with the NT hash. The LM hash is extremely easy to break and then could then be used to crack the NT hash and recover the password. With the password, an attacker could completely spoof the authentication process. Utilities such as anger (http://www.securiteam.com/windowsntfocus/2TUQBR5SAW.html) perform the attack on MS-CHAPv1 enabled PPTP VPNs. It collects the challenge and response packets that are exchanged for use in a cracking utility and it also provides the active attack using the change password messages.

In MS-CHAPv2, the change password message was altered to eliminate the vulnerabilities that tools like anger took advantage of. Since the LM hash is no longer sent along with the NT hash, it is more difficult to break. That is not to say that it is secure. The attack that can be performed on MS-CHAPv2 is described in the "EAP-LEAP" section. Ettercap (http://ettercap.sourceforge.net) is another utility that can be used to exploit weaknesses in PPTP. It has a number of plugins which automate the process of recovering passwords from PPTP MS-CHAP authentication.

4.3   Denial-of-Service Background and Attacks

Denial of service (DoS) and distributed denial of service (DDoS) attacks can render networks useless and are some of the hardest attacks to thwart. Though computers and networks have become faster and more reliable, they still have practical limits.

All available network bandwidth may be easily consumed by DoS and DDoS attacks, whether the network is wired or wireless.

The network clients count on the ability to access network resources. It is generally easier to perform a DoS attack on a wireless network than it is on a wired one. 802.11 networks broadcast data over a limited range of radio frequencies. All wireless networks within range compete for those frequencies. Attackers can take advantage of this fact by creating signals which saturate the network resources. This can be done with a powerful transmitter that broadcasts interfering signals or by low-tech approaches to RF-jamming like placing metal objects in microwaves that use the same frequency.

Other attacks can be performed at the link layer with disassociation and de-authentication frames that control the communication. If such frames were spoofed, connections could be manipulated without consent. Programs such as FakeAP (http://www.blackalchemy.to/project/fakeap), Void11 (http://forum.defcon.org/showthread.php?t=1427), and File2air (http://sourceforge.net/mailarchive/forum.php?thread_id=3164707&forum_id=34085) perform such attacks.

One strategy would be to send an authentication frame with an unrecognizable format which would cause the client to become unauthenticated because the access point would be confused. This attack has been implemented in the tool fata_jack (http://www.networkchemistry.com/news/whitepaper.pdf) which is meant to be used with AirJack (http://sourceforge.net/projects/airjack/). It sends an authentication frame to the access point with the sequence number and the status code both set to 0xFFFF. This frame is spoofed so that the access point believes it comes from a node that has already connected. This results in a fractured connection. If this attack is repeated, the real client will no longer have the ability to connect to the access point.

When a wireless client associates and authenticates with the access point, the access point must store information about the client in an internal state table. This includes the client's MAC address, IP address, etc. Since the memory of the access point is finite, it is possible to fake enough connections that the state table overflows. Depending on the access point, this could produce a crash or lock-up thereby blocking legitimate future authentications. Either way the attacker has successfully terminated the wireless connection. Joshua Wright wrote a Perl script called macfld.pl (http://home.jwu.edu/jwright/perl.htm) that will perform this attack. It works by flooding the access point with a large number of MAC addresses. Before WPA was implemented, the way that 802.11 checked the integrity of the packets that were received was through the CRC. If the CRC didn't match the value that was calculated by the wireless device, the packet was dropped. If, on the other hand, the packet was received correctly, an acknowledgement frame was sent so the sender could delete the transmitted frame from its send queue. This can be exploited by corrupting a frame as it was transmitted so that the receiver would drop it. The attacker could then spoof an acknowledgement from the receiver saying that the frame was successfully received. The sender would then delete it from the queue and the frame would disappear from the datastream.

While DoS attacks don't allow an attacker to steal data or get access to the network, it does create significant chaos to the network resources. It is very difficult to stop and has disastrous consequences on affected networks.

4.4 Man-In-The-Middle Attacks

An effective man-in-the-middle (MITM) attack is one in which the attacker positions him/herself between the victim and the device with which the victim is trying to communicate. In this capacity, the attacker can control the information between the two devices. All traffic is re-routed through the attacker's computer where it can be manipulated or simply inspected. The attacker can then gather login information such as keys and passwords. In a wireless environment, the situation is more threatening because information that is transmitted over a wireless network is by definition available to all who have the ability to translate the RF signals to data. This might involve the injection of malicious code into the datastream to further compromise of the network and network nodes.

In the infrastructure mode of wireless networking, clients or stations all connect to central access points. One MITM strategy is to spoof an access point by de-authenticating and disassociating a client, neutralizing the AP with a DoS, and then re-authenticating the client with a clone under the control of the attacker. A number of MITM attack tools are widely available. Quite often the setup consists of a software access point and DoS software. An attacker's computer would usually have two separate wireless cards to handle both jamming and cloning functions. Some of the software access point programs that are available are: HostAP (http://hostap.epitest.fi) and HermesAP (http://hunz.org/hermesap.html).

5. Conclusion

It has been said that Wireless Networks will never be secure as long as radio frequencies fail to observe property lines. The validity of this claim lies in the fact that the physical security of the communication technology is for all intents and purposes absent in wireless environments (cf. also [9]). Though the physical security of a building is not a fault-proof barrier, it is at least a practical one. Wireless technology, even if properly configured, is not even a practical barrier. Even the most risk-averse can "sniff" transmissions with little chance of detection by using free software that is easily found on the Internet. The plain truth is that wireless technology encourages digital eavesdropping. The World Wide Wardrive (http://www.worldwidewardrive.org) and Wigle (http://www.wigle.net) Websites are obvious illustrations. Wigle maintains a database of nearly four million active wireless networks in its online database. The World Wide Wardrives are network discovery contests.

In this chapter we have sought to identify some of the wireless insecurities that loom largest in today's increasingly wireless world. To the inattentive, the deployment of wireless can create the loss of trade secrets, the loss of personal privacy, theft of services, and unwitting participation in information warfare. For the attentive, the watch phrase must be "danger lurks within."

Appendix A: Wireless Security Utilities by Operating System and Function

Utility name	OS	Use
WEPcrack	Any platform (if Perl is available)	Finding WEP keys
AirSnort	Linux, Windows	Finding WEP keys
dwepcrack	BSD	Finding WEP keys
reinj	BSD	Packet Injection tool
WEPWedgie	Linux	Packet Injection tool
wep_tools	Linux	Finding WEP keys
asleap	Linux, Windows	Finding LEAP passwords
Leapcrack	Any platform (if Perl is available)	Finding LEAP passwords
leap	Linux	Finding LEAP passwords
L0phtcrack	Windows	Password cracking
ettercap	Linux	
fata_jack	Linux	Denial of service
macfld.pl	Linux	Denial of service
dinject	Linux	Denial of service
airjack	Linux	Drivers for MITM, DoS, etc.
File2air	Linux	Denial of service
Void11	Linux	Denial of service
omerta	Linux	Denial of service
HostAP	Linux	Software Access Point
HermesAP patch	Linux	Software Access Point
WPA Cracker	Linux	WPA-PSK password cracking
FakeAP	Linux, BSD	Random AP frame generation
WepAttack	Linux	Enhanced WEP cracking
aircrack	Linux	Enhanced WEP cracking
chopchop	Linux	Packet by packet decryption
chopper	Linux	POC WEP cracker
coWPAtty	Linux	WPA cracker

Appendix B: KoreK's New WEP Cracking Code

```
/*
    This code was written by KoreK and published on the
NetStumbler.org forums
    (http://www.netstumbler.org/showthread.php?t=11869)
*/


/* This code runs the KSA algorithm */
for (i=0; i<256; i++) S[i]=i;     /* initialize the S[]
                                   array */
for (i=0,j=0; i<p; i++)           /* run the loop until the
                                   unknown byte */
{
    j=(j+K[i & 0x0f]+S[i]) & 0xff;
    swap(S+i,S+j);
}
/* at this point, the attacks can be run. Depending on how
the weak IVs setup the S[] array, we can extract
information about the unknown key byte */
/* Original FMS attack which has a 5% chance of working */
if ((S[1] < p) && ((S[1]+S[S[1]]) == p))
{
  jp=o1; /* o1 is the first byte of the keystream (z) */
  stat1[(jp-j-S[p]) & 0xff]++; /* extract the info and
                                keep track of it */
}

/* The following attacks were developed by KoreK and work
in much the same way.
    That is, depending on how the S[] is setup, the values
give away information about the unknown key byte.
*/

/* Second type of attack -- 13% chance of working */
if (S[1] == p) /* S[1] is equal to the byte location we're
            looking for */
 {
   for (jp=0; S[jp]!=0; jp++); /* find the first index, i,
                                where S[i] isn't 0 */
       if (o1 == p) /* if the unknown key byte is the same
                     as the first byte of the cipher (z) */
          {
          stat2[(jp-j-S[p]) & 0xff]++; /* extract the info and
                                        keep track of it */
          }
       // for statistical purposes
       pstat2[(jp-j-S[p]) & 0xff]++;
```

```
   }
   /* A third attack -- This one works if the second byte of
   the cipher (z) is 0, the value of the S[] array at
   location p (the unknown key byte were looking for) is 0,
      and the third (index=2) element of the S[] array isn't
   zero */
      if ((o2 == 0) && (S[p] == 0) && (S[2] != 0))
         {
           stat3[(2-j-S[p]) & 0xff]++;   /* extract the info and
                                          keep track of it */
         }
   // and two more (well there are still about 10 of 'em left:)
   /* The next two start with the same requirements. The
second element (index=1) of S[] must be greater than the
value of the unknown key byte we're searching for and
      the second (index=1) element of S[] plus the third
(index=2) minus the value of p (the unknown key byte
we're searching for) must be zero
   */
   if ((S[1] > p) && (((S[2]+S[1]-p) & 0xff) == 0))
     {
     /* once this condition is met, one of two more
   conditions are needed to qualify */
     /* The first is the second byte of the keystream (z)
   should be equal to S[1] */
      if (o2 == S[1])
         {
       /* Now find the first value in the S[] array that
   doesn't have a value
         of S[1] - S[2]. Save that index
       */
       for (jp=0; S[jp] != ((S[1]-S[2]) & 0xff); jp++);
         /* As long as that index isn't 1 or 2, we can do an
   extraction and save it */
         if ((jp!=1) && (jp!=2)) stat4[(jp-j-S[p]) & 0xff]++;
         }
      else
         {
       /* The other option is to see if the second byte of
   the keystream (z) is
         equal to 2 minus the third value in the S[] array
   (index=2)
       */
       if (o2 == ((2-S[2]) & 0xff))
         {
           /* Find the first index of the S[] array where
         the value isn't the same as the second byte of
         the keystream (z)*/
```

```
        for (jp=0; S[jp] != o2; jp++);
        /* As long as that index isn't 1 or 2, extract
      the byte and save it */
        if ((jp!=1) && (jp!=2)) stat5[(jp-j-S[p]) & 0xff]++;
        }
      }
    }
    // inverted attack
    /* This attack is useful in determining false positives. As
      the byte values get placed in the stat6[] bin, there is
      a chance that that value is not correct. KoreK placed a
    threshold on this at 32. If any byte appears in
    the stat6[] bin more than 32 times, it must not be the right
    value. These tests are pretty straight forward. Just
    remember that o1 is the first byte of the keystream.
    */
    if (S[2] == 0)
      {
      if ((S[1] == 2) && (o1 == 2))
        {
        stat6[(1-j-S[p]) & 0xff]++;
        stat6[(2-j-S[p]) & 0xff]++;
        }
      else if (o2==0)
        {
        stat6[(2-j-S[p]) & 0xff]++;
        }
}
if ((S[1] == 1) && (o1 == S[2]))
  {
    stat6[(1-j-S[p]) & 0xff]++;
    stat6[(2-j-S[p]) & 0xff]++;
  }
if ((S[1] == 0) && (S[0] == 1) && (o1 == 1))
  {
    stat6[(-j-S[p]) & 0xff]++;
    stat6[(1-j-S[p]) & 0xff]++;
  }
```

REFERENCES

[1] Barkin L., *How Secure is Your Wireless Network?*, Prentice Hall PTR, Upper Saddle River, 2004.

[2] Berghel H., "Wireless infidelity I: War driving", *Commun. ACM* **47** (9) (2004) 21–26.

[3] Berghel H., Uecker J., "Wireless infidelity II: Air jacking", *Commun. ACM* **47** (12) (2004) 20–25.

[4] Berghel H., Uecker J., "WiFi attack vectors", *Commun. ACM* **48** (8) (2005) 21–27.

[5] Fluhrer S., Mantin I., Shamir A., "Weakness in the key scheduling algorithm of RC4", http://www.cs.umd.edu/~waa/class-pubs/rc4_ksaproc.ps, 2001.

[6] Giller R., Bulliard A., *Wired Equivalent Privacy*, Swiss Institute of Technology, Lausanne, 2004.

[7] Hulton D., "Practical exploitation of RC4 weaknesses in WEP environments", http://www.dachb0den.com/projects/bsd-airtools/wepexp.txt, 22 Feb. 2002.

[8] Meetinghouse Data Communications, "802.1X—still evolving as a standard", http://www.mtghouse.com/8021X.pdf, 28 Aug. 2004.

[9] Mikhailovsky A., Gavrilenko K., Vladimirov A., *Wi-Foo: The Secrets of Wireless Hacking*, Addison–Wesley, Boston, 2004.

[10] Moskowitz R., "Weakness in passphrase choice in WPA interface", http://wifinetnews.com/archives/002452.html, 04 Nov. 2003.

[11] Newsham T., "Cracking WEP keys", Presentation: Black Hat, 2001, http://www.blackhat.com/presentations/bh-usa-01/TimNewsham/bh-usa-01-Tim-Newsham.ppt.

[12] Peikari C., Fogie S., *Maximum Wireless Security*, Sams Publishing, Indianapolis, 2002.

[13] Sankar S., Sundaralingam S., Balinsky A., Miller D., *Cisco Wireless LAN Security*, Cisco Press, Indianapolis, 2005.

[14] Schneier B., Mudge, "Cryptanalysis of Microsoft's PPTP authentication extensions (MS-CHAPv2)", http://www.schneier.com/paper-pptpv2.html, 19 Oct. 1999.

[15] Stevens R.W., *TCP/IP Illustrated*, vol. 1, Addison–Wesley, Boston, 1994.

[16] Strand L., "802.1X port-based authentication HOWTO", http://ldp.hughesjr.com/HOWTO/8021X-HOWTO/intro.html, 18 Oct. 2004.

[17] Stubblefield A., Ioannidis J., Rubin A.D., "Using the Fluhrer, Mantin, and Shamir attack to break WEP", http://www.isoc.org/isoc/conferences/ndss/02/proceedings/papers/stubbl.pdf.

[18] Vladimirov A., Gavrilenko K., Mikhailovsky A., *Wi-Foo*, Addison–Wesley, Boston, 2004.

[19] Wright J., "Weaknesses in LEAP challenge/response", Presentation: Defcon, 2003, http://asleap.sourceforge.net/asleap-defcon.pdf.

The State of the Art in Digital Forensics

DARIO FORTE

CISM, CFE,
University of Milano at Crema
Italy

Abstract

We are in an historical moment where computing is part of the social life. It does mean that computers are also part of crimes, both physical and virtual. In this an idea of the state of the art of the digital forensic will be provided, with special emphasis on UNIX operating systems and log file management. Included will also be an overview of current scientific research on the topic and illustrations of a number of potential issues that are often the subject of discussions in courtrooms the world over.

ADVANCES IN COMPUTERS, VOL. 67
ISSN: 0065-2458/DOI 10.1016/S0065-2458(05)67006-4

253

1. Introduction

We find ourselves at a juncture where interest in digital forensics is skyrocketing. This is essentially due to a series of high profile court cases and the enactment of some quite important legislation (such as the Sarbanes-Oxley Act) that are bringing digital forensics into mainstream and obligatory use. It has become a crucial tool for coping with the continual changes in the nature of the objects of its investigations. Using Digital Forensic, as basic part of an incident response procedure, will also help companies to be ready to deal with attackers, Trojan horses, frauds and so on. Furthermore, an effective forensic analysis will help companies to not repeat IT Management Mistakes.

Before starting with the chapter, I would like to give some definition about the topic we are gonna talk about.

– *Forensics*—The recreation of a crime scene after a crime has been committed in order to determine what happened so that the evidence can be used in a court of law.

– *Digital forensics*—When a crime has been committed using a computer, recreating the evidence on the computer.

1.1 Some Basics of Digital Forensics

The principles that comprise forensic operations are essentially platform independent, though some file systems are not. In keeping with the rules of due diligence contained in the IACIS (International Association of Computer Investigative Specialists— http://www.cops.org) code of ethics, it is important to clarify what is meant in digital forensics by "investigative process." Such a process comprises the sequence of activities which should be performed by the forensic examiner to ensure compliance with juridical requirements now common to all countries.

For the purposes of this document, the investigative process is subdivided into six phases as illustrated in Fig. 1.

Notification. This first report occurs when an attack is detected by an automatic device, by internal personnel, or through external input (for example by a system administrator in another company, or by another business unit in the same company). The action taken is usually to create or activate a response team, whose first task is to confirm that an attack has occurred.

Preservation. This is a critical phase in incident response and the first bona fide digital forensic action. The main objective here is to make sure that the scene of

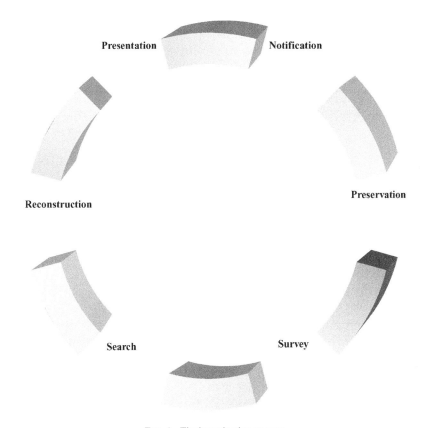

FIG. 1. The investigative process.

the crime is left intact so as not to preclude any future investigative or analytical measures. The "digital crime scene" is usually duplicated, i.e., an image disk is created, so that detailed analyses may be performed in a properly equipped laboratory.

Survey. This is the first evidence collection step. The objective here is to examine the scene of the crime for any *obvious digital evidence* and to develop hypotheses that will orient further investigation.

Search. The hypotheses developed in the Survey stage are investigated with the help of analysis tools as needed. In this more detailed evidence collection phase, the "cold" trails are abandoned and the "hot" ones followed.

Reconstruction. This phase comprises detailed testing to connect the pieces of evidence and reconstruct the event. In many cases this activity may indicate the need for or reveal further evidence.

Presentation. The final act in this process is to collect all the findings and present them to those who requested the investigation.

A forensic analysis is indicated in two fundamental cases: (1) reconstruction of an attack (Post Mortem Analysis); (2) examination of a computer that may have been used to carry out some sort of criminal violation. In the first case, the examined computer is the *target* of a violation, in the second it is a *tool* used to commit a crime. The job of the Forensic Examiner is to carry out the investigative process.

2.   Tools and Techniques for Forensic Investigations

This section addresses investigation methodologies as they apply to the various investigation phases described above. The objective here is to provide the reader with the initial guidelines needed to approach the problem.

2.1   The Preservation Phase: Imaging Disks

For the purpose of this chapter, we will talk about UNIX. The generation of an image disk under UNIX is an essential part of the Preservation phase. We have chosen to work with UNIX because, as we will see later, it is one of the few platforms that allow user interaction with hidden areas of the disks, especially latest generation disks. One of the most common errors involves making a "non-forensically reliable" copy of disks. This obviously would be the lesser of two evils if we consider the fact that there are still quite a few operators who work (and often even write) on the original disks. While it may be admissible to work on non-rewritable CD-ROMs, the same can certainly not be said for hard drives. For this reason, the first necessary step is to make a copy, or "image disk," of the original disk, which thereafter is referred to as the "*source*." There are various methods and tools for accomplishing this, as we will see below.

There are guidelines regarding preparations for doing the imaging. In most cases, the machine is delivered to the incident response investigator turned off. It may also be left on but disconnected from the network. In the former case, the computer must not be turned on except by trained operators, otherwise data may be modified in a way that compromises the investigation. When in doubt, the golden rule is "if the machine is off it has to stay off; if it is on it has to stay on; *until further orders*."

It goes without saying, but I will say it anyway: The original support must be carefully protected (for example, apply write-protect where possible).

The image of the support is obtained using software tools, described below, to create a bit by bit image. The preferred method is to use a trusted workstation for the acquisition whether the source disk is a single hard disk, a floppy or a CD. Otherwise, if conditions permit, the investigated computer may be booted from a floppy (drive A:) rather than from the hard disk. In this case the computer boots up with a minimal operating system that contains additional programs and drivers so that the computer recognizes an external memorization device as a removable hard disk. Then a program is booted from the floppy that creates the image of the hard disk(s) on the external device. This image will include both visible and hidden files, the parts of the disk that contain information on details of the directories (file name, dimension, date and timestamp) and also certain other fragments of files that had been previously deleted but not yet overwritten. The image file can be easily read or examined, although in some cases (especially during the Reconstruction phase) it may be necessary to carry out a reverse procedure on a second computer with similar characteristics to the first, i.e., an exact clone of the original disk so that all details can be completely reproduced. In any case, the images are copied onto *Write Once Read Many* CD ROMs that cannot be altered.

As a preliminary, remember: the disk image destination drive must be *wiped*. The procedure involves the complete cancellation of the entire contents of the hard disk. There are a number of ad hoc tools for this purpose, including one known as "Wipe." Keep in mind that the wiping operation must be documented in the forensic analysis report whether or not the report relates to incident response operations. It is recommended that the disk image destination hard disk be wiped upon completion of an examination. In any case it must be done (and documented) prior to any subsequent image acquisition.

2.1.1   Disk Imaging Tools

Forensic analysis operations require a number of software tools and dedicated hardware devices. The tools have different functions, such as backup and restore, file comparison, checking and comparison of encrypted checksums, system setup check, list of services and processes, systems for backtracing the attacking sites and their ISPs.

We shall proceed by examining the tools that preserve evidence by creating an image of it.

2.1.2   Creating Disk Images in a UNIX Environment

I personally believe that in addition to ensuring the integrity of the evidence base, one of the main objectives of the Preservation phase is to allow for the image to be examined on the greatest possible variety of investigation tools. To this end, the format I prefer for the image disk is DD. This tool has been tested by the National Institute of Standards and Technologies as part of their Computer Forensics Tool Testing (CFTT) project, thus guaranteeing that it will enjoy some recognition in court. For further information on DD, check out the website at http://www.opengroup.org/onlinepubs/009695399/utilities/dd.html.

DD copies a file (by default from the standard input to the standard output) with preset input and output block dimensions, and may convert the file. It reads the input one block at a time according to the dimensions specified for input blocks (default value is 512 bytes). If the **bs** = *byte* option is present and no conversion other than **sync**, **noerror** or **notrunc** is required, it writes the data (which might be less than required) into a separate output block. This output block has the same length as the input block, unless the **sync** option is specified, in which case spaces are added to the end of the data.

Otherwise, the input, read one block at a time, is processed and the resulting output is collected and written in blocks having the specified dimension. The final output block may be shorter.

The numerical operations that follow (bytes and blocks) may be followed by a multiplier: $k = 1024$, $b = 512$, $w = 2$, $c = 1$ ("w" and "c" are GNU extensions; "w" should never be used: it means 2 in System V and 4 in 4.2BSD). Two or more of these expressions may be multiplied by placing an "x" between them.

It is possible to import the images created with DD using the most recent versions of the best known forensic investigation tools, both GNU and commercial, such as FTK, Encase, or Smart. The basic concept is that DD makes a bit-by-bit copy from one location to another using the syntax:

```
dd if=<src> of=<dst>
```

where, <src> and <dst> may be files, file system partitions or an entire hard drive. DD is not a network program; you can use 'netcat' to extend it to a network. Netcat is used to make TCP/UDP connections to a server and is also an excellent diagnostic tool. Netcat typically works in two modes, Server and Client:

```
server% nc -l -p 30000      ==>   (Awaiting input via port 30000 on <server> )
client% nc <server> 30000   ==>   (Connection to <server> via port 30000)
```

Getting back to the topic of acquisition tools, granted that a computer forensics investigation is carried out on copies and not on the originals, the tools must still not alter the evidence. Even with copies you have to make sure that their content is not altered during the investigation. To ensure this you have to have a checking mechanism that lets you be sure that the evidence (and copies of it) has not been altered or damaged. The best technique is to create a hash of the image produced.

A *hashing algorithm*, starting from a data sequence of any length, such as the entire contents of a disk, generates another, much shorter data sequence called a *hash* whose contents strictly depend on the original data. The feature of the hashing algorithm that makes them so useful is that even minimal changes in the input data will produce a completely different hash. There are many hash generating algorithms. The most important and widely used are SHA-1 (Secure Hash Algorithm, RFC 3174) and MD5 (Message-Digest Algorithm, RFC 1321). The critical issue with these algorithms is not so much a question of generating a hash that does not let you get back to the original data but that of avoiding overlapping results, i.e., making the relationship between the input data and the hash as unambiguous as possible. In this moment, a group of Chinese Cryptologists has presented a paper related to MD5 and SHA-1 cracking. The paper can be found at http://www.iacr.org/conferences/crypto2004/. However, we are pretty far from a practical implementation of the proof of concept expressed in the paper itself. The forensic community advice examiners to perform either SHA-1 and MD5 on the same image file. In any case, while we wait for NIST to come up with its final pronouncement on a new hashing standard, many laboratories are carrying out tests with RIPEMD160.

There are many tools, both freeware and commercial, that can generate hashes of files. For example, a tool included in F.I.R.E. (Forensic and Incident Response Environment) generates images of disks and a hash of the file created. The tool in question is called DCFLDD (or EDD for "Enhanced DD"). This software was specially created for F.I.R.E. and is a tool that extends the potentials of DD (the basic tool) with a feature that allows the creation of an MD5 hash of the disk image. Depending on the options, it is possible to create the hash in a separate output file. It can also create hashes of subsections of disks (or in general of input data flows) specifying the dimension of the hash window, i.e., specifying the data intervals at which hashes should be created. We will get into a little more depth on F.I.R.E in the section on First Response CDs.

DCFLDD, hence, is a modified version of DD that calculates the hash value of the created image. Example:

```
# dcfldd -hashwindow=BYTE -hashlog=FILE if=Dev of=dev
```

Hashwindow indicates the number of bytes for which a hash should be created and Hashlog generates the text file containing the calculated values.

Another handy freeware tool for generating hashes is Hashish. This tool has the sole objective of generating a hash on the basis of an input file or a simple data string. The potentials of this tool derive from the number of its algorithms. It is a complete and easy-to-use tool with a GUI. And the fact that it can run both under Windows and LINUX/UNIX is nothing to turn your nose up at.

DD, furthermore, may be used also in the event of memory dumping. This occurs when the machine is still on when delivered to the forensic examiner. In this case the procedure is as follows:

```
dd if= /dev/kmem of=output
dd if= /dev/mem of=output
```

Regarding how to handle memory images, it should be mentioned that a number of examiners have provided feedback speaking of systems freezing up following the above-described procedure. As an alternative, *Memdump*, written by Wietse Venema can be used. The MemDump utility is designed to dump any part of 4GB linear memory address space under MS-DOS and Windows 9x DOS to a console or a text file. This utility provides transparent access to memory with or without installed memory managers. The software can be downloaded from http://www.porcupine.org/forensics/memdump-1.0.README

To dump physical memory:

```
memdump | nc host port
memdump | openssl s_client -connect host:port
```

In the meantime, research is looking into alternative methods for acquiring the memory contents based on hardware cards [Carrier02]. These cards would dump the memory without performing any operations on it and without interacting with the operating system kernel of the compromised machine, and might solve a lot of problems. However, from the practical point of view there are a lot of limitations, mainly in the deployment phase.

At any rate, the memory dump is generally more useful in the "pure" investigation phases, rather than for subsequent appearances in court. Whatever the case, do not forget that all imaging operations, including the description and specifications of the tools used, must be documented in the report.

2.2   Survey and Search Phase: Seeking Evidence under UNIX

This section cover issues and techniques in performing digital forensics, including searching, file recovery techniques and other topics.

There are certain basic differences, as I mentioned above, between a forensic exam done on a target platform such as UNIX and one done under Windows. The problems that are often encountered regard mainly the reconstruction of data that has been deleted or scattered around the file system. These problems are even more noticeable when you are dealing with tapes and/or various types of backup units, often containing only distributed portions of backup. In UNIX, furthermore, a term may not mean the same thing it would in a Windows-based operating system. The concept of *Slack Space*, for example, is slightly different in UNIX. Since UNIX files are stored compactly, except for the unavoidable wastage in the last block or fragment, it might be said that UNIX has no slack. However, certain ISV forensic analysis software producers also identify this type of space as "slack."

A forensic analysis under UNIX may have two main goals: (1) reconstruction of events (e.g., an attack); (2) search for evidence of other violations (e.g., pedophilia or any other abuse of the technology). Depending on the reason for acting, investigators will carry out searches that may be focused on log files rather than fragments of evidence. Usually, following an intrusion, the decision is made whether to turn off and disconnect the compromised system. If the system is left on and on line to collect more information on the intrusion and the intruder, it is good to keep in mind that the system could be or could have been used as a stepping stone for attacking another site. In such case, it is very important that the police be contacted immediately and that the recommended measures be taken to decrease the likelihood of this happening. In many cases, when the system cannot be turned off, another machine is "associated" on the same network segment, set up in promiscuous mode with TCP dump, in order to monitor network traffic in and out of the target in question.

At any rate, one of the first things that has to be decided regards turning off the system prior to actually seizing it. The turning off procedure under UNIX has always been a source of debate among operators; there is no common agreement, at least not among the community of practitioners, on what operations have to be carried out. Hence it is recommended that the Standard Operating Procedures (SOP) of one's agency or office be followed. Some, for example, believe that before you turn off a UNIX machine, you should change the root password, if the user is logged as root. The reasoning is that it would otherwise be extremely difficult to recover the root password later on. This procedure is a part of rather outdated SOP; it is currently common opinion that any operations carried out on the "original" machine may compromise the integrity of the evidence and hence should be avoided. In the jargon, a machine that has been altered is known as *tainted fruit*.

Other operators think that the best thing to do is turn off the machine simply by pulling the plug. This is a rather widespread practice even though it has certain contraindications, not least among them the loss of critical information or the risk of irreparable damage to the file system. In many cases, however, the swap file remains unaltered, and may contain very important information.

An alternative method for "crystallizing the scene of the crime" often used by certain investigators is the following:

- Photograph the screen and document which programs are running;
- Right click on the menu;
- Select **Console**;
- If the prompt is not on the user root, get there by typing **su** – ;
- If the root password is not available, pull the plug on the computer;
- If the root password is available, enter it. At the pound sign (#) type **sync; sync; halt** and the system will shut down;
- Unplug the machine.

The sequence **sync;sync;halt** is often discouraged since it might write something. However, numerous guidelines [DoE01] indicate this as the most suitable option.

As always, whatever approach is taken, it is critical that all operations be documented in a report.

2.2.1   Search Tools and Data Left in the System by an Intruder

Intruders generally install customized tools to enable them to monitor the system and/or access the machine in the future.

The main tool categories are the following:

- Network sniffer;
- Trojan horse;
- backdoor;
- vulnerability exploit;
- other (Denial-Of-Service, use of processing resources);
- communication systems with other compromised systems.

When a system is compromised, the intruder may install a network monitoring program (on UNIX systems) commonly known as sniffers or packet sniffers, with the goal of intercepting information regarding user accounts and passwords. The first step in determining whether there is a sniffer in the system is to check if there is a process that uses a network interface in promiscuous mode. It is not possible to detect promiscuous mode interfaces if the machine has been rebooted after the discovery of the intrusion or if it is operating in single user mode. It should be kept in mind that certain legitimate network monitors and protocol analyzers could set the network interface to promiscuous mode. Thus, the discovery of a promiscuous interface does not necessarily mean that a non-legitimate sniffer is at work in the system.

Another aspect to consider is that the log files of a sniffer tend to grow quickly; hence a utility like *df* might come in handy for determining whether a part of the file system is bigger than expected. Remember that *df* is often replaced by a Trojan horse in cases where a sniffer has been installed; so make sure you've got a clean copy of the utility before you use it. If a sniffer is found in the system you should examine the output files to determine what other machines are at risk, i.e., what other machines appear in the destination field of the intercepted packets. In cases where the same passwords are used, or the source and destination machines have a trusted relationship, the source machine is at risk nevertheless. In certain cases the sniffers encrypt their logs; hence it is important to check files that increase rapidly in size. Also keep in mind that there may be other machines at risk in addition to those that appear in the sniffer log. This is because the intruder may have obtained previous logs from the system or through other types of attack.

Another operation is the search for files that are open at a specific time. This may be useful (especially on a machine that has not yet been turned off) to check for backdoors, sniffers, eggdrop IRC bots, port redirectors like "bnc," etc. The program that may be used for this purpose is called LSOF (LiSt of Open Files). It is advisable to run it from a CD-ROM with statically precompiled binaries, in order not to fall into an attacker's booby trap, making a trojanized version of this tool "available" to investigators.

There are also tools that are used to search for *rootkits*, i.e., tool that are installed by the attacker after the target machine has been compromised. One of the most widely used tools is *chrootkit* (http://www.chrootkit.org) that has a list of rootkits of varying degrees of sophistication that it should be able to recognize.

For certain types of analysis, in order to identify the features of rootkits or other tools installed by the attacker, a debugging or even a reverse engineering operation may prove necessary. This type of activity may require some minimum legal assessment, to ensure that no laws prohibiting reverse engineering are broken, such as DMCA.

3. Logs: Characteristics and Requirements

The issues highlighted above regarding UNIX are only one side of the coin. There are also a number of very important problems regarding log file integrity and management.

Every IT and network object, if programmed and configured accordingly, is capable of producing logs. Logs have to have certain fundamental requisites for network forensics purposes. They are:

- *Integrity*: The log must be unaltered and not admit any tampering or modification by unauthorized operators;
- *Time Stamping*: the log must guarantee reasonable certainty as to the date and hour a certain event was registered. This is absolutely essential for making correlations after an incident;
- *Normalization* and *Data Reduction*. By *normalization* we mean the ability of the correlation tool to extract a datum from the source format of the log file that can be correlated with others of a different type without having to violate the integrity of the source datum. *Data Reduction* (a.k.a. *filtering*) is the data extraction procedure for identifying a series of pertinent events and correlating them according to selective criteria.

3.1 The Need for Log Integrity: Needs and Possible Solutions

A log must guarantee its integrity right from the moment of registration. Regardless of the point of acquisition (Sniffer, Agent, Daemon, etc.) a log usually flows like this (Fig. 2).

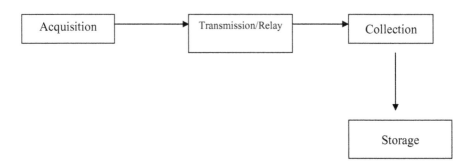

FIG. 2. Log flow.

Acquisition occurs the moment a network sniffer, a system agent or a daemon acquires the event and makes it available to a subsequent transmission process directed to a machine that is usually different from the one that is the source of the event. Once the log has reached the destination machine (called the *Log Machine*) it may be temporarily memorized in a pre-assigned slot or input to a database for later consultation. Once the policy-determined disc capacity has been reached, the data are stored in a predetermined location. The original logs are deleted to make room for new files from the source object. This method is known as *log rotation*.

Log file integrity can be violated in several ways. An attacker might take advantage of a non-encrypted transmission channel between the acquisition and destination points to intercept and modify the transiting log. He might also spoof the IP sending the logs, making the log machine think it is receiving log entries and files that actually come from a different source.

3.2 An Example of Log File Integrity Problem: Syslog

The basic configuration of *Syslog* makes this a real possibility. The RFC 3164 states that *Syslog* transmissions are based on UDP, a connectionless protocol and thus one that is unreliable for network forensic purposes, unless separate LANs are used for the transmission and collection of log files. But even here there might be some cases that are difficult to interpret.

So, Despite its popularity and widespread use, the *syslog* protocol is intrinsically insecure. Indeed the protocol specifications themselves cite gaps in the definition of the standard. Although some of these shortcomings are remedied in RFC 3195, this standard is far from being widely implemented and the majority of logging systems do not conform with its recommendations.

For this reason we should list the main drawbacks involved in using this protocol to collect and maintain a consistent series of data to be used following an incident or for routine log reviews.

For clarity we should break the problems down into 3 categories:

- Transmission related problems.
- Message integrity problems.
- Message authenticity problems.

For each of these categories we will look at examples of possible attacks which highlight the dangers associated with using this logging protocol.

3.2.1 Syslog: Transmission Related Problems

As we know, *syslog* relies on UDP to transmit messages. This makes communication between the two parties unreliable by definition. On top of this, messages generated during network transmission between the source host and the destination host may be lost entirely. This can only be solved by using as a transport substrate a reliable protocol like TCP which uses transmission notification, following an initial handshake phase. Some implementations of the *syslog* daemon (e.g., *syslog-ng*) allow you to choose the underlying communication channel to be used. Another solution is to use a point-point connection (e.g., serial line) or a dedicated subnet to collect system logs, but this option is rarely adopted, for obvious reasons. Let's take an example of a hacker with access to the communication network between source and destination. The attacker could passively listen to the communication channel and delete any messages that reveal their presence. This cannot be detected because there is no notification mechanism or sequential numbering of the messages sent.

3.2.2 Syslog: Message Integrity Problems

A second intrinsic problem with the protocol is that it does not provide, except at the IP packet level, any mechanism to safeguard the integrity of the message produced. This means an attacker can capture, change and reintroduce into the network a message in transit from the source host to the destination host without leaving any trace. Note that merely adding a field for a checksum or a hash to the message doesn't solve the problem. Sticking with the same example, all the hacker needs to do is recalculate the error control code or the message hash and overwrite the existing one to avoid suspicion on the part of the destination host.

3.2.3 Syslog: Message Authenticity Problems

Finally, there is no mechanism to verify the source of the messages. In effect the remote log collector does nothing more than listen to the specific port and write the messages it receives to disk. This opens the door to a range of problems linked to the possibility to exploit such 'trust' in the source to cause disservice or introduce false information into the system. One possible scenario might be as follows: once the hacker has gained access to the system, he generates false alerts and transmits them to the remote host until its disk space is full. Having done that, he could then operate on the system safe in the knowledge that his activities, though monitored, are not being registered on the remote host. This type of intrusion does not require any special expertise. We could illustrate a possible program designed to create a disservice of this type on a remote host log with few lines of pseudo-code such as:

```
while (true){
    ip.addr = ip.log_host;

    udp.dport = 514;

    udp.data = random_string();
}
```

The packet is not even required to contain all the fields it previously contained. This makes it even easier to produce harmful messages.

Another way of taking advantage of the lack of message authenticity control might be to forge ad hoc messages to distract the attention of the system administrator from real threats taking place.

Once collected, *syslog* data must be stored safely to be used as proof in any investigation of a system violation. However forensic analysis requires that the proof, i.e., the logs, satisfies the following criteria:

- Admissible: they must conform with certain legal requisites to be valid in court,
- Authentic: it must be possible to prove that the logs contain evidence of the incident in question,
- Complete: the logs must represent the entire history of the incident and not just a part,
- Trusted: there must be no doubts about how the data was collected, its authenticity and its subsequent movements,
- Credible: they must be easily understandable in court.

To bring the *syslog* system closer into line with the above requirements various versions have been developed that furnish new implementations regarding both the secure transmission of the data and its integrity and authenticity.

Currently numerous such implementations exist, including: modular *syslog*, *SDSC Syslog*, *Syslog Ng* and *Kiwi*. Each of these has its strengths and weaknesses (especially for implementation in a distributed environment).

Nevertheless they are all vulnerable to attack once the attacker identifies the type of traffic involved and can then threaten the integrity of the entire system. We will introduce to those further problems in the following paragraph.

3.3   More Integrity Problems: When the Logs Arrive on the Log Machine

Another integrity problem regards the management of files once they have arrived on the log machine. If the log machine is compromised there is a very high probability of integrity violation. This usually happens to individual files, whose content is modified or even wiped. The integrity issue also regards how the *paternity* of log files is handled; in many juridical contexts, you have to be certain as to which machine generated the log files and who did the investigation.

There are several methods for resolving the problem. The first is specified in RFC 3195, which identifies a possible method for reliable transmission of *syslog* messages, useful especially in the case of a high number of relays (intermediate record retransmission points between the source and the log repository). The main problem in this case is that RFC 3195 has not been incorporated into enough systems to be considered an established protocol.

Hence, practically speaking, most system administrators and security analysts view SCP (Secure Copy) as a good workaround. The most evident contraindication is the unsuitability of such a workaround for intrusion detection purposes, since there is no real time assessment of the existence of an intrusion via log file reading. And the problem remains of security in transmission between the acquisition and the collection points. In response to the problem, in UNIX-based architectures the practice of using *cryptcat* to establish a relatively robust tunnel between the various machines is gaining wider acceptance.

The procedure is as follows:

On log-generating host:

1. you must edit /etc/syslog.conf in this mode:

```
*.*                           @localhost
```

2. then run command:

```
# nc -l -u -p 514 | cryptcat 10.2.1.1 9999
```

On log-collecting host:

1. run syslog with remote reception (-r) flag (for Linux)
2. run command:

```
# cryptcat -l -p 9999 | nc -u localhost 514
```

The above configuration will establish an encrypted connection among the various transmission nodes. An alternative would be to use a *Syslog* replacement such as *Syslog-ng*, which performs relay operations automatically and with greater security potentials.

From the practical standpoint, the methods described above offer a good compromise between operational needs and the theory that a hash must be generated for each log entry (something which is impossible in a distributed environment). The objective still remains of achieving transaction atomicity (transactions are done or undone completely) and log file reliability. The latter concept means being sure that the log file does not get altered once it has been closed, for example via interception during the log rotation phase. The most important aspect of this phase is the *final-record message*, indicating the last record written in the log, which is then closed and hashed. This sequence of processes may turn out to be critical when, after correlation, a whole and trustworthy log has to be provided to the judicial authorities.

3.4   Log Time Stamping Management: Problems and Possible Solutions

Another problem of a certain importance is managing log file time stamping. Each report has to be 100% reliable, not only in terms of its integrity in the strict sense (IP, ports, payloads, etc.), but also in terms of the date and time of the event reported. Time stamping is essential for two reasons: atomicity of the report, and correlation. The most common problems here are the lack of synchronization and the lack of uniformity of the time zones.

The lack of synchronization occurs when the acquisition points (network sensors and *Syslog* devices) are not synchronized with an atomic clock but only within small groups. Reliance is usually placed on NTP in these cases, but this may open up a series of noted vulnerabilities, especially in distributed architectures connected to the public network. Furthermore, the use of NTP does not guarantee uniformity unless a series of measures recommended by certain RFCs is adopted for certain types of logs as we will describe below. Some technology manufacturers have come out with appliances equipped with highly reliable processors that do time stamping for every entry, synchronizing everything with atomic clocks distributed around the world. This sort of solution, albeit offering a certain degree of reliability, increases design costs and obviously makes management more complex. In a distributed architecture, a time stamping scheme administered by an appliance is set up as in Fig. 3.

The appliance interacts with a PKI that authenticates the transaction nodes to prevent the problem of report repudiation.

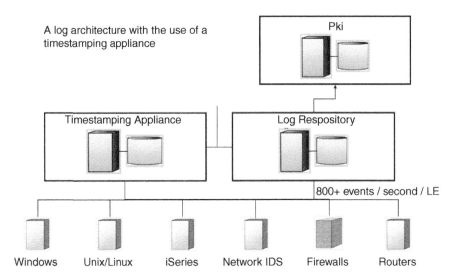

FIG. 3. Log architecture with time stamping machine.

While this type of architecture may be "easily" implemented in an environment with a healthy budget, there are applications for less extensive architectures that may be helpful in guaranteeing a minimum of compliance with best practices.

Granted that one of the most commonly used log format is *Libpcap*-compatible (used by TcpDump, Ethereal) over TCP connections (hence 3-way), it is possible to attribute a further level of timestamping, as per RFCs 1072 and 2018, by enabling the Sack OK option (Selective Acknowledgement OK). This option can return even a 32 bit time stamp value in the first 4 bytes of each packet, so that reports among transaction nodes with the Sack OK option enabled are synchronized and can be correlated. This approach may be effective provided that the entire system and network is set up for it.

Another factor that is not taken into consideration are *Time Zones* (*TZ*). In distributed architectures on the international scale, some information security managers believe it is wise to maintain the time zone of the physical location of the system or network object. This choice has the disadvantage of making correlation more complicated and less effective because of time zone fragmentation. We are currently witnessing an increase of times zones being simply based on GMT, which has the plus of simplifying management even though it still requires that the choice be incorporated into a policy.

3.5   Normalization and Data Reduction: Problems and Possible Solutions

Normalization is identified in certain cases with the term *event unification*. There is a physiological need for normalization in distributed architectures. Numerous commercial systems prefer the use of XML for normalization operations. This language provides numerous opportunities for event unification and management of digital signatures and hashing. There are two basic types of logs: system logs and network logs. If the reports all had a single format there would be no need for normalization. In heterogeneous architectures it is obvious that that is not the case. Let us imagine, for example, an architecture in which we have to correlate events recorded by a website, by a network sniffer and by a proprietary application. The website will record the events in w3c format, the network sniffer in LibPcap format, while the proprietary application might record the events in a non-standard format. It is clear that unification is necessary here. The solution in this case consists of finding points in common among the various formats involved in the transaction and creating a level of abstraction according to the diagram in Fig. 4.

It follows in this case that an attacker can once again seek to violate log integrity by zeroing in on the links between the various acquisition points and the point of normalization. We will discuss this below. Regarding the correlation, the point of normalization (normally an engine) and the point of correlation (an activity that may be carried out by the same module, for example, in an IDS) may be the same machine. It is clear that this becomes a potential point of failure from the perspective of network forensics and thus must be managed both to guarantee integrity and to limit possible losses of data during the process of normalization. For this purpose the state-of-the-art is to use MD5 and SHA-1 to ensure integrity and to perform an in-depth verification of the event unification engine to respond to the data reduction issue, keeping the "source" logs in the normalized format. In Fig. 5, where each source log is memorized on ad hoc supports, another layer is added to Fig. 4.

In order to manage the secure repository section and still use a series of "source log files" that guarantee a certain reliability, the machines in the second line of Fig. 5

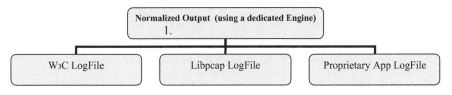

FIG. 4.   Normalization.

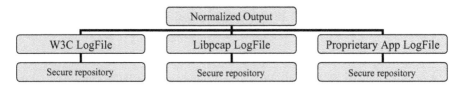

FIG. 5. Multi-layered log architecture.

have to be *trusted*, i.e., hardened, and have cryptosystems that can handle authentication, hashing and reliable transmission as briefly discussed in Section 2.1.

3.6   Correlation and Filtering: Needs and Possible Solutions

In performing log correlation and filtering, the Security Architect and the Manager have to deal with the problems described above. Here, the perspective on the problem shifts to the architecture.

3.6.1   Correlation and Filtering: Some Definitions

> Correlation—"A causal, complementary, parallel, or reciprocal relationship, especially a structural, functional, or qualitative correspondence between two comparable entities." Source: http://dictionary.com

In this article we use *Correlation* to mean the activity carried out by one or more *engines* to reconstruct a given complex event, that may be symptomatic of a past or current violation.

By *filtering* we mean an activity that may be carried out by the same engines to extract certain kinds of data and arrange them, for example, by protocol type, time, IP, MAC Address and so on.

A fairly complex architecture may be set up as follows.

As may be observed from Fig. 6, and assuming the necessary precautions indicated in the above sections have been followed, if data is collected at the individual acquisition points (i.e., *before* the logs get to the normalization engines) by methods such as SCP, the very use of this method might slow down subsequent operations since these activities require a greater dynamism than the "simple" acquisition and generation of logs. Hence in this phase you have to use a Tunneling and Authentication (T_p) system based on a secure communication protocol that might be a level 3 ISO/OSI.

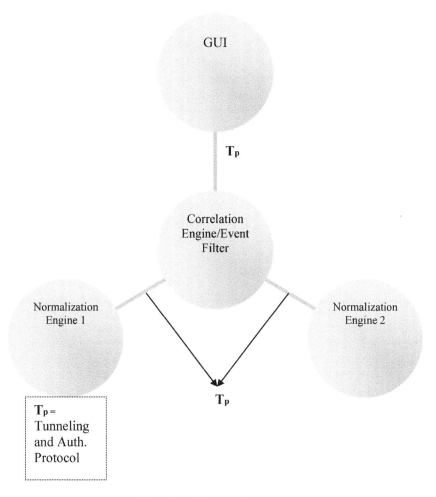

FIG. 6. Correlating normalized events.

3.6.2 Interpretation of Log Files

In most cases the security administrator reads the result of a correlation done by a certain tool, but he only sees the tip of the iceberg. If you look at the figures in this chapter, the set of processes upstream of the GUI display is much more complex. Whatever the case may be, the literature indicates two basic methods for analyzing logs, called *approaches*.

3.6.3   Top Down Approach

This is the approach most frequently used in network forensics when the examiner is working with an automated log and event correlation tool. While in intrusion detection a top-down approach means starting from an attack to trace back to the point of origin, in network forensics it means starting from a GUI display of the event to get back to the source log, with the dual purpose of:

1. Validating the correlation process used by the engine of the automatic log and event correlation tool and displayed to the Security Administrator;
2. Seeking out the source logs that will then be used as evidence in court or for subsequent analysis.

In reference to Fig. 6, we have a top-down approach to get back to the source logs represented in the previous figures. Once retraced, the acquired logs are produced and recorded onto a CD-ROM or DVD, and the operator will append a digital signature.

3.6.4   Bottom-Up Approach

This approach is applied by the tool starting from the source log. It is a method used by the IDS to identify an ongoing attack through a real time analysis of events. In a distributed security environment the IDS engine may reside (as hypothesized in Section 2.2) in the same machine hosting the normalization engine. In this case the IDS engine will then use the network forensic tool to display the problem on the GUI. You start from an automatic low level analysis of the events generated by the points of acquisition to arrive at the "presentation" level of the investigative process. Such an approach, furthermore, is followed when log analysis (and the subsequent correlation) is performed manually, i.e., without the aid of automated tools. Here, a category of tools known as *log parsers* comes to your aid. The purpose of these tools is to analyze source logs for a bottom-up correlation. A parser is usually written in a script language like Perl or Python. There are however parsers written in Java to provide a cross-platform approach to network forensics examiners, perhaps on a bootable CD-ROM (see Section 5 for examples).

3.7   Requisites of Log File Acquisition Tools

Regardless of which vendor is chosen to represent the standard, the literature has identified a number of requisites that a logging infrastructure must have to achieve forensically compliant correlations:

- TCPdump support, both in import and in export;
- Use of state-of-the-art hashing algorithms;

- Data reduction capabilities as described in previous sections;

- Data Recovery. This feature comprises the ability to extract from the intercepted traffic not only the connections but also the payloads for the purpose of interpreting the formats of files exchanged during the transaction;

- Ability to recognize covert channels (not absolutely essential but still highly recommended);

- Read Only During Collection and Examination. This is an indispensable feature for this type of tool;

- Complete Collection. This is one of the most important requisites. It is important that all packets are captured or else that all losses are minimized and documented;

- Intrinsic Security, with special emphasis on connections between points of acquisition, collection repositories, administrative users, etc.

4. Experimentation: Using GPL Tools for Investigation and Correlation

So far we have introduced logs, correlation techniques and the associated security issues. Regarding the tools used for this type of analysis and investigation, there are GPL or open source projects with the main goal of providing the necessary tools for a bottom-up investigation, which is a less costly and less complicated alternative to the top-down approach based on automated correlation and GUI display techniques. In this section we will introduce some projects and tools that may be used for the purpose at hand.

4.1 The IRItaly Project

IRItaly (Incident Response Italy) is a project that was developed at the *Crema* Teaching and Research Center of the Information Technology Department of the *Università Statale di Milano*. The main purpose of the project is to inform and sensitize the Italian scientific community, small and large businesses, and private and public players about Incident Response issues.

The project, which includes more than 15 instructors and students (BSC and MSC), is divided into two parts. The first relates to documentation and provides broad-ranging and detailed instructions. The second comprises a bootable CD-ROM. The issues addressed regard information attacks and especially defensive systems, computer and network forensics on incident handling and data recovery methods.

Regarding response procedures to information incidents, best practices are presented for analyzing the victim machines in order to retrace the hacking episodes and understand how the attack was waged, with the final aim of providing a valid response to the intrusion. This response should be understood as a more effective and informed hardening of the system to reduce the possibility of future attacks. It does not mean the generation of a counterattack.

All the operations described so far are carried out with special attention to the method of identification, storage and possible use of evidence in a disciplinary hearing or in court. The unifying theme of the CD-ROM is the set of actions to undertake in response to an intrusion. It contains a number of sections offering a detailed analysis of each step:

- the intrusion response preparation phase;
- the analysis of available information on the intrusion;
- the collection and storage of associated information (evidence);
- the elimination (deletion) of tools used for gaining and maintaining illicit access to the machine (rootkits);
- the restoration of the systems to normal operating conditions.

Detailed information is provided on the following:

- management of different file systems;
- procedures for data backup;
- operations for creating images of hard and removable discs;
- management of secure electronic communication;
- cryptographic algorithms and their implementation;
- tools for the acquisition, analysis and safeguarding of log files.

The CD also proposes a number of standardized forms to improve organization and facilitate interactions between organizations that analyze the incident and the different targets involved in the attack. Specifically, an incident report form and a chain of custody form are provided. The latter is a valuable document for keeping track of all information regarding the evidence.

The CD-ROM may be used to do an initial examination of the configuration of the compromised computer.

The tools included offer the possibility to carry out analyses of the discs, generate an image of them and examine logs in order to carry out a preliminary analysis of the incident. The IRItaly CD-ROM (http://www.iritaly.org) is bootable and contains a series of disc and log analysis tools. All the programs are on the CD in the form of static binaries and are checked before the preparation of the magnetic support.

After booting, the tool launches a terminal interface that the examiner can use to start certain applications such as TCPDump, Ethereal, Snort, Swatch and so on.

The CD can thus be used for a preliminary analysis of the logs present on the machine or for an analysis of the machine using the TASK/autopsy tool, which is more specific to the analysis of the hard disc. The correlation process, in this case, involves the comparison of logs present on the machine with others on other machines. In this case, the IRItaly CD essentially works in very small environments or even in one-to-one contexts, as illustrated in Fig. 7.

Here, T_1, T_2 and T_3 represent various targets that may be booted with the IRItaly CD and connected to the main forensic workstation with the aid of Netcat or Cryptcat. As stated above, the main limitation of the use of the completely functional CD is that it cannot be used in a distributed architecture due to obvious management difficulties. However, the IRItaly workgroup is carrying out a series of tests of a new version of the CD that should resolve some of the above problems with the aid of other tools.

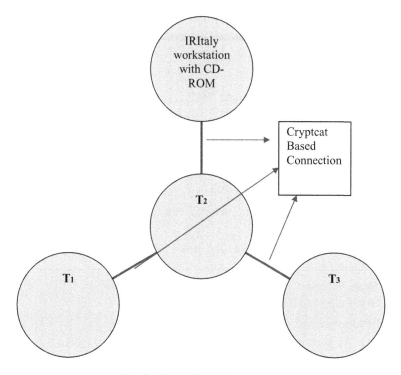

FIG. 7. IRItaly CD-ROM normal use.

4.2   Further Developments: IRItaly Version 2

The IRItaly Project has already begun work on two fundamental tasks for the resolution of several of the issues illustrated in this chapter. The first regards the release of a new version of the CD-ROM, which will contain a full implementation of Python FLAG.

According to the Project Documentation, FLAG was designed to simplify the process of log file analysis and forensic investigations. Often, when investigating a large case, a great deal of data needs to be analyzed and correlated. FLAG uses a database as a backend to assist in managing the large volumes of data. This allows FLAG to remain responsive and expedite data manipulation operations.

Since FLAG is web based, it is able to be deployed on a central server and shared with a number of users at the same time. Data is loaded into cases which keeps information separated. FLAG also has a system for reporting the findings of the analysis by extensively using bookmarks.

FLAG started off as a project in the Australian Department of Defence. It is now hosted on sourceforge. PyFlag is the Python implementation of FLAG—a complete rewrite of FLAG in the much more robust python programming language. Many additional improvements were made. Some of the most obvious features are:

- Disk Forensics
  - Supports NTFS, Ext2, FFS and FAT.
  - Supports many different image file formats, including sgzip (compressed image format), Encase's Expert Witness format, as well as the traditional dd files.
  - Advanced timelining which allows complex searching.
  - NSRL hash support to quickly identify files.
  - Windows Registry support, includes both win98 variant as well as the Window NT variant.
  - Unstructure Forensics capability allows recovery of files from corrupted or otherwise unmountable images by using file magic.
- Network Forensics
  - Stores tcpdump traffic within an SQL database.
  - Performs complete TCP stream reconstruction.
  - Has a "knowledge base" making deductions about network communications.
  - Can construct an automatic network diagram based on TCPDump, or real time.

- Log analysis
  - Allows arbitrary log file formats to be easily uploaded to database.
  - GUI driven complex database searches using an advanced table GUI element.

The ultimate objective is to integrate PyFlag into IRItaly's CD-ROM, in order to provide first responders with a tool that can guarantee a minimum of correlation that is significantly broader than that offered by the current version.

Another research project included in the IRItaly CdRom, and related to Log Analysis, is called SecSyslog. As stated in the first part of this chapter, one of the most critical problems related to Syslog is Integrity. This part of the CIA Paradigm (Confidentiality, Integrity Availability) could be violated by compromising authentication between machines, even spoofing addresses and intercepting traffic. SecSyslog wants solve this problem using covert channels. In a hypothetical scenario where the machine "A" is syslog sender and the machine "B" is receiver/daemon, SecSyslog would use the following factors:

(1) tcp in addition to the "simple" and inadequate UDP to establish connection between the machines;

(2) the "syslog" packets are encapsulated in particular fields of the UP packets using crypto. In this way, even an interception would not be able to understand which kind of traffic is passing the line;

(3) Once at destination, the syslog packets are "decrypted" by the SecSyslog Daemon and the messages can be analyzed.

It is clear that with the use of SecSyslog (which has many differences rather than solutions such as Syslog NG and so on) is an example of a "good dual use" of hackers techniques. Using SecSyslog could solve many integrity and confidentiality problems, related to the lack of security and the "forensic compliance" of many logging architectures.

5. SecSyslog and Covert Channels in Detail: Introduction and Definition

The commonly accepted definition states that a covert channel is "any communications channel which can be used to transmit information using methods that violate existing security policies.[1]"

---

[1] *Department of Defense Trusted Computer System Evaluation Criteria.* The translation is ours.

A second definition similarly describes a covert channel as "any method that allows the transmission of information via one or more global system variable not officially designed for that purpose.[2]"

5.1   Categories

Covert channels can be divided into two main categories: *storage channels* and *timing channels*. Their purpose is basically the same; they differ only in how the information is made available.

The first category uses a shared *global variable* (an area of memory for IT specialists, for example, or a letter for a prisoner) which acts as a transmission channel in which one of the two communicating parties can make changes to be read directly or indirectly by the other. The second category allows us to transmit information by modulating use of particular system resources (CPU time, receipt of a packet and the relative response and so on), so as to exploit the differences from normal operation to codify the information transmitted. We can also create hybrid covert channels combining the two methods described above to make the hidden channel even more difficult to detect.

Where earlier research focused on covert channels that allowed information flows between different processes in the same system, more recently interest has shifted to allowing information to be sent from one host to another using channels exploiting various possibilities offered by network protocols that are today the basis of the Internet.

5.2   Network Covert Channels: Current Use

TCP/IP protocols offer many ways to establish covert channels and transmit data between hosts. Such methods can then be used for the following purposes (see next page):

- To by-pass perimeter security devices;
- To implement techniques to evade network sniffers and NIDS;
- To encapsulate information, encrypted or otherwise, in ordinary packets for secret transmission in networks that prohibit such behavior (this is known as *TCP/IP Steganography*).

Here we will not only discuss techniques for manipulating TCP/IP headers, but also those used for the ICMP protocol and higher levels such as HTTP and DNS.

---

[2] *Estimating and Measuring Covert Channel Bandwidth in Multilevel Secure Operating Systems*, by *Shiuh-Pyng Shieh*. The translation is ours.

Let us now turn to some of the common techniques used to create covert channels and describe the tools to implement them.

5.2.1 Information Coding in IP Headers

TCP and IP headers provide numerous fields in which information can be sent secretly. Figure 8 shows the header format for the IP protocol.

In this case the only field that can be used to set up a covert channel that is not easy to detect is the *Identification* field, which we will look at more closely below.

The header of the TCP protocol provides several possibilities, but again the covert channel must be difficult to detect and the best field to use for this is the *SN* (*Sequence Number*) field. The TCP header looks like in Fig. 9.

We can use the Sequence Number field in two ways: using the Initial Sequence Number or the Acknowledge Sequence Number.

0	4	8	16	19	24	32

VERS	HLEN	Service Type		Total Length	
Identification			Flags	Fragment Offset	
Source IP Address					
Destination IP Address					
IP Options				Padding	
Data					

Fig. 8.

0	4	8	16	19	24	32

Source Port		Destination Port	
Sequence Number			
Acknowledgment Number			
HLEN	Reserved	Code Bits	Window
Checksum		Urgent Pointer	
Options			Padding
Data			

Fig. 9.

5.2.2 Manipulating the IP ID Field

The ID field of the IP protocol is used by routers and hosts to reassemble the packets received. It works by giving a unique value to every packet so that they can be reassembled correctly after fragmentation.

This method substitutes the ID field for a value that represents the information (for simplicity we can use an ASCII character) to be coded and sent. The transmission is not altered in any way, only what is transmitted, and the recipient only has to read the ID field and translate it, using a decoding algorithm, into the ASCII value which the source intended to transmit.

Here is a brief example of traffic received by *Tcpdump* showing how the text string ("MICKEY") can be transmitted to a Web server. The decoding algorithm subtracts one from the ID field and then performs Mod 256 to obtain the original ASCII value.

```
        Ascii('M') = 77    Ascii('I') = 73    Ascii('C') = 67
        Ascii('K') = 75    Ascii('E') = 69    Ascii('Y') = 89

10:38:59.797237 IP (ttl 47, id 26702) foo.bar.com.57459 >
test.bar.com.www: ...
Decoding: ... (26702 - 1)  mod 256 = 77 = 'M'

10:39:00.797237 IP (ttl 47, id 34378) foo.bar.com.48376 >
test.bar.com.www: ...
Decoding: ... (34378 - 1)  mod 256 = 73 = 'I'

10:39:01.797237 IP (ttl 47, id 36164) foo.bar.com.17583 >
test.bar.com.www: ...
Decoding: ... (36164 - 1)  mod 256 = 67 = 'C'

10:39:02.797237 IP (ttl 47, id 23884) foo.bar.com.26587 >
test.bar.com.www: ...
Decoding: ... (23884 - 1)  mod 256 = 75 = 'K'

10:39:03.797237 IP (ttl 47, id 27206) foo.bar.com.18957 >
test.bar.com.www: ...
Decoding: ... (27206 - 1)  mod 256 = 69 = 'E'

10:39:04.797237 IP (ttl 47, id 20048) foo.bar.com.31769 >
test.bar.com.www: ...
Decoding: ... (20048 - 1)  mod 256 = 79 = 'Y'
```

This method uses a forged ad hoc packet with correct destination and source fields and the coded information contained in the ID field. The remote host receives the data by listening to port 80 with a daemon that can distinguish the covert channel packets from regular HTTP requests, decode the former and send the latter to the Web server.

The method is fairly robust and easy to implement, but we can see that it is also fragile and vulnerable to failure if there is a firewall or a natting machine in place between the two hosts. In that case the IP header could be altered with a resulting loss of data. In addition this system can easily be detected because the ID field values are not randomly calculated but pre-determinable.

5.2.3 Initial Sequence Number Method

In the TCP protocol the ISN value guarantees flow reliability and control. Every byte transmitted by the TCP stream has an 'assigned' sequence number. Each connection (defined as a pair of sockets in communication) can be used for several flows and the stronger the ISN calculation algorithm the more streams are available. At the moment of connection the client host must determine the ISN value and launch the so-called "three-way handshake."

The ISN field is ideal for transmitting clandestine information because of its size (32 bit). We can exploit this field in a similar way to the example given above. An ISN value is generated from the ASCII character that we wish to code and transmit. The packet with just the SYN flag active is the one that contains the coded data. The recipient only has to read the ISN value and, in the following example, divide this by $65\,536 * 256 = 16\,777\,216$. Below is an example showing transmission of the string "MICKEY."

```
Ascii('M') = 77   Ascii('I') = 73   Ascii('C') = 67
Ascii('K') = 75   Ascii('E') = 69   Ascii('Y') = 89

12:11:56.043339 foo.bar.com.57645 > test.bar.com.ssh: S
1300938487:1300938487(0)
Decoding: ... 1300938487 / 16777216 = 77 = 'M'

12:11:57.043339 foo.bar.com.46235 > test.bar.com.ssh: S
1235037038:1235037038(0)
Decoding: ... 1235037038 / 16777216 = 73 = 'I'

12:11:58.043339 foo.bar.com.46235 > test.bar.com.ssh: S
1140809246:1140809246(0)
Decoding: ... 1140809246 / 16777216 = 73 = 'C'
```

and so on.

Note that the calculated ISNs are very close to each other and this could raise suspicions in anyone paying close attention. However, with 32 bits available, one could adopt ISN calculation algorithms that produce much more random results. Such values would be more credible making the covert channel less likely to be detected.

5.2.4 Acknowledge Sequence Number Method

This method depends on the use of IP spoofing allowing the sender to 'bounce' the packet off a remote server and on to the proper destination. The technique fools the recipient into thinking that the server off which the packet was bounced is actually the source host, thus achieving an anonymous communication, but only in one direction. This type is covert channel is very difficult to detect, especially if the bounce-server is heavily loaded.

This technique rests on a particular feature of TCP/IP protocols whereby the destination server responds to the connection request by sending a packet with an ISN increased by one. The sender needs to forge an ad hoc packet changing the following fields:

– Source IP;
– Source port;
– Destination IP;
– Destination port;
– TCP Initial Sequence Number containing the coded data.

The choice of the destination and source ports is entirely arbitrary. The destination IP must be that of the bounce-server, and the source IP that of the destination host. The packet is thus sent by the client to the bounce-server, which proceeds to forward it to the destination machine (with the ISN increased by one) for decoding.

A correctly configured router/firewall should not allow a packet with the ACK flag active to pass, if it does not recognize that the destination host is responsible for opening the connection. Widespread use of stateful racket filters means that this method is becoming increasingly ineffective, but it may still work if the configuration can be altered. Using known bounce-servers (.mil, .gov web sites, for instance) may also block other types of filters which might be applied on the destination host network.

5.3   Covert Channels Using ICMP Tunnels

Even today many systems are vulnerable to this type of covert channel which were discovered as long ago as 1996. The only requirement in order to send clandestine information via ICMP packets is that the system permits ICMP_ECHO traffic.

Many consider this kind of traffic benign, as indeed it is in scope, the ICMP protocol being used to test or measure network performance or for network management. ICMP packets are encapsulated in the IP datagrams. The first 32 bits of the ICMP header are always the same and the rest of the header may contain any of fifteen different types of message allowed by the protocol.

The ICMP messages that are vulnerable to this 'defect' are ICMP_ECHO (query) and ICMP_ECHOREPLY (reply). But while we can send queries and get responses, the protocol's design also makes it a potential vehicle for hidden data-streams. The utility *Ping*, for example, sends and receives just such messages. So how can we send and receive data using an ICMP tunnel?

ICMP_ECHO messages allow you to enter information in the Data field, normally used to hold information on delay times and so on. However, the Data field is not subject to control by any particular device and can therefore be used to send arbitrary data thus creating a covert channel.

5.3.1   HTTP/S Tunnel

Various factors may be taken into consideration when designing a covert channel based on HTTP, and there is no one way to do it. For instance one could look at the server model to be implemented (such as http daemon, proxy or CGI); how to confuse the traffic so as to disguise the channel further (proxy chains, generation of noise, etc.); or the type of functionality required. Having examined these aspects, we can turn to actually applying the model in practice; what http methods to use (GET, CONNECT, POST . . .).

It may be useful, as with any covert channel implementation, to consider steganographic or cryptographic techniques to further confuse anyone observing the traffic generated and render the communication even more invisible.

In principle, though, there must be two processes capable of working in synchrony: one inside the network from which we wish to obtain information (or the network into which we want to intrude) and another on the outside. The external server should be accessible from the inside and if contacted must not raise the suspicions of any controlling mechanism, whether automatic or not. Typically, given that we are dealing with HTTP requests, the server must act as if it is capable of processing such requests, while the client should send suitably coded information formally presented as normal HTTP requests.

HTTP-based covert channels can therefore take many forms, making the protocol the ideal vehicle for anyone wishing to hide illicit traffic.

Many open-source and closed-source tools use HTTP tunnels for a wide variety of purposes. For example, tools designed to "track a stolen computer, wherever it is, as soon as it is connected to the network" will send the necessary locating information by, say, e-mail invisibly using covert channels based on TTP tunnels. The SOAP protocol (RPC over HTTP) is itself based on the use of HTTP tunnels.

So covert channels are not used exclusively for illicit purposes. Studying the loopholes which network protocols involuntarily leave open can provide valuable input for useful projects.

Two tools we might mention whose function is worth examining, even for merely academic purposes, are **hcovert** and **GNU http-tunnel**, whose code is freely available over the Internet. To find out more about HTTP tunneling and see a few of the possible techniques it affords, readers should go to *Exploitation of data streams authorized by a network access control system for arbitrary data transfers*: *tunneling and covert channels over the HTTP protocol*, available to read at the site http://www.gray-world.net.

5.4   DNS

The possibility of using ordinary DNS requests/responses to send all kinds of data has aroused great interest recently. In 2004 Dan Kaminsky demonstrated tools that allowed him to achieve SSH sessions and to transmit/receive audio traffic via normal DNS servers, though he is not the first to exploit the weaknesses of the DNS protocol.

DNS manages a hierarchical naming system (.com; .bar.com; .foo.bar.com) and this leads us to a number of interesting considerations. If we can control a DNS server, thanks to the authority granted by a certain name domain, we can change the tables which provide the information needed to satisfy the client requests.

Exploiting this feature it is clearly possible to create a covert channel using certain records from the DNS table. What is surprising is the 'bandwidth' available. Using the CNAME record to code transmitted information we can send/receive 110 bytes per packet, while the TXT record gives a full 220 bytes per packet. This is an enormous amount of data when compared with that offered by TCP and IP headers.

Many tools use this technique. We should just mention NSTX and note that rumors abound that botnets and other malignant codes may be able to exploit DNS servers to exchange clandestine data. It will surprise no-one if the next generation of viruses and worms use precisely this method to synchronize themselves and receive the command to launch another DDoS of the sort we have become used to in recent years.

The DNS protocol does however share a number of similarities with the HTTP protocol:

– DNS works on blocks of data;
– DNS does nothing until the client submits a specific request;
– DNS works on character sets (Base32/Base64).

As we have seen above, many tools have been developed to exploit HTTP tunnels. Given the similarities between the two protocols, there must be numerous ways of using DNS for our purposes and tools similar to the existing ones for HTTP. The effective implementation of these techniques can be studied in the work of Dan Kaminsky, who developed the OzyManDNS, a proof-of-concept downloadable off the Internet.

A final remark on this technique regards the fact that whereas for HTTP and numerous other protocols the first products to filter requests are becoming available, this is not yet possible for DNS and for various reasons it is quite unlikely to happen near term. Meanwhile, intense DNS traffic could easily raise suspicion. This is only partly counter balanced by the high bandwidth (max 220 bytes per packet) the method offers. From this standpoint, it is still far more effective to use a HTTP tunnel when a sizable transmission bandwidth is required.

5.5   SecSyslog: Proposal for a Syslog Daemon Using Covert Channels

There are numerous open and closed-source implementations of the *syslog* protocol available. Each of these adds functionality to the protocol's original features and answers specific known weaknesses. Today, given the importance of logs both for troubleshooting and for legal purposes, it is widely considered essential, for instance, to guarantee that messages reach their destination, and that the communication remains unaltered, secure and secret. Each version brings both advantages or disadvantages over the others, so the choice is purely a matter of personal preference based on a detailed understanding of the particular version and additional features it offers, weighed against the added complexity of configuration.

In this section we wish to describe a possible implementation of a new system logging solution using covert channel communications and list the advantages and disadvantages it offers over other softwares.

5.6   Why Use DNS Covert Channels?

Why might it be useful to use a covert channel? Let's imagine the case of a company that has many branch offices and needs to centralize its logs. How can it send these without keeping the *Syslog* service publicly open?

Some *syslog* daemons allow you to authenticate the clients that are allowed to send messages. Although this is easy to configure, the *syslog* messages are still transmitted in the clear and require the log service to be public on the net. It might be a good idea to tunnel the messages in SSH encrypted sessions, but this simply shifts the problem onto another service that you may want to close with a firewall. Another solution could be to use a VPN, but configuration is expensive and in some cases costly to maintain.

None of the above ideas is inherently wrong. Any decision has to take into account a variety of factors: simplicity, cost, availability, and so on. What advantages does a covert channel offer in this case, especially considering the peculiarities of the DNS service?

If we want to implement a project using covert channels we have to consider the task to be performed. By analyzing the requisites we can decide which techniques are best suited to provide the desired solution. We could start by examining the data transmission bandwidth required.

What kind of data does a *syslog* client transmit to the server? How frequently are log messages sent to the server? As we mentioned earlier, if we need to contact the server many times it might be a good idea to mask the covert channel in a very common type of traffic, like HTTP GET or DNS queries. This would make the communication less visible and suspect.

Syslog is simply a system for exchanging text strings. This does not exclude *a priori* the use of HTTP tunneling, but this offers a huge amount of bandwidth, most of which is unnecessary. The *syslog* daemon does not make very heavy demands since it only needs to send strings of a few characters at a time. On the other hand, techniques using TCP and IP headers are hardly suitable either. They provide limited bandwidth so that a single message might generate an enormous volume of traffic which would quickly attract attention.

Furthermore, DNS tunneling techniques are interesting and as yet little used. The fact that there are still no application filtering techniques (unlike those for HTTP) gives this method a big advantage. Indeed it is likely that viruses and worms in the future, if not already, will base their communications on DNS covert channels.

One other advantage is the very widespread availability of DNS servers. Every medium/large company has one or more internal DNS server, some of which are also accessible to various clients in the subsidiaries. Often the service is not even filtered.

In practical terms, a DNS covert channel can be used to send logs invisibly from branch systems to a centralized SecSyslog server at another site miles away, by simply 'bouncing' the data off the DNS at the second branch's premises. What better solution to send *syslog* messages between geographically distant locations transparently and almost invisibly? What better way to hide a data flow than passing under the nose of anyone wishing to intercept the messages?

Such considerations explain why sending logs with SecSyslog via a covert channel is so powerful, and why DNS tunneling provides an excellent solution to the problem.

5.7 Suggested Implementation

Figure 10 shows a rough diagram of how the SecSyslog project might work. Below we describe the problems faced and the solutions that we are examining to resolve them. As the project is still only at the design stage, these might not be the best or most workable solutions, but it illustrates a possible application of DNS to establish a covert channel.

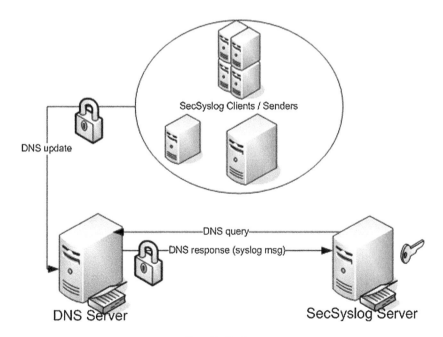

FIG. 10. Project.

Basically the idea is to achieve communication by bouncing the information off a DNS server on which certain hosts (SecSyslog clients, the sources of information) may write the data to be sent by modifying the tables on a particular area managed by the server. Meanwhile, the real destination—the SecSyslog server—makes a number of queries to obtain records from the DNS server which in turn will answer these by forwarding the data originally transmitted by the client.

The first problem to be addressed is to ensure that the requests sent to the DNS server reach their destination, i.e., to guarantee the integrity of the transmission. DNS is based on UDP but it can also answer TCP requests. In the DNS communication mechanism the client tracks all UDP requests and waits for the answer 'task executed.' If no answer is forthcoming within a given timeframe the client sends a second identical request through a TCP session.

At the moment of writing we have demonstrated that, in any case, if the dimension of the packet containing the request is higher than 512 octets, it is immediately sent via TCP. In this way the problem is resolved by the DNS service protocol itself.

5.8   Authentication of Clients

Interaction with the DNS server involves modifying its tables, but we cannot allow a situation where the DNS server is open to editing by anyone. Basic principles of security require that we look at a way to authenticate and authorize specific subjects to make the necessary changes.

In solving this problem implementation of the Dynamic Update mechanism on the domain name servers can be of use to us. By configuring the system accordingly (using allow-update{} inside the zone definition) we can declare that, among the various queries received from the clients, only update requests with specific signatures may be successfully executed. In effect, the DNS server defines, for each zone managed, who can alter the tables and who cannot.

We can also use the allow-query{} construct to define which hosts may request to read records for a specific zone and get their queries answered. Such mechanisms (or DNS server equivalents other than BIND, which we use) allow us to control who can send and who can receive SecSyslog messages.

5.9   Authenticity and Integrity of Messages

In order to guarantee the legal validity of the logs transmitted, we must be able to guarantee the authenticity and integrity of the *syslog* messages received through the covert channel. SecSyslog provides these guarantees via DNS Security Extensions, using asymmetric key cryptography and various hashing algorithms. Encryption also provides a further level of secrecy to the message and prevents unauthorized publication of the logs.

The DNS server publishes the public key for write access via specific records (KEY and SIG), thus allowing the clients to download it and control its authenticity by verifying the signature. The DNS server may periodically adopt a new key, so it is helpful to implement a mechanism to synchronize the key updating event with the downloading by the clients.

Once the *syslog* message is encrypted, the results of the three most widely used hashing algorithms—MD5, SHA1 and RIPE-160—are added, in specific order, below the message. The encrypted message and the three hash values thus constitute the effective payload which is sent to the DNS.

5.10   How Communication Works

Figure 11 illustrates the communication algorithm for publication of the *syslog* message and downloading by the server. Each passage is described in detail below.

These are the steps taken by the SecSyslog client to publish the messages.

1. The client encrypts the message to be sent and calculates the three hashes, adding them at the bottom to complete the payload.
2. The client updates the message header inserting the timestamp of the previous packet, the length of the encrypted message, the number of parts contained within it, the current part number and the message ID.
3. The client updates the DNS zone publishing the header and payload in a TXT field for the host by the name of <HOSTID><timestamp>, where the timestamp is the current time (calculated at the moment the packet is composed) in tai64 format. This value must be stored for inclusion in the header of the packet to be sent later, so as to recreate the full list of packets transmitted.
4. When the last packet containing the last part of the *syslog* message has been published to the DNS, the client must update its own CNAME field, the <HOSTID>LW. This record is used as a list 'index,' i.e., a starting point for reading the messages to be downloaded by the server. In other words the timestamp of the header represents the 'marker' for the previous item.

The tasks performed by the SecSyslog server to download the messages are as follows.

1. For the controller host, the server asks the DNS for the alias corresponding to the last published message, sending a query to <HOSTID>LW.
2. The server now knows the last message published by that client and can thus query the TXT record to download the last packet sent, requesting the <HOSTID><timestamp> corresponding to the alias.

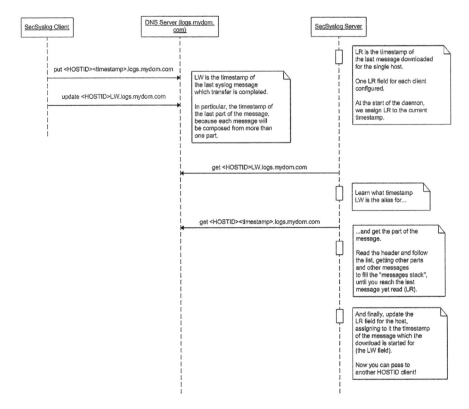

FIG. 11. Syslog communication.

3. The server reads the packet header, finds the timestamp of the previous packet and continues to download packets corresponding to that timestamp, in effect repeating step 2, until it reaches the timestamp of a message already downloaded.

4. Having filled the message stack, the server can now process the data received to write the messages into log files for the configured host.

5. After a brief wait, the server can check another of the configured hosts and download new *syslog* messages. The waiting time must be brief enough to enable it to check all the hosts before the DNS cache expires (TTL).

Note that with a little tuning of the TTL, the DNS server cache will not be unnecessarily overpopulated since the old *syslog* messages sent to the client are automatically deleted from the DNS daemon when the cache expires.

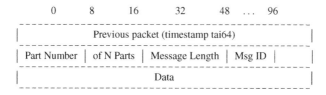

FIG. 12.

In Fig. 12 we can see the format of the packet sent by the client and published to the DNS server. This example uses the TXT record which allows it to publish 220 bytes, 18 of which for the header.

6. The State of the Art in Research; Solving Emerging Issues

The internal tool validation process remains one of the most pressing problems in digital forensics, including the tools we discussed in this chapter. The validation process that the IRItaly Project, for example, is seeking to complete offers as a deliverable a checklist of tools that comprise the daily toolset of a forensic investigator, according to master documents in the literature. The ultimate purpose of this deliverable is a checklist to ensure that the tools used are state-of-the-art. The priority is to guarantee a minimum of compliance with best practices and a solution to the problems of integrity and security defined in this article. This is currently not possible since the issues expressed regard the acquisition phase and not the analysis phase, which is essentially done off-line with the tools cited above.

To date we have completed the daemon architecture and we are writing the code to be submitted for in-depth testing at the IRItaly laboratory (Incident Response Italy) located at the DTI in Crema. Implementation studies will be largely geared to verifying in practice what we have described above, with particular reference to the forensic compliance of the daemon we have decided to implement. We believe this project may represent a valid alternative to advanced syslogging systems such as those cited at the top of this chapter and that SecSyslog, as described, can guarantee reliability for a system that was not developed for digital forensic purposes, but which can satisfy these functions when circumstances require it. In most criminal trials in which we have been called as expert witnesses, the defense attorney has questioned the integrity of the *syslog* produced as evidence, citing its vulnerability to interception and attack by hackers. We believe that, after satisfying certain implementation requirements, the SecSyslog daemon will be ready for peer review (we are aiming to publish our results on sourceforge by the end of 2005) and stable implementation in architecture requiring secure and forensically compliant stealth-based syslogging. Following you have the test bed graphical representation of the SecSyslog model (Fig. 13).

We decided to install a SecSyslog implementation in our TestLab placed at University of Milano at Crema. It will help us in integrating our existing Honeynet with two more modules.

In any case, the objective of this chapter is to act as a tutorial for log and event correlation. To ensure that the operations comply with the general principles of digital forensics, the tools used have to meet a series of requisites. The IRItaly Project is currently seeking to achieve precisely this objective. At the moment, the most important problems to resolve are the manageability of distributed architectures, with particular emphasis on top-down and real time approaches. We currently see a gap between the two approaches, which are pursued, respectively, by ISVs and by the GPL world. The latter is famously less well financed than the former, and for this reason cannot use the same methodology. In any case, the hope is to guarantee a minimum of autonomy to those operators who are not able to invest large sums in complex distributed systems.

A number of current scientific conferences are unquestionably important. Some of them deal with applied digital forensics, others delve into forensic engineering. The most recent Digital Forensics Research Workshop (http://www.dfrws.org), for example, hosted a series of innovative papers discussing how the investigative paradigm is changing, needs that have developed over time, and past experiences.

There are studies that show the effectiveness of network forensics and correlation tools, at least in the prototype stage, supported by advanced display tools. Researchers at the Iowa State University Department of Electrical and Computer Engineering have developed a prototype network forensics analysis tool that integrates presentation, handling and automated analysis of intrusion evidence. In this case, the evidence graph was proposed as a novel graphic tool to facilitate the presentation and handling of intrusion evidence. For automated evidence analysis, a hierarchical reasoning framework that includes local reasoning and global reasoning has been developed. In local reasoning, a Rule-based Fuzzy Cognitive Map (RBFCM) was deployed to model the evolving state of suspicious hosts. In global reasoning, the project aims to identify groups of strongly correlated hosts involved in the attack and determine their relationships within that scenario.

While part of the scientific community is engaged in creating new tools, another part concentrates on investigative methods. One of the most frequently reported problems is the high percentage of errors in the so-called incident reproduction phase. According to the dominant doctrine, there are three types of reproduction: Physical, Logical, and Theoretic. The first is when investigators succeed in wholly reproduc-

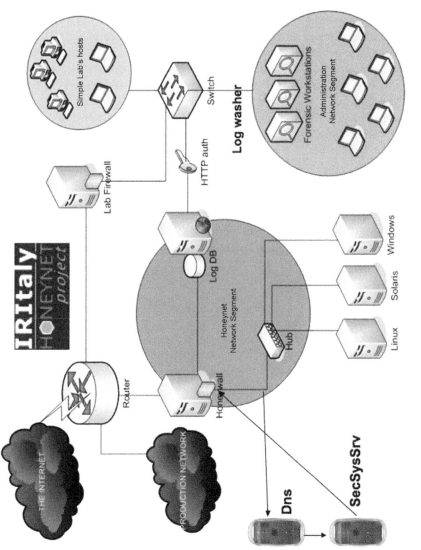

FIG. 13. SecSyslog implementation.

ing (even using identical hardware) an event or chain of events. Logical reproduction refers to the situation where the reproduction environment is completely or partially similar to the original but not identical physically. Lastly, "theoretical" reproduction comprises revealing a pattern of abstract reasoning in order to identify a possible set of events that led to the current state of a specific piece of evidence.

A group of researchers has presented a three-component model of a digital investigation which comprises: determination of input-output layers, assignment of read and write operations associated with use of forensic tools, and time-stamping of read and write operations. This builds on work of several authors, culminating in the new model presented at DFRWS which is generic, scalable, compatible with all functions in the system, and guaranteed to produce high quality reproducibility. It uses scientifically derived and proven methods for the collection, identification, validation, preservation, analysis, interpretation, documentation, and presentation of digital evidence derived from digital sources for the purpose of facilitating or furthering the reconstruction of events found to be criminal, or helping to anticipate unauthorized actions shown to be disruptive to planned operations.

While the above research has focused on the incident reproduction phase or at least on the findings, another group of researchers has dedicated their attention to the search step. Before I go on, however, I should point something out. There is an important difference between the "survey" phase and the "search" phase. The latter, also known as the "analysis phase," has two infungible requisites:

1. The work is much more meticulous and in-depth than the survey phase. Automated tools may be used, but in cases where special skills are required for the reconstruction of scattered digital evidence (a procedure known as "chaining") human intervention is vital;
2. In many cases the search phase requires greater expertise than the survey phase, which is usually the purview of the so-called community of practitioners. That is why we are beginning to see a gap between "simple" digital investigators and the true computer forensic analysts.

Having said this, at Purdue University automated search functions have been developed. It is almost a countertrend to the preponderance of manual activity seen over the past three years. The research presented in DFRWS 2005 starts from a practical experience with the Honeynet Project. In the research paper, authors introduce techniques to automate the searching process by suggesting what searches could be helpful. Researchers also use data mining techniques to find files and directories created during the incident. The results from using these techniques on a compromised honeypot system were pretty good and showed that the data mining techniques detect a higher percentage of files than a random sampling would, but there are still many false positives. More research into the error rates of manual searches is needed to fully understand the impact of automated techniques.

Managing digital forensics cases is becoming more and more complex in a way that is directly proportional to the capacity of the media that are the objects of investigation. As has been said before, it is not possible to create a complete image of the file system of Google. For this reason, in any forensic investigation, planning and analysis activities are required in order to determine what digital media will be seized, what types of information will be sought in the examination, and how the examination will be conducted. Existing literature [Bogen and Dampier] and suggested practices indicate that such planning should occur, but few tools provide support for such activities. Planning an examination may be an essential activity when investigators and technicians are faced with unfamiliar case types or unusually complex, large-scale cases. In complex, large-scale cases it is critical that the investigators provide computer forensics technicians with the appropriate amount of case data supplemented with keyword lists; too much case data or too little case data can make the forensics technician's task very difficult.

Bogen and Dampier's paper presents the concept for a novel application of ontology/domain modeling (known as case domain modeling) as a structured approach for analyzing case facts, identifying the most relevant case concepts, determining the critical relationships between these concepts, and documenting this information. This method may be considered as a foundational analytical technique in computer forensics that may serve as the basis for useful semi-automated tools. The approach sounds very interesting but, like every model related paper, it lacks implementation.

6.1   AntiForensic Tools

So far we have talked about what the scientific community is doing to improve digital forensics techniques and management on a large scale. The Black Hat community, on the other hand, is researching tools and processes for obfuscating data that the investigators would like to analyze. At the Black Hat Conference 2005, the Metasploit Anti-Forensic Investigation Arsenal (MAFIA) was presented. It is a multilevel tool which claims to be able to modify a range of information that is usually sought both in the survey and in the search & analysis phases. The Timestomp module, for example, is a first-ever tool that can modify all four NTFS timestamp values: modified, accessed, created, and entry modified. Another component of MAFIA is Slacker, another first ever tool that allows you to hide files within the slack space of the NTFS file system.

It is clear that there are potential problems of obfuscation here, not only at this level but also at others. There are tools, in fact, that do the same thing as Slacker but hide data in the so-called HPA (Host Protected Access) area and manipulate the De-vice Configuration Overlay (see below) maliciously. HPA is defined as a confidential area for data storage outside the normal operating file system. This area is hidden from the operating system and file system, and is normally used for specialized applications. Systems may wish to store configuration data or save memory to the hard disk drive device in a location that the operating systems cannot change. If an HPA area exists on a suspect's drive, tools for forensic seizure operation will detect this area and copy all the contents of the suspect's hard disk drive sectors, including all the HPA hidden sectors, to the evidence drive.

6.2   Device Configuration Overlay (DCO)

DCO allows systems to modify the apparent features provided by a hard disk drive device. It provides a set of commands that allow a utility program to modify some of the commands, modes, and feature sets reported as supported by the hard disk drive. It can be used to hide a portion of the hard disk drive capacity from being viewed by the operating system and the file system. If DCO is detected on a suspect's drive, tools for forensic seizure operation will copy all the contents of the suspect's hard disk drive sectors including all the DCO hidden sectors to the evidence drive.

Unlike MAFIA, these tools are independent of the operating system and hence even less controllable. While HPA activities are becoming worrisome, the first tools are appearing that are designed to counter certain other tools such as Transmogrify, a first ever tool to defeat EnCase's file signaturing capabilities by allowing users to mask and unmask user's files as any file type, and Sam Juicer, a Meterpreter module that dumps the hashes from the SAM, but does it without ever hitting disk.

7.   Conclusions

We have talked about a number of general issues in this chapter and listed those which are still unresolved. We have introduced forensic imaging under UNIX, with emphasis on dd, which is currently one of the few tools able, at least on paper, to recognize and create an image of the HPA and DCO on a 2.6 or higher Linux kernel. Based on my personal experience, I believe that the above listed issues are something to keep an extremely careful eye on, especially in distributed environments and re-garding remote forensics since there is currently little practical experience with them and a need to find a more organized approach. Hopefully the technical community will soon deploy valid countermeasures. An appropriate awareness of the potential threats may help greatly in preventing the recurrence of a gap between attacks and countermeasures that not so very long ago caused a great host of problems for businesses and other institutions.

FURTHER READING

[1] IETF, "RFC 791: Internet Protocol", http://www.ietf.org/rfc/rfc0791.txt.

[2] IETF, "RFC 793: Transmission Control Protocol", http://www.ietf.org/rfc/rfc0793.txt.

[3] U.S. Department of Defense, "Trusted computer system evaluation criteria", 1985.

[4] Comer D.E., *Internetworking with TCP/IP*, vol. 1, Prentice Hall, New York, 1995.

[5] Szor P., *The Art of Computer Virus Research and Defense*, Addison–Wesley, Reading, MA, 2005.

[6] Rowland C.H., "Covert channels in the TCP/IP protocol suite", *First Monday* (1997), http://www.firstmonday.org/issues/issue2_5/rowland/.

[7] Owens M., "A discussion of covert channels and steganography", http://www.sans.org/rr/whitechapters/covert/678.php, 2002.

[8] Murdoch S., Lewis S., "Embedding covert channels into TCP/IP", http://www.cl.cam.ac.uk/users/sjm217/chapters/ih05coverttcp.pdf, 2005.

[9] "Simple Nomad", README for the ncovert2 tool, http://ncovert.sourceforge.net/, 2003.

[10] Bejtlich R., *The TAO of Network Security Monitoring*, Addison–Wesley, Reading, MA, 2005, pp. 505–517.

[11] Alhambra and daemon9, "Project Loki: ICMP tunneling", *Phrack Magazine* **6** (49) (1996), http://www.phrack.org/phrack/49/P49-06.

[12] Carrillo J.F., Ospina C., Rangel M., Rojas J.A., Vergara C., "Covert channels sobre HTTP", http://www.criptored.upm.es/guiateoria/gt_m142m.htm, 2004.

[13] Dyatlov A., Castro S., "Exploitation of data streams authorized by a network access control system for arbitrary data transfers: tunneling and covert channels over the HTTP protocol", http://www.gray-world.net/projects/chapters/html/covert_chapter.html, 2003.

[14] Kaminsky D., "Black Ops of DNS", http://www.doxpara.com/dns_bh, 2004.

[15] IETF, "RFC 2136: Dynamic Updates in the Domain Name System", http://www.ietf.org/rfc/rfc2136.txt.

[16] IETF, "RFC 2535: Domain Name System Security Extensions", http://www.ietf.org/rfc/rfc2535.txt.

[17] Albitz P., Liu C., *DNS and BIND*, fourth ed., O'Reilly, 2001.

[18] Forte D., "Analyzing the difficulties in backtracing onion router traffic", http://www.ijde.org/archives/02_fall_art3.html. The International Journal of Digital Evidence, Utica College, United States, http://www.idje.org, JDE 2002 1:3.

[19] Forte D., "The art of log correlation, tool and techniques for log analysis", in: *Proceedings of The ISSA Conference 2004, Johannesburg, South Africa, Digital Crime and Forensic Science in Cyberspace*, Idea Publishing, Greece, 2005.

[20] Forte D., et al., in: Th.A. Johnson (Ed.), *Forensic Computer Crime Investigation, Forensic Science*, CRC Press, November 2005.

[21] Forte D., et al., "Forensic analysis of UNIX systems", in: H. Bidgoli (Ed.), *Handbook of Information Security*, Wiley, New York, November 2005.

[22] Forte D., Zambelli M., Vetturi M., Maruti C., "SecSyslog: an alternative approach based on covert channels", in: *Proceedings of the First International Workshop on Systematic Approaches to Digital Forensic Engineering (SADFE 2005)*.

[23] Chuvakin A., "Advanced log processing", http://www.securityfocus.com.

[24] Wang W., Daniels Th.E., "Network forensics analysis with evidence graphs (demo proposal)", Department of Electrical and Computer Engineering, Iowa State University, *DFRWS Proceedings*, 2005, New Orleans.

We suggest to read also the chapter "Wireless insecurities" by Michael Sthultz, Jacob Uecker and Hal Berghel in this volume of the "Advances." That chapter describes ways to break into wireless networks.

Author Index

Numbers in *italics* indicate the pages on which complete references are given.

Subject Index

Contents of Volumes in This Series

Printed and bound by CPI Group (UK) Ltd, Croydon, CR0 4YY

03/10/2024

01040415-0007